FREE PAGES AND OTHER ESSAYS

Anarchist Musings

FREE PAGES AND OTHER ESSAYS
Anarchist Musings

Manuel González Prada

Translated from the Spanish by
FREDERICK H. FORNOFF

EDITED WITH AN INTRODUCTION AND CHRONOLOGY
BY DAVID SOBREVILLA

OXFORD
UNIVERSITY PRESS

2003

OXFORD
UNIVERSITY PRESS

Oxford New York
Auckland Bangkok Buenos Aires Cape Town Chennai
Dar es Salaam Delhi Hong Kong Istanbul Karachi Kolkata
Kuala Lumpur Madrid Melbourne Mexico City Mumbai Nairobi
São Paulo Shanghai Taipei Tokyo Toronto

Copyright © 2003 by Oxford University Press, Inc.

Published by Oxford University Press, Inc.
198 Madison Avenue, New York, New York 10016

www.oup.com

Oxford is a registered trademark of Oxford University Press

Library of Congress Cataloging-in-Publication Data
González Prada, Manuel, 1844–1918.
[Selections. English. 2002]
Free pages and other essays : anarchist musings /
by Manuel González Prada ; translated from the Spanish
by Frederick H. Fornoff ; edited with an introduction
and chronology by David Sobrevilla.
p. cm.—(Library of Latin America)
ISBN 0–19–511687–9—ISBN 0–19–511688–7 (pbk.)
1. González Prada, Manuel, 1844–1918—
Translations into English.
I. Fornoff, Frederick H.
II. Sobrevilla, David, 1938–
III. Title. IV. Series.
PQ8497.G6 A24 2002 861'.5—dc21 2002025114

1 3 5 7 9 8 6 4 2

Printed in the United States of America
on acid-free paper

Contents

Series Editors' General Introduction   *vii*

Criteria for This Edition   *xi*

Biographical Note on Manuel González Prada   *xiv*

Chronology of Manuel González Prada   *xv*

Introduction by David Sobrevilla   *xxiii*

Selected Bibliography   *lviii*

About the Editor and Translator   *lxiii*

Free Pages and Other Essays: Anarchist Musings   1

Series Editors'
General Introduction

The Library of Latin America series makes available in translation major nineteenth-century authors whose work has been neglected in the English-speaking world. The titles for the translations from the Spanish and Portuguese were suggested by an editorial committee that included Jean Franco (general editor responsible for works in Spanish), Richard Graham (series editor responsible for works in Portuguese), Tulio Halperín Donghi (at the University of California, Berkeley), Iván Jaksić (at the University of Notre Dame), Naomi Lindstrom (at the University of Texas at Austin), Francine Masiello (at the University of California, Berkeley), and Eduardo Lozano of the Library at the University of Pittsburgh. The late Antonio Cornejo Polar of the University of California, Berkeley, was also one of the founding members of the committee. The translations have been funded thanks to the generosity of the Lampadia Foundation and the Andrew W. Mellon Foundation.

During the period of national formation between 1810 and into the early years of the twentieth century, the new nations of Latin America fashioned their identities, drew up constitutions, engaged in bitter struggles over territory, and debated questions of education, government, ethnicity, and culture. This was a unique period unlike the process of nation formation in Europe and one which should be more familiar than it is to students of comparative politics, history, and literature.

The image of the nation was envisioned by the lettered classes—a minority in countries in which indigenous, mestizo, black, or mulatto peasants and slaves predominated—although there were also alternative nationalisms at the grassroots level. The cultural elite were well educated in European thought and letters, but as statesmen, journalists, poets, and academics, they confronted the problem of the racial and linguistic heterogeneity of the continent and the difficulties of integrating the population into a modern nation-state. Some of the writers whose works will be translated in the Library of Latin America series played leading roles in politics. Fray Servando Teresa de Mier, a friar who translated Rousseau's *The Social Contract* and was one of the most colorful characters of the independence period, was faced with imprisonment and expulsion from Mexico for his heterodox beliefs; on his return, after independence, he was elected to the congress. Domingo Faustino Sarmiento, exiled from his native Argentina under the presidency of Rosas, wrote *Facundo: Civilización y barbarie*, a stinging denunciation of that government. He returned after Rosas' overthrow and was elected president in 1868. Andrés Bello was born in Venezuela, lived in London where he published poetry during the independence period, settled in Chile where he founded the University, wrote his grammar of the Spanish language, and drew up the country's legal code.

These post-independence intelligentsia were not simply dreaming castles in the air, but vitally contributed to the founding of nations and the shaping of culture. The advantage of hindsight may make us aware of problems they themselves did not foresee, but this should not affect our assessment of their truly astonishing energies and achievements. It is still surprising that the writing of Andrés Bello, who contributed fundamental works to so many different fields, has never been translated into English. Although there is a recent translation of Sarmiento's celebrated *Facundo*, there is no translation of his memoirs, *Recuerdos de provincia (Provincial Recollections)*. The predominance of memoirs in the Library of Latin America series is no accident—many of these offer entertaining insights into a vast and complex continent.

Nor have we neglected the novel. The series includes new translations of the outstanding Brazilian writer Joaquim Maria Machado de Assis's work, including *Dom Casmurro* and *The Posthumous Memoirs of Brás Cubas*. There is no reason why other novels and writers who are not so well known outside Latin America—the Peruvian novelist Clorinda Matto de Turner's *Aves sin nido*, Nataniel Aguirre's *Juan de la Rosa*, José de Alencar's *Iracema*, Juana Manuela Gorriti's short stories—should not be read with as much interest as the political novels of Anthony Trollope.

A series on nineteenth-century Latin America cannot, however, be limited to literary genres such as the novel, the poem, and the short story. The literature of independent Latin America was eclectic and strongly influenced by the periodical press newly liberated from scrutiny by colonial authorities and the Inquisition Newspapers were miscellanies of fiction, essays, poems, and translations from all manner of European writing. The novels written on the eve of Mexican Independence by José Joaquín Fernández de Lizardi included disquisitions on secular education and law, and denunciations of the evils of gaming and idleness. Other works, such as a well-known poem by Andrés Bello, "Ode to Tropical Agriculture," and novels such as *Amalia* by José Marmol and the Bolivian Nataniel Aguirre's *Juan de la Rosa*, were openly partisan. By the end of the century, sophisticated scholars were beginning to address the history of their countries, as did Joao Capistrano de Abreu in his *Capitulos de historia colonial*.

It is often in memoirs such as those by Fray Servando Teresa de Mier or Sarmiento that we find the descriptions of everyday life that in Europe were incorporated into the realist novel. Latin American literature at this time was seen largely as a pedagogical tool, a "light" alternative to speeches, sermons, and philosophical tracts—though, in fact, especially in the early part of the century, even the readership for novels was quite small because of the high rate of illiteracy. Nevertheless, the vigorous orally transmitted culture of the gaucho and the urban underclasses became the linguistic repertoire of some of the most interesting nineteenth-century writers—most notably José Hernández, author of the "gauchesque" poem "Martin Fierro," which enjoyed an unparalleled popularity. But for many writers the task was not to appropriate popular language but to civilize, and their literary works were strongly influenced by the high style of political oratory.

The editorial committee has not attempted to limit its selection to the better-known writers such as Machado de Assis; it has also selected many works that have never appeared in translation or writers whose work has not been translated recently. The series now makes these works available to the English-speaking public.

Because of the preferences of funding organizations, the series initially focuses on writing from Brazil, the Southern Cone, the Andean region, and Mexico. Each of our editions will have an introduction that places the work in its appropriate context and includes explanatory notes.

We owe special thanks to the late Robert Glynn of the Lampadia Foundation, whose initiative gave the project a jump start, and to Richard Ekman of the Andrew W. Mellon Foundation, which also generously supported the project. We also thank the Rockefeller Foundation for funding the 1996 symposium "Culture and Nation in Iberoamerica," organized by the editorial board of the Library of Latin America. We received substantial institutional support and personal encouragement from the Institute of Latin American Studies of the University of Texas at Austin. The support of Edward Barry of Oxford University Press has been crucial, as has the advice and help of Ellen Chodosh of Oxford University Press. The first volumes of the series were published after the untimely death, on July 3, 1997, of Maria C. Bulle, who, as an associate of the Lampadia Foundation, supported the idea from its beginning.

—*Jean Franco*
—*Richard Graham*

Criteria for This Edition

The only books in prose that Prada published during his life-time were *Pájinas libres* [Free pages] (1894) and *Horas de lucha* [Times of struggle] (1908). The rest were organized by his son Alfredo González Prada and Luis Alberto Sánchez on the basis of articles that don Manuel published in newspapers and magazines and those he left unpublished. The dates that appear at the end of the articles are in general supplied by Alfredo González Prada or Luis Alberto Sánchez.

The translations of this English-language edition are based on the edition of the *Obras of González Prada* published in three tomes and seven volumes by Luis Alberto Sánchez. The first four of these volumes are dedicated to his prose writing. The notes, either by Alfredo González Prada (A.G.P.) or Luis Alberto Sánchez (L.A.S.), are also from this edition. Only when it has seemed necessary has the editor or the translator supplied an additional note. I wish to thank the Instituto Luis Alberto Sánchez in Lima for permission to reproduce many of the helpful notes taken from the *Obras* in this selection.

The texts included in this volume were selected with the intention of offering a thorough panorama of the thought of González Prada, bearing in mind that readers will come primarily from the English-speaking academic world. For this reason, although approximately half of this volume consists of a large number of essays referring to Peruvian problems (which is inevitable for an author like González Prada), the other half consists of texts on the subject of anarchy from a more general perspective. Finally, we have included a few texts by Prada on philosophical, literary, and linguistic problems.

The order adopted for presenting the texts is derived from González Prada's books: (1) those he published during his lifetime (*Pájinas libres* and *Horas de lucha*), (2) a couple of essays from *Nuevas pájinas libres* [New free pages] chosen for their thematic relevance, (3) a text from *El tonel de Diógenes* [Diogenes' cask], most likely written between 1896 and 1898, (4) a good number of articles written for anarchist pamphlets in Peru, and (5) some of the texts that González Prada wrote toward the end of his life, which he could not publish because there was no place to publish them. They appeared after his death with the title *Bajo el oprobio* [Under opprobrium].

Since this presentation does not allow the reader to form a very clear idea of the González-Pradian vision of reality, we suggest adopting the following order for reading the texts in order to organize more clearly the main lines of thought of our author:

I. Peruvian problems
   A. Analysis of Peruvian problems and the possibilities of the Peruvian situation: "Our Mother" [Spain's legacy], "The Rotten Core," "Catholic Education," "Peru and Chile," "Our Judges," "Caporalismo," "Our Indians," "Vijil," "Grau"
   B. González Prada's Proposals
      1. Radical-positivist proposals: "Lecture at the Atheneum in Lima," "Speech at the Olympus Theater," "Speech at the Politeama Theater," "Propaganda and Attack"
      2. Radical-anarchist proposals: "The Parties and the National Union," "Tyrannicide," "The Good Revolution"
II. Anarchy
   A. Social problems
      "The Intellectual and the Worker," "Authority," "The State," "The Sword," "The Soldier's Rebellion," "Anti-Politicians," "The Police," "The Two Nations"
   B. Anarchy: Proposals
      "Anarchy," "The Responsibility of the Anarchist," "The

Individual," "Force," "Revolution," "Strikes," "The Paris Commune," "The Universal Holiday," "The Beginning," "The First of May, 1907," "The First of May, 1908 [two versions]," "Socialism and Anarchy"

III. Philosophical, literary, and linguistic problems
   "Death and Life," "A Moment of Philosophy," "Renan," "Poetry," "Notes on Language"

Biographical Note on
Manuel González Prada

M anuel González Prada was born in Lima in 1844. He came from an aristocratic family. He resided in Chile from 1855 to 1856. In 1857 his father enrolled him in the Santo Toribio Seminary in Lima. Two years later Prada left to enter the San Carlos College, where he studied sciences and law. When his father died in 1863, he left school and began to write. Between 1871 and 1879 he went to live on the Tútume farm in Mala valley to read, translate, and farm. He returned to Lima to participate in the War of the Pacific. When Lima fell in 1881, he went into seclusion in his house for three years. Then he emerged as a literary leader, married in 1887, and became a political leader, founding the National Union Party (May 1891). Shortly thereafter he left for Europe (Paris, Barcelona, and Madrid) and returned to Peru in 1898. He broke with his party in 1902, moving toward anarchy after 1904. In 1912 he was named director of the National Library, but a coup d'état caused him to resign. When democracy was restored, he was reappointed to the post (1916). He died in Lima in 1918.

Chronology of Manuel González Prada

1844   *January 5:* Born as the third child of Francisco González de Prada y Marrón y Lombera and Josefa Alvarez de Ulloa y Rodríguez de la Rosa

1851   Attends the Ferreyros sisters' elementary school

1852   Francisco González de Prada y Marrón y Lombera is minister to Echenique and ambassador to Bolivia

1855   After Castilla's victory over Echenique, Prada y Marrón y Lombera travels to Chile with his family and sets up house in Valparaíso. Manuel attends the Colegio Inglés (English High School), where he takes classes in English and German

1856   Late in the year, the family returns to Lima

1857   Francisco González de Prada y Marrón y Lombera enrolls his son Manuel (thirteen years old) in the Santo Toribio Seminary (where the future president of the Republic, Nicolás de Piérola, and the future bishop, Agustín Obín y Charún, are also studying)

1857–1858   Francisco González de Prada y Marrón y Lombera, mayor of Lima and (after 1858) dean of the College of Law in Lima

1859	Manuel González Prada leaves the seminary and enrolls in San Carlos College
1862	He begins his study of law
1863	He studies sciences (specializing in chemistry)
1863	His father dies; he leaves school and announces that he intends to study engineering in Belgium, but he encounters opposition from his mother
1867	*September 18:* He publishes his first poem in *El Comercio*
1868	*August:* An earthquake levels the south of Peru. He travels to Arequipa and to Cerro de Pasco. He writes his theatrical works "Love and Poverty" and "The Aunt and the Niece" (both lost)
1871	The Bolivian writer José Domingo Cortés publishes *Parnaso peruano,* an anthology in which he includes some compositions by Prada and an autobiographical note in which the author eliminates the honorific *de* from his name He is a founding member of the Círculo Literario. He participates in the Arts and Letters section *September 16:* He begins to collaborate in the first issue of *El Correo del Perú* [Mail from Peru] He goes into seclusion on the Tútume farm in the Mala valley, where he devotes himself to reading, translating, and farming
1873	He publishes some Indian ballads in *El correo del Perú*
1877	*August 20:* Birth of Mercedes González Prada y Calvet, illegitimate daughter of González Prada and Veronica Calvet Child is reared by her maternal grandmother, Carolina Bolívar de Porras
1879	*January 15:* Prologue to the book by the poet V. Mérida (Aureliano Villarán), *Cuartos de hora* *December 26:* Obligatory military service decreed by Piérola González Prada enlists
1880	*December:* Quartered in the Second Division on San Francisco hill. Prada is named garrison commander on El Pino hill

1881   *January 13:* Battle of San Juan
        January 15: Battle of Miraflores
        Prada goes into seclusion in his house

1882   *October 20:* Treaty of Ancón ending the War of the Pacific

1882   *October:* The Chileans leave Lima

1883   *August 27:* Cáceres attacks Lima
        September 11: Prada considers joining the "revolution" with
        Cáceres, but finally does not

1884   Text on "Grau"
        Text on "Victor Hugo"
        The Club Literario changes its name to the Ateneo de Lima
        [Atheneum of Lima]
        December 25: Letter from Palma to Prada, enclosing his
        translations of Heine

1885   *January 30:* Lecture at the Athenaeum of Lima at the in-
        auguration of the section on "Literature and Fine Arts"
        August: He publishes his study "Fragments of Lucifer" in
        the *Revista social* under the pseudonym "Justino Franco"
        October: Luis A. Márquez founds the Círculo Literario and
        invites González Prada to be a member, which he accepts
        (at the time he was second vice president of the Club
        Literario)
        He is elected vice president of the Circulo Literario as well

1886   *April 16:* Approval of the statutes of the Ateneo de Lima
        Prada is named librarian
        Midyear: Death of Josefa Alvarez de Ulloa, González Prada's
        mother
        September 11: He marries Adriana de Verneuil
        September 26: He is elected president of the Círculo Literario
        September 27: Speech in the Palace of Fine Arts

1887   *April:* Death of Luis A. Márquez
        Speech at the funeral of Luis A. Márquez
        July 29: Speech at the Politeama Theater
        October 30: Speech at the Olympus Theater
        November 10: Rebuttal article, "The Propaganda of Defa-

mation," appears in *El trabajo*
November 13: "The Propaganda of Defamation," by R.
Palma (who does not sign it), appears in *El Comercio*
November 15: Correction by Prada in *El Comercio*
November 19: Attack by Nicolás Augusto González against
Palma in *El Comercio*
December 4: Editorial in *El Comercio* putting an end to the
polemic
"Propaganda and Attack," an article in *La luz eléctrica*
Death of Cristina González Prada de Verneuil, daughter of
GP (Prada wants to commit suicide)

1888   *January 18:* Cristina González de Prada de Ulloa dies
"Peru and Chile"

1889   "The French Revolution"
"Notes on Language"
"Freedom to Write"

1890   *February 9:* His son Manuel is born
February 19: Manuel dies
"The 15th of July"
"Death and Life"

1891   Visit to Cañete to see Cerro Alegre, the estate of Francisco
González de Prada de Ulloa
May 16: The platform of the Unión Nacional [the National
Union Party] is published in *Integridad*
Proposal by the administration of Morales Bermúdez for a
senatorship (rejected)
May: He embarks for France
June: He rents an apartment at Number 47, rue de Lourmel,
in the district of Grenelle
October 16: Julio Alfredo is born
He attends courses by Renán (semiweekly) and Louis
Ménard
He meets Gastón de Costa, former communist and former
secretary of Raoul Rigault

1892   *October 2:* Renán dies; González Prada attends his funeral
"Secular Education"

1894   *Midyear:* First edition of *Pájinas libres*

1895   *March:* Piérola's coup against Cáceres; several members of the Unión Nacional change parties

1896   *Early:* He attends the funeral of Verlaine
They leave for the south of France, following this itinerary: Orleans, Blois, Tours, Poitiers, Anguléme, Burdeos, Biarritz
They decide to go to Barcelona first, since there is an epidemic of smallpox in Madrid. Itinerary: Bayona, Pau, Lourdes, Tolosa, Carcasonne, Narbonne, Perpignan, and Port Bou
December: They arrive in Barcelona

1897   Because of the detour, their mail from Lima does not reach them for two months, so they decide not to travel to Italy
He meets Odón de Buen, professor at the University of Barcelona who is affiliated with the republicans
February: De Buen takes Prada to a republican assembly in Reus. Prada spends his time looking for refrains to the Virgin, to Jesus, to the saints, etc.
Adopts the pseudonym "Luis Miguel," which he subsequently uses to sign in *Germinal* and *The Pariahs*
June: They leave for Madrid, following this itinerary: Zaragoza, Calatayud, Guadalajara, and then Madrid
They take an apartment on La Montera Street
Through a relative of Odón de Buen, Fernando Lozano, Prada meets Francisco Pi y Margall, with whom he visits the Royal Spanish Academy
According to Luis A. Sánchez, he met Campoamor and Menéndez Pelayo in the Fernando de Fe bookstore
August: Assassination of Antonio Cánovas del Castillo by Miguel Angiolillo. Prada approves of the act
He visits the Escorial
December: They set out on their return journey, traveling first to Burdeos

1898   *January 6:* They celebrate Manuel's birthday in Burdeos
March 28: Departure from Burdeos for Lima
May: Arrival in Lima

August 21: Speech in Matavilela: "The Parties and the National Union"

August 28: Piérola succeeds in preventing Prada from giving the speech, "Free Thought in Action"

1899   *January:* Prada founds the newspaper *Germinal,* which is shut down by a legal maneuver by Piérola

August: He founds the newspaper *El Independiente*

López de Romaña lets Prada know through his brother Francisco that he will pay whatever he asks if he will refrain from criticizing him. Prada rejects the proposition

Prada continues to publish in *La idea libre* and *El Comercio*

September: He opposes the merger between the National Union and the Pierolists

1900   *March:* He stops attending meetings of the National Union

1901   Adriana and Alfredo print a hundred copies of *Minúsculas* [Lowercase] on a port card printer at home

1902   *May 3:* Confrontation between the journalists of *La idea libre* and *El Comercio.* As a result, Luis Pazos Varela is killed. Criminal charges are brought against Glicerio Tassara. Prada defends Tassara

April 11: He breaks with the National Union over its merger with the Pierolists. He feels that the coordinating committee of the National Union is accommodating the Pierolists, whereas they should be blocked

1903   He takes part in conversations in the name of the National Union with the Pierolists and the Liberal Party. He refuses to continue participating when the liberals withdraw the candidacy of Augusto Durán, which results in the candidacy of Colonel Seminario

1904   He begins to collaborate with anarchist publications such as *Los parias* [The pariahs]

He writes "Our Indians"

1905   He delivers the speech "The Intellectual and the Worker" before the Union of Bakery Workers

1906   He publishes in *Los parias* the Indian ballad, "Song of the Indian Girl"

1908   He publishes *Horas de lucha* [Times of struggle]
          President Augusto B. Leguía offers him the directorship of
          Guadalupe High School and subsequently that of the School
          of Fine Arts, both of which he rejects

1909   He publishes *Presbitarianas* [Presbyterians] anonymously

1911   He publishes *Exóticas* [Exotics]

1912   *March 6:* He is appointed director of the National Library
          April 30: Prada's report on the library
          October 25: Palma, *Notes on the Library of Lima*

1913   *July 14:* Memoir as director of the library

1914   *February 15:* Prada resigns as director of the National Library
          in protest over Benavides's coup d'état
          May 23: Benavides's administration refuses to accept Prada's
          resignation, firing him instead
          Prada publishes the first and only issue of *La lucha*, which
          is banned

1915   *February 1:* The new president, José Pardo y Barreda, reap-
          points Prada to the position of director of the National
          Library
          Second edition of *Páginas libres* (with the original spelling
          altered) prepared in Madrid by Rufino Blanco-Fombana,
          who writes the prologue

1916–1918 Interviews with Prada

1917   *July:* He publishes his memoir as director of the National
          Library

1918   *July 22:* He dies of heart failure

Introduction

The Radical Thought of González Prada

In 1918, when he died, don Manuel González Prada was famous in Peru and very well known in Spanish America. In the last two years of his life he was interviewed by some of the best young Peruvian writers and journalists—José Carlos Mariátegui, Abraham Valdelomar, César Vallejo, Félix del Valle, and others.[1] Among his foreign admirers he counted writers of the stature of Miguel de Unamuno in Spain and Rufino Blanco-Fombona in Venezuela. This despite the fact that at the time he had published only two books in prose and three books of poetry.[2] He had written many articles and poems that appeared in newspapers, a poetry anthology in Peru, and journals. Beyond this, he was a man who was celebrated, criticized, and even vehemently attacked in Peru. Among those who wrote about him (either praise or criticism) were José de la Riva Agüero (1905), Ventura García Calderón (1910, 1914), and V. A. Belaunde (1917). In 1895 a priest writing under the pseudonym of F. B. González published *Pájinas razonables,* a refutation of *Pájinas libres;* several newspapers had been shut down for daring to publish articles by him, and during the regime of Colonel Oscar R. Benavides (who came to power in a military takeover) Prada had nowhere to publish. Rumor has it that many copies of *Pájinas libres* were burned along with the effigy of the author when they reached Arequipa (the book had been printed in Paris).

We now know much more about the vicissitudes of Prada's life—thanks to *Don Manuel*, Luis A. Sánchez's fictionalized biography (1930), *Mi Manuel*, by his widow, Adriana de Verneuil (1947), and the portrait of the González Prada family, also written by Sánchez (1977); about his work—thanks to studies like the one by Hugo García Salvatecci, *El pensamiento de González Prada*.[3] We now have access to his complete texts—thanks to the admirable publication of his manuscripts by his son, Alfredo González-Prada, and the edition by Luis A. Sánchez of all the *Obras* of González Prada (in seven volumes that appeared between 1985 and 1989).[4] A study and anthology titled *El anarquismo en América Latina*, edited by the scholar Angel J. Cappelletti, gives Prada a preeminent position within this movement.[5]

Not all the secrets of his biography have been resolved for us; on the contrary, part of its trajectory is still shrouded in confusion. Contrary to what authors such as Sánchez and García Salvatecci have claimed—that Prada was a radical almost from the beginning of his career—it has recently been argued to some effect that for a period of fifteen years (between 1873 and 1888) he was allied with the intellectuals of the Civilist Party.[6] Almost eighty years after his death Prada continues to arouse irritation and polemics. In a text published as recently as 1997 it is argued that the greater part of his critique of religion was "crude" and never rose above the level of insult and defamation and was meant only to scandalize and offend his contemporaries, that his vision of the Indian was stereotyped, and that his position on the problem of the national tradition was essentially nihilistic and destructive.[7] And in another text, also from 1997, it is argued that the author was an apologist for violence (i.e., a defender of fanaticism), that he employed a sarcastic or mocking tone that betrayed a certain insensitivity, and that he used specious and alarmist rhetoric to justify individual action.[8] Even though today we know considerably more about the life of Prada than we did earlier, we are still in the dark concerning certain aspects. Despite the years that have passed since his death, his work continues to arouse anger and opposition, as it did when he lived. Prada endures as an author about whom there is still much to investigate and who continues to foster debate.

This volume is a collection of the essays of González Prada, not his poetry. We can divide the evolution of his thought (modifying slightly a proposal by García Salvatecci)[9] into four major periods: (1) the formative years (1844–1879), (2) the radical-positivist period (1879–1891), (3) the European years (1891–1898), and (4) the radical-anarchist period (1898–1918). Following Prada's formative years, the central characteristic of his ideas is his radicalism. Radical ideas do not appear at the end of the nineteenth century in Peru as an absolute novelty, but rather have their origin in the radicalism already existing at midcentury. At that time radicalism developed as the third of the major political options (there were also a few minor options that were less important) that emerged following independence. The first of these was *conservative thought,* the second *liberal,* and the third *radical.* Radicalism was introduced into Peru by the Chilean Francisco Bilbao (1823–1865), a man who had lived in Lima from 1851 to 1855, with an intermediate residence in Guayaquil from 1852 to 1853. It was taken up by Enrique Alvarado (1835 or 1837 to 1856) and further developed by Mariano Amézaga (1834–1882).[10] Radicalism has been viewed both negatively and positively: negatively for its anticlericalism, its anti-Spanish attitude, and its denunciation of the moral and economic problems of Peru; positively for being an extreme left option opposing the bourgeoisie, capitalism, and nascent imperialism and favoring a broad-based egalitarianism.

The following section is organized in terms of the four stages through which González Prada's thought passed.

The First Period (1844–1879)
The Formative Years

José Manuel de los Reyes González de Prada y Alvarez de Ulloa, or more simply, Manuel González Prada—as he came to be known—or even more simply, Manuel G. Prada—as he signed his name—was born in Lima on January 5, 1844. His family was aristocratic: his father, Francisco González de Prada y Marrón y Lombera, was a lawyer and conservative politician, and his mother, doña Josefa Alvarez de Ulloa y Rodríguez de la Rosa, an Arequipa matron. Manuel was the third of four children.

Prada began school in Lima in 1851 and four years later moved with his family to Chile. As his father had been minister of state under President Echenique, he feared reprisals from the victorious revolution of General Ramón Castilla, who led the uprising against Echenique.

The González Prada family set up house in Valparaíso, and there Manuel attended the English High School, making good progress in English and German. At the end of 1856 the family returned to Lima, and don Francisco became so close to Castilla that he ended up serving as mayor of Lima from 1857 to 1858. He was also named dean of the College of Lawyers during those same years.

In 1857 don Francisco enrolled his son Manuel in the Seminary of Santo Toribio, which he quietly abandoned two years later to enroll in the liberal San Carlos School. During those years he developed an anticlerical spirit as a reaction against the excessive religiosity (or worse, the sanctimoniousness) of his family. There, he studied sciences (especially chemistry) and law—this at his father's behest. He may have read certain positivist writers at San Carlos.

In 1863, don Francisco died and Manuel left the school. Apparently he intended to travel to Belgium to study engineering, but he ran into opposition from his mother. At this time he began to cultivate his literary aptitude, translating and writing. In 1867 he published his first *letrilla*—a humorous poem—in the newspaper *El Comercio*.

In 1868 he traveled to Arequipa and then to Cerro de Pasco. During this period he must have written two theatrical pieces, which have been lost. In 1871 he was included in the anthology *Parnaso peruano* (Peruvian Parnassus) and decided to go into seclusion at Tú
tume, the family farm in the valley of Mala—south of Lima—to read, translate, write, and farm. During those years he translated Goethe, Uhland, Heine, and Lessing from German, and Victor Hugo, Dumas, and Mérimée from French, experimenting with poetic forms that were hardly known in Spanish and trying to introduce the ballad genre.

He continued to make trips to Lima and on those trips he met and began a relationship with Veronica Calvet y Bolívar, resulting in the birth of their daughter, Mercedes, on August 20, 1877. He never acknowledged her, though, and apparently never saw her. His trips to Lima also allowed him to stay in touch with the literary scene. In 1873 he helped found the Club Literario, which brought together the most renowned literary figures of the moment, among whom Ricardo Palma, author of the "traditions," was the most distinguished.

The Second Period (1879–1891)
The Radical-Positivist Years

The Transformation of Prada: From Literary Leader to
Political Leader

Prada returned to Lima to take part in the War of the Pacific, which was declared in 1879, and fought in the battles of San Juan and Miraflores in January 1881. When the capital fell, he went into seclusion in his house for three years because he did not want to run into a single Chilean on the streets.

A year after peace with Chile was decreed in 1883 in the Treaty of Ancón, Prada considered joining the guerrilla forces of General Cáceres, who had led the uprising against General Iglesias, head of government, but in the end he decided against it.

In 1886 the Círculo Literario, a group of young writers, was formed, and Prada was invited to participate in it. He accepted and was elected vice president. At the time he was also second vice president of the Club Literario (which had in the meantime changed its name to the Ateneo de Lima, or Athenaeum of Lima), indicating his wide support. Prada gave a speech at the Athenaeum that was a kind of manifesto for the young writers of the Círculo Literario. This situation became even clearer when they elected him president the following year. During this period his mother died and Prada married Adriana de Verneuil, a young Frenchwoman who was living with his family in Lima.

The year 1888 was of key importance in Manuel's life. Successive speeches—one in the Politeama Theater condemning the course of the history of the republic, in which he pronounced his famous distich ("Old men to the grave, and young men to the task at hand!"), another at the Olympus Theater in which he attacked Palma and the members of the Athenaeum, and the articles "Propaganda and Attack" and "Peru and Chile"—transformed him from a literary leader into a political leader. His first daughter died during the same year, and a year later his son, both soon after birth.

The Literary Circle was the origin of the National Union Party, whose political program was published in May 1891. According to Prada it ought to have been a "radical party" and named that, but the timidity of its followers caused its character to be blurred under the other name.

To the surprise of the young members of the National Union, Manuel left for Europe that same month.[11] The articles that he had been writing during this period were revised and published in Paris in 1894 under the title *Pájinas libres.*

The Radical-Positivist Thought of González Prada

Because *Pájinas libres* consists of texts reworked after Prada's trip to Europe, we are compelled to be very cautious in evaluating them as being illustrative of the thinking of don Manuel between 1879 and 1891, since they may very well have been rewritten under influences or experiences subsequent to this period. The very title—Free Pages—indicates the clear intention of the author to place them at least in proximity to the later, anarchist stage of Prada's thought. Next we will examine the following aspects of the intellectual posture of the author: (1) his literary proposals, (2) his role as a writer and an intellectual committed to action, (3) reality and the problems of Peru, (4) his radical-positivist proposals, (5) his attitude toward death, and (6) his orthographic reform.

THE LITERARY PROPOSALS

As already noted, Prada began as a leader of the Literary Circle. He made his literary proposals in his lecture at the Athenaeum of Lima (1886).[12] Initially the speech had been intended to focus on Heinrich Heine, but it ended up treating other topics as well. It took up the problem of imitation in literature and, more concretely, in Peruvian literature, in which imitators are imitated (e.g., imitations of Bécquer, who imitated Heine). It examined the virtues of Heine's poetry and recommended assimilating objectivism from German poetry. It criticized those who try to pass as Germanists or Germanizers, when in reality they are only Teutomaniacs, like Palma.[13] He declared war on the kind of improvisation found in newspapers, as well as archaism and purism. He expressed surprise that Peru had achieved political emancipation but had not sought stylistic independence from Spain, especially since Spain was a country so dependent in literary matters. And, finally, he proposed several grand ideals for Peruvian literature of the moment: to learn science, to seek inspiration in classical Greek literature, and to come to terms with neologism, foreignism, and provincialism that rejuvenate and enrich the language, and to work for tomorrow. He insisted on the necessity of working and studying and on the right of the country to expect something from its citizens. He ended the speech with an expression of confidence in the existence of talented persons in Peru and a recommendation that in the aftermath of the war with Chile it was necessary to forget the horrible nightmare of blood and to undertake reconstruction from the ruins. The speech was a kind of literary manifesto for the young writers of the Círculo Literario against the consecrated authors of the Club Literario.[14]

In "Speech in the Palace of Art" (September 27, 1887) Prada claims that it is only from the young that one can expect forthright freedom in the expression of ideas and a democratic elevation in style; a literature that is afraid to proceed from the deductions of positivist science is little more than archaeological restoration; art is on a par with religion and science, even surpassing them in certain respects; and the Círculo Literario is destined to become the "radical party of our literature."

THE WRITER'S ROLE AND COMMITMENT TO ACTION

González Prada alludes to the writer's commitment in "Speech at the Olympus Theater" (October 30, 1888). He is aware that the Círculo Literario is destined "to become a nucleus for militant political action." As for the group's program, he asks rhetorically how strong they are, who should guide them, and what kind of resistance they will confront. He notes that it will be impossible to measure their strength with precision, because they will grow day by day in their war against everything that smacks of "regression in Science, in Art, and in Literature." They should seek orientation from no national or Spanish writers but should seek out the most stimulating sources from France (Fourier and Comte), and especially Germany (Hegel and Schopenhauer) and England (Darwin and Spencer). Prada thinks that there will be little resistance: in Peru there is no educated clergy, no bourgeoisie as in Europe, nor any reactionary parties, but only a malevolent, secular clergy and a mendacious and deceitful religious press.

Three things that the members of the Círculo Literario should not forget are the honesty of the writer, truth in style, and in truth ideas. Language has become prostituted in contemporary Peru. "Truth in style and language is as important as truth in substance" (*Obras*, 1:71). As for truth in ideas, it belongs to positivist science today, while theology and metaphysics have a monopoly on falsehood: "the diagnosis of Peruvian literature can be summed up in one phrase: congestion of words, anemia in ideas" (*Obras*, 1:166). It is time for the reign of truth to begin in literature, time to break the infamous pact of speaking softly.

González Prada appears even more radical in his 1888 "Propaganda and Attack" (*Obras*, 1:163–177), in which he characterizes the writer as an antithesis of the politician and a forerunner of the figure of the anarchist intellectual:

> A difficult job awaits the writer who hopes to counter the influence of the corrupt politician: his work must consist of propaganda and attack. It may be that this is not the time for trying collective action, but for solitary, individual effort; perhaps we don't need the book so much as the pamphlet, the newspaper, the broadside. But whether we act individually or collectively, the most fiery propaganda is of little value unless it goes hand in hand with a determined assault on politics and politicians. (*Obras*, 1:171).

The reason for this is that politics, particularly Peruvian politics, has always been the art of governing men the way you run a machine or control a herd of sheep; politicians behave like a syndicate of people sick with ambition. Politics has corrupted everything. "We shook off the tutelage of the viceroys only to vegetate under the tyranny of military strongmen, so our true form of government is caporalism" (*Obras*, 1:172). If politics is in fact the evil, the writer has to take an active part in it so as to "discredit it, dissolve it, and destroy it" (*Obras*, 1:175).

REALITY AND THE PROBLEMS OF PERU

Narciso Aréstegui initiated indigenist prose in Peru in 1848 with his novel *Father Horan,* and Juan Bustamante Dueñas claimed in 1867 that it wasn't those living on the coastal plain but the Indians who basically constituted the republic.[15] But it was González Prada's reaffirmation of that fact in 1888 in "Speech at the Politeama Theater,"[16] which impressed on Peruvian consciousness that the real Peru consists fundamentally of Indians, not *criollos* (*Obras*, 1:89). In that speech he expressed his outrage that the tyrannical brutalizing of the Indian is carried out by the justice of the peace, the governor, and the priest. The Indian is, according to Prada, the basic reality of Peru as well as one of its essential problems. "If we make the Indian a slave, what country will he defend?" (*Obras*, 1:88). In many of his poems published prior to 1888 as *Baladas peruanas*,[17] Prada had already addressed the problem of injustices committed against the natives.

The main problem of Peru is that we're dealing with an organism so sick that "wherever we poke our finger, pus comes out" (*Obras*, 1: 171). This crisis explains the defeat in the war with Chile, and not the other way around. To what must we attribute our moral crisis? To a multiplicity of mutually reinforcing causes: the degenerate, shabby descendants that the Spanish nobility left us as a legacy and the swarm of soldiers and clerks bequeathed to us by independence (*Obras*, 1:88). The fact that after we emancipated ourselves, our universities continued teaching theology and metaphysics without accepting positivist science (*Obras*, 1:89). The sealing off of our decrepit institutions, preventing enlightened foreigners from reinvigorating them as happened in Chile (*Obras*, 1:97). The pernicious system of looking to the government and the capital for our only direction (*Obras*, 1:100). The fact that we have no genuine parties of ideas—liberals, conservatives, not even reactionaries—and that we lack national unity (*Obras*, 1:88). The fact that politics among us has been practiced as a game of vested interests and improvisations (*Obras*, 1:17ff.). The presence of a legion of improvised measures in all spheres of our national life (*Obras*, 1:87). The fact that the Church has preached respect and resignation, which have acted on us like narcotics to discourage action (*Obras*, 1:166ff.).

These were circumstances that brought about the defeat in the war with Chile, which has left us not only dazed and discouraged but, more than that, intimidated, shrunken in spirit, and resigned to the defeat, all of which makes us incapable of reacting. Hence, at the national and international level as well, we are afflicted with an enormous sense of servility (*Obras*, 1:170). If we go on like this, being what we were and what we are, Chile will conquer us again tomorrow and forever (*Obras*, 1:95).

THE RADICAL-POSITIVIST PROPOSALS

If what affects Peru is a moral crisis, the only possible way to restore health is to regenerate the diseased body. "The strength of nations comes from themselves, it comes from their moral elevation" (*Obras*, 1: 95). To attain such regeneration, writers especially must show people the horror of such debasement so as to awaken them and move them to act (*Obras*, 1:176). Because our education has been dominated by theology and metaphysics, we should make the "grand effort to secularize life" (*Obras*, 1:120)—an enterprise that Virgil embarked on long ago—and to cultivate positivist science (*Obras*, 1:90). To fulfill this task we must refuse to put our hope in the older generation and turn to the young: "Old men to the grave, and young men to the task at hand!" (*Obras*, 1:90). We have to renounce any expectation that the solution will come from the government or the capital: we must do away with centralism (*Obras*, 1:100). And, of course, we have to regard politics as evil and politicians as the true enemy (*Obras*, 1:175). Finally, we must never forget the injury and damage that Chile has inflicted on us, waiting our turn quietly and patiently and preparing our vengeance (*Obras*, 1:106).

Contrary to the widely accepted notion that Prada evinced great negativism against the past, the present, and the future of Peru, in *Pájinas libres* this is not so. In this book he thoroughly vindicates men such as Vigil, Grau, and Bolognesi as paradigmatic figures; he argues that Peru has very impressive material (*Obras*, 1:90) as well as spiritual (*Obras*, 1:91) potential, and that if indeed the history of many of Peru's governments can be summed up in three words—"imbecility in action"—it is also true that "the entire life of the [Peruvian] people can be characterized by three different words: "versatility in motion" (*Obras*, 1:91). The proposal that don Manuel makes is to accept almost any government "with the greatest number of individual rights and the least possible administrative action" (*Obras*, 1:175). National regeneration demands coherence among the guarantees established in the Constitution and their implementation: "the republican structure will continue to be a gratuitous phrase in a stillborn Constitution as long as the lowest Peruvian lacks freedom to express his ideas or is prevented from enjoying the right to confront those in power and censure them for their acts of extortion, their violations of law, and their injustices" (*Obras*, 1:162). The government must guarantee freedom for all and especially for the most helpless (*Obras*, 1:89). The degree of development of Peruvian society should be measured not by the wealth of a few and the distinction of a few others, but by the general well-being and the intellectual level of the masses (*Obras*, 1:172). To break with the injurious traditions of the past, Prada views revolution as the ideal path (*Obras*, 1:270), which to him means a violent step to emancipate humanity from religion (*Obras*, 1:275–276).

The political platform of the National Union published in the news-paper *Integridad* (May 16, 1891) includes a number of Prada's demands: the state should maintain the same centralized form as before but should gradually move toward federalism and decentralization, making ever more real the obligations of the executive and legislative power (I–III). The tax system should be reformed, giving preference to indirect taxes (VI), raising the social condition of the worker (VII), and return-ing lands taken from indigenous communities (VIII). The army should be brought closer to the nation (X). Freedom of conscience, freedom of the press, the right to vote, freedom to hold meetings, and freedom of association should be guaranteed (IX).

These proposals did not really go beyond those of Francisco Bilbao, who in his pamphlet *Gobierno de la libertad* (1855) proposed far more radical principles, such as a government without a representative system but based instead on committees. Prada's program was far more mod-erate and attainable, although it too was in the radical line.

His Attitude toward Death

What coherent attitude should we adopt in life toward death, given our anticlerical position? According to González Prada, we should not delude ourselves about some imagined transcendence, and we should accept "the universe in all its beauty but also in its implacable reality"— in which death figures as a natural event.

> We didn't ask for existence, but by living, we accept life. Let's accept it then without monopolizing it or wanting to eternalize it for our exclusive benefit; we laugh and make love on our parents' tombs; our children will laugh and make love on ours. ("Death and Life," in *Pájinas libres* [*Obras,* 1:287])

The Orthographic Reform of González Prada

In "Lecture at the Athenaeum of Lima" (1886), González Prada de-fended an orthographic reform and put it into practice in the first Paris edition of *Pájinas libres*. According to Julio Díaz Falconi, who has stud-ied the subject (1960), don Manuel's reform was a response to the Hispanic ideal of orthographic simplicity. He tied his reform to two postulates: (1) phonetic, which allowed him to write the way he pro-nounced *(estraño, trasporte, i, hoi, pájinas),* and (2) euphonic, which led him to exploit to the maximum the aesthetic values of Spanish orthography, reestablishing the apostrophe and contractions. In the Gonzalo-Pradian system, orthographic unity prevails because it does not eliminate vanished Spanish sounds (z, ll, v) to the advantage of others that were thought to be more genuinely Spanish American (s, y, b). Prada's reform was neither radical nor violent because it preserved both what was correct and what was common, the learned and the popular, the general and the local. It was linked to the Chilean reformist movement, especially that of Bello, and cannot be regarded as a mere act of antiacademic insubordination (*Obras,* 1:36–37).

Third Period (1891–1898)
The European Years

Residence in Europe and the Return to Lima

Prada lived in Paris from the middle of 1891 to the beginning of 1896. His son Alfredo was born on October 16. In Paris he was able to visit libraries, attend the College de France twice a week to hear Ernst Renan, whom he greatly admired, and audit classes of the positivist philosopher Louis Ménard.

Later the González Prada–de Verneuil family traveled to the south of France and from there to Barcelona, arriving there in December 1896. There Manuel met the republican Odón de Buen, who took him to the university and to a republican assembly in Reus.

The Pradas arrived in Madrid in 1897 sometime after the middle of the year. There Manuel met Pi y Margall, with whom he visited the Royal Spanish Academy, and he established contact through letters with Unamuno.

Toward the middle of December, they traveled to Burdeos, setting sail from there to Lima on March 28, 1898.

Influences on González Prada through Personal Contacts and Readings in France and Spain

The French authors of his time who exerted the greatest influence on González Prada were connected with positivism, a movement to which he himself had belonged in an earlier period. They reinforced the earlier irreligious attitudes of our author, leading him to an extreme position. Among these authors, the most important and most admired by Prada was Joseph-Ernst Renán, whose lectures on the history of the Israeli people he was able to attend twice a week.[18] Prada wrote four pieces on Renán: "Renán" (1893),[19] "El entierro de Renán [Renan's funeral]" (1899),[20] "Junto a Renán [In the company of Renán]" (1903, 1912),[21] and "Renán" (n.d.).[22] Another author from the circle of French positivism who made a great impression on Prada was Jean-Marie Guyau. Guyau wrote— among other things—*Esquisse d'une morale sans obligation ni sanction* (1885), *L'irreligion de l'avenir* (1887), and *L'art au point de vue sociologique* (1889). The first two of these are praised without restraint by González Prada, who remarks that compared with them, the writings of Renán seem old-fashioned and reactionary.[23] He cites the third in connection with an appraisal by Guyau on the novel as a genre, which González Prada thinks could be extended to poetry.[24] Elsewhere he defends Guyau (and Comte) against what he regards as unwarranted attacks by Valera.[25]

Finally, I would like to add that according to V. A. Belaunde, it was the French positivist philosopher Louis Ménard who was responsible for the paganism in *Pájinas libres* and *Exóticas*.[26]

A French writer for whom González Prada felt great admiration— an admiration that surfaced in an article he wrote on the occasion of the writer's death in 1885, prior to his trip to Paris—was Victor Hugo.[27] He also makes numerous references to Voltaire,[28] whom he regarded as Victor Hugo's seventeenth-century equivalent. He felt that he had the advantage of having written at the risk of his freedom and his life and the disadvantage of sacrificing everything for the sake of making a good joke and of exposing his adversaries' weaknesses.[29]

Among the French anarchists, González Prada mentions only, and rarely, P.-J. Proudhon,[30] E. Reclus,[31] Jean Grave,[32] and S. Faure.[33] On the other hand, he wrote an article focusing on Luisa Michel.[34] Of all these authors it is only Proudhon who seems to have had an important influence on his ideas.[35]

In France, Prada must have read the Russian anarchists Bakunin and Kropotkin, whom he also quotes on several occasions.[36] The Peruvian writer must have been drawn to Bakunin for his antireligious, antistatist, and violentist tendencies. According to Angel J. Cappelletti,

Prada's debt to Kropotkin must have been even greater: several paragraphs from his 1905 speech, "The Intellectual and the Worker," were probably little more than glosses on *La conquista del pan* [Winning one's bread]; and I would suggest that he must have borrowed some of Kropotkin's ideas on mutual aid in developing his own general notion of evolution.[37]

As for the German socialists, Hugo García Salvatecci claims that González Prada wrote his essay "The Individual"[38] under the influence of the German anarchist Max Stirner, which is quite likely. Prada must have read *Der Einzige und sein Eigenthum* (1845) in France.[39] Although no references to Marx by name occur in Prada's work, there seems to be an indirect reference (in 3:302), and there is a reference to the Marxist socialists (3:244)—at any rate the distinction that our author makes between anarchy and "depressing" socialism (as he calls it) shows that he knew his work.[40] One social democrat to whom he refers on two occasions[41] is Karl Liebknecht (1871–1919).[42]

In Spain our author had a relationship with republicans such as Odón de Buen (whom he mentions in a text from *Anarchy*[43] quoting one of his texts from 1905, indicating that he followed his development) and with Francisco Pi y Margall, a distinguished figure throughout the Iberian Peninsula because he had been president of the legislative chambers.

Another politician and publicist for the Spanish Republic who attracted Prada's attention and about whom he wrote an essay was José Nakens. In 1906 Nakens was accused of hiding the terrorist Mateo Morral, who tried to assassinate Alfonso XIII and his fiancée, Victoria Eugenia, on their wedding day and was condemned to a nine-year prison term, though he was given a pardon in 1908. Prada's 1907 article details the international pressure in favor of freeing Nakens and the paradox that in one of his newspapers, *El motín,* Nakens had spoken out against anarchist terrorist acts.[44]

With regard to the Spanish anarchists, González Prada wrote a piece on Fermín Salvochea (or Salvoechea) on the occasion of his death on September 28, 1907,[45] recalling his life and actions. He also mentions the Italian terrorist Miguel Angiolillo[46] and Mateo Morral, as already noted.

Among Spanish writers, González Prada fixed his attention on Valera, Castelar, and Núñez de Arce, dedicating an article to each of them.[47] He has reservations about the three,[48] though he acknowledges

Valera's merits as a translator and indicates that Núñez de Arce impresses him as being "the true standard bearer of Castilian poetry."[49] On the other hand, his judgment of Castelar is totally negative. He finds him guilty of three great sins: ruining the language, history, and politics of Spain.[50]

Among the British writers and intellectuals whom Prada cites are Shakespeare, Spencer, and Darwin; and among the Germans, Goethe, Heine, and Schopenhauer.[51] Although he surely read many of these authors in Peru, others he must have read for the first time especially in France and Spain.

Final Period (1898–1918)
The Radical-Anarchist Years

From Leader of the National Union Party to Anarchist Leader: The Directorship of the National Library

On August 21, 1898, Prada gave his speech "The Parties and the National Union." A second speech scheduled for August 27, "Free-Thought in Action" was blocked by Piérola. Since there were no journalistic publications available to Prada, he founded the newspaper *Germinal* and then *El Independiente*, both of which were shut down.

In 1902 Prada resigned from the National Union and after 1904 began to associate and collaborate with anarchist groups. In 1908 Prada published *Horas de lucha, Presbiterianas* the following year, anonymously, and in 1911 his collection of poems, *Exóticas*.

Don Manuel was appointed director of the National Library of Peru on March 6, 1912, following a minor scandal in which Ricardo Palma resigned from the post. Prada in turn resigned from the position on February 15, 1914, as a protest against the coup d'état by Colonel Oscar R. Benavides. He was reappointed on February 1, 1916, shortly after the restoration of constitutional government in Peru.

Manuel González Prada died of heart failure on July 22, 1918.

The Radical-Anarchist Thought of González Prada

THE BREAK WITH THE NATIONAL UNION

On his return from Europe, Prada gave his speech "The Parties and the National Union" (August 21, 1898) attacking the inept leaders who had ruled Peru as well as the existing parties; he distinguished between the socialist concept of revolutions, which views them as a product of profound, sorrowful action by the people, events that "spill blood but create light," and the concept of revolution that existed in Peru, in which neither Pardo nor Piérola managed to change anything, in don Manuel's opinion. For these reasons Prada urged the National Union to distinguish its actions from those of the existing parties. Evincing a perceptible anarchist influence, he suggested that the program of the National Union could be summed up in two phrases: "evolution in the direction of the highest freedom for the individual, valuing social reforms over political transformations" (*Obras*, 3:32). Paraphrasing the social democrat Karl Liebknecht, he argued that "the world today tends to be divided, not between republicans and monarchists or between liberals and conservatives, but into two great segments: the haves and the have-nots, the exploiters and the exploited" (*Obras*, 3:33). Because of this, the members of the National Union should not be dazzled by political events such as elections. He argued that on the international level it was necessary to see things clearly: to demand justice with regard to the hostile attitudes of the Chileans and to prepare for a possible confrontation—this last notion evincing a perspective different from that of the anarchists.

Prada was forced to acknowledge that many of the members of the National Union were unwilling to postpone their political ambitions for the sake of working for social reforms and, consequently, that they were even disposed to collude with clerics and pierolists. Because of this, early in 1902 he distanced himself from the National Union.[52] Later he said in an interview with Félix del Valle (1916) that he never deluded himself or had any faith in the members of his party. He knew them well enough to know that they were not men of ideas or ideals but men of appetites, without loyalty or honor (in *Obras*, 7:484).

The Analysis of Peruvian Problems: Our Miseries

Prada was not a social researcher nor did he have any scientific methodology that would have allowed him to conduct an objective analysis of the reality of Peru. Rather, he was a great writer who, as such, could only achieve such an analysis by describing and critiquing what he observed based on the reading he had done. This analysis makes up a fundamental part of his work, and this second period of his production is to be found in particular in the second part of *Horas de lucha*, which offers a crushing inventory of Peruvian miseries. To conduct this analysis, he selects different social and political types and catalogs their weaknesses with passionate fervor.

In this way he describes the *journalists* who, though they hold no administrative posts or public functions, nonetheless influence public opinion decisively. Peruvian journalists embody no principles, only corruption, ignorance, and a total lack of honor and sincerity (*Obras*, 3: 89–97). Our *conservatives* are marked on the one hand by sterility of science and poverty of literature, and on the other by fecundity and wealth of insolence, insult, mendacity, and calumny (3:99–108). Our *liberals* have held firmly to a zigzagging line and have been deficient in brain power, so their party has died (3:109–119). Our people live deceived, like all the peoples of the world, thinking that the parliamentary system is the beginning and guarantee of the kingdom of freedom. The truth is that living more than eighty years under this system demonstrates to us that Peru's greatest ignominy is not that we lost the war with Chile but that we have had to put up with so many speechmakers with nothing to say, so many moralizers without morality, and so many sages without the least bit of sagacity—our *legislators* (3:131–36). Our *aristocrats* are adherents of Catholicism, a real stigma: they are totally plebian (3:137–142). Our *bedouins* are the *evil politicians* who have ruined Peru (3:143–46). Our *tigers* are the military and police, who have been granted a monopoly in the use of force—real monsters who have perpetrated bloody crimes (3:147–154). Above all, Lima is full of *gluttonous oligarchs* who purchase their prosperity from the misery of the people (3:155–160). Like our bullfighting fans, who neither love nor sympathize with animals, they don't harbor any tender feelings toward human beings (3:173–78). Our public men are veritable *glass lawyers,* who cover up their real vices, feign false virtues, and fear criticism, showing that they are made of fragile, brittle glass, so they have to curtail the rights of their critics (3:185). Finally, the *Church* has opposed every great reform and blocked any separation between itself and the state as well as the process of secularization (3:211–18).

Unlike the behavior and character of the types and institutions mentioned above, the Indians—the true Peruvians according to Prada— have real virtues, not the racial or cultural inferiority attributed to them by so-called scientific sociology. The solution to the problem of the

Indian does not lie in educational measures—as don Manuel believed earlier in *Pájinas libres* (1:89)—but in economic measures (3:209). The liberation of the Indian must come about as a result of his own efforts, not those of his oppressors.

González Prada wrote many texts opposing clericalism, but it is not worthwhile to reiterate them: the main points have been made. On the other hand, for him, one of the greatest miseries of Peru is centralism. Lima is a suck hole that swallows down all the country's resources; simultaneously, it is a "rotten core" that corrupts all the provincials who come there and spreads all kinds of sick germs throughout the republic. Hence, the act of disinfecting the national body cannot come from Lima but only from the provinces (*Obras*, 2:462).

The Analysis of the Peruvian Problems: Caporalism

We have seen that already in *Pájinas libres* Prada claimed that "Caporalismo," the tyranny of the military, is our true form of government. His reflections on militarism in Peru were set down in thematic form in the articles that he wrote in 1914 in response to the coup d'état by Colonel Oscar R. Benavides.[53] The author was prevented from publishing these articles during his lifetime.[54]

According to Prada, Peru has been pervaded by a mentality that looks to the benevolent dictator as the panacea for all our ills. If the deification of brute force is perhaps comprehensible in the military, it being an atavistic entity adhering to cave man–style justice, it doesn't work for civilized persons. Tyrannies boast of honor and economy but are corrupt; they work on behalf of a particular class, caste, or family to the detriment of the masses; they try or pretend to solve problems, but only resolve them in appearance and only temporarily, leaving a legacy of national and international wars; they corrupt either through servility or fear; and they weaken the will of the people, stifle free expression, and impose the silence of the tomb (*Obras*, 2:426). To this we might add that, because there has never existed a Caesar or a classical tyrant in Peru, what we get are petty tyrants who loot the Constitution and the Treasury.

Caporalism represents a degradation of militarism, or militarism elevated to the power of two: if the military man is a professional of death, the *caporal* is nothing but the upholder of illegal governments. Yet this has been the customary phenomenon in Latin America, where the lowest foot soldier dreams of becoming another Porfirio Díaz (*Obras*, 2:427). Moreover, the *caporales* are ignorant, primitive brutes who never back away from any crime, as in the case of Suleiman II—the nickname Prada gives to Benavides.

What factors produce a mentality that facilitates the seizure of power by a *caporal?* Who makes caporalism possible? The gamut of those responsible is broad and varied, according to Prada. Among them we find "honest Catholic matrons, incapable of infidelity to their husbands, but who are distinguished professors of household immorality" and who educate their children in the most odious kind of servility and pragmatism, whose emblematic instructional motto is "shut up and eat, dummy" (*Obras*, 2:437–440); venal journalists who lavish praise on anyone in power or any powerful entrepreneur in exchange for subventions from the government, banks, or corporations and who, given the chance, will play the role of secret police, *agents provocateurs*, and even pose as moralists; "men dedicated to this profession [journalism], no matter how much talent and dignity they have, inevitably end up cheapening, prostituting, and debasing themselves" (2:420–21); Congress too—the ultimate sinkhole for all the sewer rats in the republic—is made up of "honorable men" with a hankering for everything who sell themselves and defer to the executive branch, as happened with the representatives who "elected" Benavides; and, finally, the professors who rather than genuine educators or shapers of souls are enthusiasts of the common soldier—hence it comes about that the primary schools, lyceums, and universities produce "a swarm of intellectual and moral savages" (2:433).

Caporalism breeds pseudo-revolutions which are never more than military uprisings that perpetuate and even worsen the exploitation of the Indian (the republic included blacks and Chinese in that exploitation), which according to Prada has made Peru the most debased nation in all of South America (*Obras*, 2:446).

The Anarchy of González Prada

Prada begins his treatment of the topic by removing two negative meanings from the word "anarchy": (1) the state of habitual disorder, permanent war, and the return to primitive savagery; and (2) the act of individual or collective violence. Those ideas must be distinguished from the anarchist ideal, which can be "summed up in two phrases:

unlimited freedom and the greatest possible good for the individual, brought about by the abolition of the State and private property" (*Obras,* 3:228). This ideal rests on a premise that may be suspect: the optimism and the faith that the anarchist places in the natural goodness of the human being.

The anarchist conducts an implacable critique of all authority because he sees that its use is perverse: "Nothing is so corrupting or debasing as the exercise of authority, however brief and minimal it may be" (*Obras,* 3:251). Moreover, "authority implies abuse, and obedience implies degradation" (3:228). Authority most commonly presents itself is in the guise of God-state (2:247, 347). But there are other forms as well, including that of God-Church (3:242, 347). In this regard Prada writes that "anarchy is neither religious nor irreligious. It merely wishes to extirpate atavistic religiosity, that perverse regressive factor, from the human brain" (3:242). There is also God-humanity as preached by Comte and even the sovereignty of the people (God-People), which according to Prada is the most absurd of all (3:228).

The anarchist also combats the institution of private property, which (as Proudhon argued) is theft (*Obras,* 3:240). But there is really no need to resort to such an extreme point of view, since even the declared enemies of anarchy today deny the *traditional and sacred* right of the individual to own property. The reason is clear enough: if it was the entire human race that conquered and urbanized the earth and accumulated capital, then it is the human race in its entirety that should inherit that legacy: what belongs to everyone belongs to everyone (3: 240–41). Just as it's ridiculous for me to speak of *my* steamship, *my* electricity, *my* Parthenon, and so on, it's a mistake for people to refer to *their* forest, *their* estate, *their* factory, or even *their* house. Thus it is necessary to criticize and abandon such extreme egotism. But anarchy does indeed acknowledge individual interests, and it seeks only to organize property and society harmoniously. It understands property as a mere social function (3:239–241).

The anarchy of González Prada makes an equally sharp distinction between anarchy and what he calls depressing, authoritarian socialism, though he argues that at times both can work together to impose certain rights, such as the eight-hour day (*Obras,* 3:288). There are six major differences between socialism and anarchy. First, socialism believes that everything can be changed through a great, sudden, and instantaneous upheaval in the social order (its notion of revolution), while anarchy thinks that the power of bourgeois society can only be overcome little by little and by virtue of many successive assaults (3:287, 239). Second, socialism is as oppressive and regimented as the state, while anarchy rejects all regimentation and subjection of the individual to the laws of the majority (3:288). Third, socialism gives highest priority to politics (i.e., to the seizing of power), while for anarchy the thing that matters most is the vast process of human emancipation, within which the social factor outweighs the political (3:243, 280, 288). Fourth, anarchy, unlike socialism, does not regard the evolution of history as a series of economic struggles (3:240). Fifth, whereas anarchy is opposed to the idea of "country" and is, hence, genuinely internationalist and thus opposed on principle to militarism, socialism sometimes tries to reconcile the irreconcilable: internationalism and nationalism (3:293, 288–89). And sixth, socialism preaches a violent, worldwide revolution that has a quasi-religious character, whereas anarchy maintains that the process of human emancipation does not involve these characteristics (3:232–233, 236–238).

Once he has established these distinctions with bourgeois individualism (i.e., liberalism) and with depressing socialism (i.e., Marxism), Prada can move on to a positive characterization of anarchy. Anarchy seeks, as already noted, the unlimited freedom of the human being. This is equivalent to saying that the individual should not be subjected to the state, nor to the Church, nor to humanity, nor to the people—as well as the greatest possible well-being, that is, individual happiness. The human being has a right to happiness that is not engraved in bibles or in laws, but in our hearts (*Obras,* 3:242). The decisive embodiment of anarchy is the individual, who rejects laws, religions, and nationalities (3:228). Until now the individual has been kept from becoming absolute master of his person through an excess of government, laws, and religions (3:244). It is necessary now that we take possession of the self (argues Prada, echoing Max Stirner) because we do not belong to mankind nor to any collectivity at all but only to ourselves (3:349). Going a step further, he points out that we can live egotistically, idolizing ourselves and making our ego the center of the universe, or altruistically sacrificing ourselves for the ones we love and to whom we give ourselves through a personal act of will. Anarchy opts for the second possibility: for mutual aid, and in this sense it expands the Christian idea as well as Darwinism properly understood. In this there's an echo of the later Kropotkin (3:228–29). Going a step even beyond Kropotkin and approaching Proudhon once again, Prada argues that reciprocal protection does not constitute a universal or cosmic law, but an act of justice exclusive to man, or to put it more precisely, to some men (3:350): the anarchists.

To summarize, anarchy does not regard evolution and revolution as two diametrically opposed concepts, but rather a single line traced in the same direction. At times it is straight and at other times curved. Since the Reformation, the civilized world has been living in a state of latent revolution: of philosophy against dogma, of the individual against the state, of the worker against capital, of woman against the tyranny of man, of both sexes against the enslavement of love and the prison of marriage (*Obras,* 3:304–305). In backward countries such as those in South America, the anarchist revolution is presented with a triple character: religious, political, and social (3:240). From the perspective of González Prada, working in this respect under the influence of Proudhon, the most important of the three is the third, as noted earlier.

The absurd and tragic dualism between theoretical man and practical man brings about the antagonism between the intellectual and the worker. Instead of moving ahead on separate paths and regarding each other as enemies, the two ought to walk together, inseparably conjoined, since both are workers: the first works with his mind, the second with his hands (*Obras,* 3:51ff., 236; 1:357). Even so, this separation necessitates a division of revolutionary labor: the intellectual comes up with the ideas that the worker must then implement, so the revolution in ideas must precede the revolution in actions (3:236). This does not imply that intellectuals should set themselves up as tutors or guides to the workers (3:53) or expect the world to move in the direction they want and as far as they dictate (3:54). If revolutions come from above, inspired by the ideas worked out by the intellectuals, they are implemented from below by the oppressed. After receiving the initial push, they follow their own course, moving far beyond the point imagined and desired by those who inspired them. "Hence, there emerges a quite general phenomenon in history: those who seem audacious and progressive in initiating a revolution, come across as timid and reactionary in the clamor of the struggle or in the hour of triumph" (3:54–55). In fact, the intellectuals are quickly overwhelmed by the masses. When Humanity moves into action, it starts beheading its leaders. With great foresight regarding what was to happen in the Russian Revolution, Prada wrote in 1905:

> Every revolution once established tends to become a government by force, and every triumphant revolutionary degenerates into a conservative. Was there ever an idea that wasn't debased when implemented? Was there ever a reformer who wasn't corrupted by power? Men (in particular political men) never give what they promise, nor does the reality of struggle ever correspond to the illusions of the dispossessed. The discredit of a revolution starts on the same day as its triumph; and those who discredit it are its own leaders. (*Obras*, 3:55)

Prada agreed with Spencer that "the great political superstition of yesterday—the divine right of kings—has been superseded by the great political superstition of today—the divine right of parliaments" (3:244). But he argued that parliamentarianism had already fallen into discredit in his epoch.

As noted earlier, don Manuel believed with Karl Liebknecht that the world today knows only two nations: the exploiters and the exploited. Those who hold power and fear some political or social convulsion provoke international crises and invoke *love of country*, meaning love of territory or love of traditions. Another pretext used to justify neglect of the demands of the oppressed is respect for *public order*. But the glorifiers of military and police forces do not deserve to be believed, and we should banish war as an act of prehistoric barbarism as well as any repressive use of police against workers (*Obras*, 3:261–265, 257–260). In order for them to have their rights guaranteed, their strikes should be, in González Prada's opinion, general and armed (*Obras*, 3:291).

Prada indicts capitalist society, in regard to both public order and social order, as a reality based on force, whereby he concludes that it ought to be opposed by another reality: its overthrow, also by force. In such a society there is latent aggression by the haves against the have-nots. Since humankind rarely sacrifices its own interest for the sake of conviction, the use of force is justified. This argument justifies individual action: violent acts against tyrants, monopolies, or unscrupulous negotiators is perfectly legitimate. Even so, it is necessary to distinguish between individual action against those who personify authority and against authority that does not impinge on them personally. "But whether we approve or disapprove of a violent act, we cannot fail to acknowledge the generosity and heroism in the propagandists for action, in the righteous avengers who offer their lives to punish atrocities not suffered by them personally" (*Obras,* 3:319). Thus "the Angiolillos, the Brescis, the assassins of the Grand Duke Sergio, and those who executed king Manuel are more deserving of our sympathy than Ravachol, Emil Henry, and Morral" (3:317).[55] When Prada learned of the actions of the Spanish anarchists and republicans, he revised his perspective on Spain, pointing out that in reality there are two Spains: the old and the new (4:409).

With Proudhon, González Prada argues that the most luminous quality of an anarchist society is justice, which consists of giving each man what legitimately belongs to him. "Tomorrow, when waves of proletariats rush into combat against the walls of the old society, the oppressors will say: *'It's the inundation of barbarians!'* But a voice, made up of the din of countless voices, will respond: *'We aren't the inundation of barbarians, we're the flood of justice'*" (*Obras,* 2:58–59).

Prada's literary diagnosis of the terrible ills besetting Peru at the beginning of the century does not mean that he was pessimistic regarding the possibilities inherent in the oppressed majority. In 1905 he denied that "our entire people are the venal rabble evoked by our electoral platforms; many are healthy and longing to direct themselves toward something new and fecund" (*Obras,* 3:255). He also believed that the terrain was ripe for the reception of anarchist ideas, since in South America and Peru there were no deeply ingrained traditions working against any germination of the new as they did in the old societies (3:256).

THE FINAL TEMPTATION: SKEPTICISM

Prada adhered to positivism almost from the beginning of the development of his thought, and thus he was subjected early on to the attack of skepticism. In "A Moment of Philosophy" (*Obras,* 1:345–351), a text written probably between 1884 and 1888, he defends the seriousness of skepticism and maintains that we do not know reality but only appearances. In a note from *El tonel de Diógenes* (published posthumously in 1945) he claims that we are only capable of grasping provisional truths. The cognitive skepticism of don Manuel, then, was profound during the later stages of the first period of his thought. Following his trip to Europe, Prada fell subject to another doubt that began to eat away at his certainty about the nonexistence of God and the impossibility of some kind of an afterlife. In another note from *El tonel de Diógenes* he writes, "With regard to dubious matters such as God and our destiny, the true thinker does not hold fast to fixed beliefs but lives his life fluctuating between successive opinions" (*Obras*, 2:198). And in an interview he gave to Félix del Valle two years before his death, he made a confession.

> Prada: A curious thing has happened to me. In my youth I was a resolute, confirmed atheist . . . Later, on my trip to Europe, I'm not sure whether because of reflection on the intractability of the convictions of the muse or for inexplicable reasons, I began to have doubts . . .
> *Del Valle: And do those doubts persist? Don't you believe in God?"*
> Prada: The truth is that there are days when I doubt and days when . . . but generally I don't believe. (7:489)

González Prada's Reception, Influence, and Legacy

There is general agreement about the literary importance of González Prada's prose (and also about his poetry, but we won't be considering that here), not only in Peru but also in Spanish America. Unamuno wrote that he knew few authors, either American or non-American, who had more power to stir the mind than Prada; Blanco-Fombana praised his sculpted prose, his marmolean, musical style, his poetic and scientific imagination; Anderson-Imbert maintained that his cutting, wiry prose had no equal in Spain and America. There is also widespread consensus about the extraordinary coherence between the life and work of Prada: Victor Andrés Belaunde, for example, claimed that in Prada there is a lovely balance between his thought and his life, as well as a princely attitude of unyielding dignity; and José Carlos Mariátegui observed that the men of his generation admired his austere moral example, his intellectual honesty, and his noble and powerful rebelliousness.[56]

Here the agreement ends and the differences of opinion and criticism begin. From the right, Riva-Agüero has argued that Prada was intransigent in literary matters, intolerant with regard to religion, and incapable of taking action in politics. V. García Calderón accused him of being the least national and representative of Peruvian writers, of having a destructive aesthetic, and of having been a revolutionary nihilist. For all that, he maintained that although his generation was closer to Prada than to Palma in emotional terms, he could not accept him as his guide. Finally, and from the center-right, the young Victor Andrés Balaunde denounced Prada's thought as a radical deviation, claiming it was the product of learned naïveté that would have led to disdain for religious anxiety, abhorrence of Christianity, and the deification of science. All this would have led to intolerance and sectarianism, creating a Jacobin cancer. Years later, Belaunde added that there is in Prada an even more essential Spanish-ness than in Palma. Prada was in the deepest sense a typical Spaniard: "This was evident by virtue of his emphatic character, his individualism, and his dogmatism."[57]

On the other hand, from the left Mariátegui concluded that Prada had constituted the "first lucid moment" in Peruvian consciousness, but at the same time he held him responsible for having failed in the organization of Peruvian radicalism, for not having conducted a study of the national reality, for having cultivated a shallow anticlericalism, and for adhering to a decrepit ideology. L. A. Sánchez saw in Prada a human being endowed with the gamut of human grandeur and misery, and among the latter he noted his racial prejudices, his easy accommodation to his role as landlord, and the individualist basis of his anarchy. The young Mario Vargas Llosa noted in his turn that Prada's merits were many (e.g., he had elaborated a conception of the writer from the point of view of what we now term *engagé*, a literature of commitment) but found it appalling that he traveled to Europe in May 1891, almost immediately after founding the National Union Party.[58]

The severest criticism comes from the historian Jorge Basadre. For him, don Manuel was a bourgeois with a chip on his shoulder of the type defined by Nietzsche and Scheler—an apostate who lived only for the destruction of the class from which he came, and displayed a strong streak of snobbishness in F. Werfel's sense of the term. In Prada there may also have existed a striking contrast between his public life of rebellious bourgeois and his private life of a methodical, dandified married man.[59]

Prada has had an enormous influence on Peruvian literature, political thought, and politics. His ideas on literature, the Indian, and anticlericalism had a vigorous effect on writers such as Mercedes Cabello de Carbonera and Clorinda Matto de Turner, both of whom belonged to the Literary Circle.[60] Prada also influenced Enrique López Albújar, who in 1898 presented his doctoral disseration, "La injusticia en la propiedad del suelo" [Injustice in land ownership], at the University of San Marcos and had it rejected as "anarchist."[61] He held great fascination for later poets and writers as dissimilar as Chocano, Valdelomar, Eguren, and Vallejo.

In Peruvian political thought, Prada's ideas on the harmful influence of Lima and on the need for decentralization had great success in the provinces, as we can easily understand. Already in 1905 José de la Riva-Agüero was astonished at the popularity of Prada's writings outside the Peruvian capital, a fact he attributed to provincial backwardness and to the destructive content of his ideas (1905: 251–53).

Finally, the thought of González Prada had a powerful influence in politics: in the anarchist groups, which had a certain viability until their disappearance after 1927 due to the split in the workers movement and harsh repressive measures by the dictator Leguía,[62] and especially in APRA, where Víctor Raúl Haya de la Torre took from Prada the idea that intellectuals as well as laborers are "workers" (the former work with their intellects, the latter with their hands). And he baptized the popular universities that he founded with the name of González Prada.[63]

How much of González Prada's thought has died, and how much lives on? (Here I apply the classic formula used for the first time by Croce to the case of Hegel.) I am referring in particular to the radical ideas of don Manuel formulated during his anarchist period. The following seem quite dead: (1) González Prada's anticlericalism, when it turns virulent.[64] (2) His excessive insistence that writers participate in politics "so as to discredit, dissolve, and destroy it," and his overestimation of intellectuals as "thinkers and isolated individuals" who are capable of discovering from their ivory towers the ideas[65] that the revolutionary masses are to implement down below. (3) The absence of a realistic political program for the division and distribution of power. (4) The absence of any economic program. (5) His overestimation of the individual and the rights of the individual. (6) His justification of violence by the individual. (7) His belief in a convergence between the trajectories of evolution and of revolution.

On the other hand, the following ideas of González Prada seem alive and viable: (1) His analysis of Peru as a country in a deep crisis of long duration, due to multiple factors, chief among which is militarism. (2) His conviction that in order to overcome these ills, it is necessary to *modernize* Peru (as we would express it today) or, to use Prada's words, to *secularize* Peru. (3) His rejection of the power incarnate in the state, in the churches, and in political dogmas, such as the unlimited sovereignty of the people. (4) His critique of the concept of property. (5) His strong critique of authoritarian socialism. (6) His idea that to revolutionize social, political, and economic structures human beings first have to transform themselves. (7) His conviction that revolution does not consist of a single upheaval in the status quo, but that since the Reformation there have been several revolutions: (*a*) philosophy against dogma; (*b*) the citizen against the state; (*c*) the worker against the exploitation of capital; (*d*) woman against the tyranny of man; (*e*) both sexes against the enslavement of love and the prison of marriage. (8) His priority of *universalism* over *communitarianism*—as we would express it now—or of *internationalism* over the idea of *country*—as Prada expressed it.[66] (9) His condemnation of war.

As we can see, Prada's thought remains profoundly alive.

—David Sobrevilla
(tr. F. Fornoff)

REFERENCES

Alarco, Luis Felipe. 1952. "Manuel González Prada." In *Pensadores peruanos,* 51–74. Lima: Sociedad Peruana de Filosofía.

Anderson-Imbert, Enrique. 1978. *Historia de la literatura hispoamericana,* 1:338–340. México: FCE.

Basadre, Jorge. 1994. *Perú: Problema y posibilidad.* Lima: Fundación Bustamante de la Fuente.

Belaunde, V. A. 1987. *Meditaciones peruanas.* In *Obras completas,* 2:187–99. Lima: Comisión Nacional del Centenario.

———. [1931] 1991. *La realidad nacional,* 109–111. Lima: Horizonte.

Blanco-Fombona, Rufino. 1915. Prologue to *Páginas libres.* In Manuel González Prada, *Páginas libres,* vii–lxxxix. Madrid: Sociedad Española del Libro.

Cappelletti, A. J. 1990. "Manuel González Prada." In *El anarquismo en América Latina,* xciv–cxii. Caracas: Ayacucho.

Cornejo Polar, Antonio. 1992. *Clorinda Matto de Turner, novelista.* Lima: Lluvia.

Díaz Falconi, Julio. 1960. *La reforma ortográfica de González Prada.* Annex 3 of *Sphinx.* Lima. 13 pp.

García Calderón, Ventura. 1910. "Un 'ensayista': Manuel González Prada." In *Del romanticismo al modernismo: Prosistas y poetas peruanos,* 387–399. París: Ollendorff.

——. 1946. *Nosotros.* París: Garnier. [On González Prada: 33–42].

García Salvatecci, Hugo. 1972. *El pensamiento de González Prada.* Lima: Arica. The second edition of this book—rewritten but not substantially changed—has been published with the title *Visión de un apóstol: Pensamiento del maestro González Prada.* Lima: Emisa, 1990.

González, F. B. 1895. *Páginas razonables.* Lima: Centro de Propaganda Católica. Two pamphlets of eighty-seven and eighty-eight pages, respectively.

González Prada, Manuel. 1985–1989. *Obras.* Edition, prologue, and notes by Luis A. Sánchez. 7 vols. Lima: COPE.

Guyau, Jean-Marie. [1889] 1943. *El arte desde el punto de vista sociológico.* Buenos Aires: Suma.

Kristal, Efraín. 1986. "Problemas filológicos e históricos en *Páginas libres* de González Prada." *Revista de crítica literaria latinoamericana* 23: 141–150.

Mariátegui, José Carlos. 1972. "González Prada" In *Siete ensayos de interpretación de la realidad peruana,* 254–265. Lima: Amauta.

Oviedo, José Miguel. 1997. "Apocalíptico de fin de siglo." *Debate* 95 (July–August): 44–46.

Palma, Ricardo. 1888. "La propaganda de la difamación." *El Comercio,* November 13, 4.

Pareja, Piedad. 1978. *Anarquismo y sindicalismo en el Perú (1904–1919).* Lima: Rikchay.

Pi y Margall, F. 1968. *Pensamiento social.* Madrid: Ciencia Nueva.

Pinto Gamboa, W. 1985. *Manuel González Prada: Profeta olvidado (seis entrevistas y un apunte).* Lima: Cibeles. Now in Manuel González Prada. *Obras,* 7:465–561. Lima: COPE, 1989.

Podestá Airaldi, Bruno. 1975. "Breve noticia sobre su vida y otras coordenadas." In *Pensamiento político de González Prada,* 17–52. Lima: INC.

Riva-Agüero, José de la. [1905] 1962. *Carácter de la literatura del Perú independiente.* In *Obras completas* 1:59–308. Lima: PUC.

Sánchez, Luis A. 1930. *Don Manuel.* Lima: Rosay. There are later editions.

——. 1977. *"Nuestras vidas son los ríos..." Historia y leyenda de los González Prada.* Lima: San Marcos. Edición definitiva: Lima: Banco de Comercio, 1986.

Sanders, Karen. 1997. "Manuel González Prada." In *Nación y tradición:*

Cinco discursos en torno a la nación peruana 1885–1930, 197–242. Lima: PUC.

Stirner, Max. [1845] N.d. *El único y su propiedad.* Valencia: Sempere.

Tamayo Herrera, José. 1982. *Historia social del indigenismo en el Altiplano.* Lima: Treintitrés.

Unamuno, Miguel de. [1906] 1962. "Manuel González Prada." In "Consideraciones sobre la literatura hispano-americana." In J. de la Riva-Agüero. *Obras completas,* 1:357–362. Lima: PUC, 1962.

Tamayo Vargas, Augusto. N.d. *Literatura peruana.* Lima: Godart.

NOTES

1. These were collected by Willy Pinto G. (1985).

2. *Pájinas libres,* 1894 and 1915 (actually, it was Rufino Blanco-Fombona who published this second edition), and *Horas de Lucha,* 1908; *Minúsculas,* 1909, in an edition of only a hundred copies, *Presbiterianas,* 1909, anonymously, and *Exóticas* in 1911.

3. García Salvatecci (1972, 1990).

4. *Obras* (Lima: COPE, 1985–1989). This edition is divided into three tomes and seven volumes. It poses a number of problems (discussed in part by Efraín Kristal in his note, "Problemas filológicos e históricos en *Pájinas libres* by Manuel González Prada" (Kristal 1986, 141–150). I will, however, be using and citing from this edition. As no reason for its division into tomes is apparent, I will simply refer to the volume and the page number, separated by a colon.

5. Cappelletti 1990. The author discusses González Prada on pages XCIV–CXII and anthologizes his works on pages 266–331.

6. Such is the claim of Efraín Kristal in the note cited earlier, especially on pages 144–148.

7. Sanders 1997, 215, 225, 240.

8. Oviedo 1997, 44–46.

9. García Salvatecci 1972, 18–20.

10. The ideological options following the independence of Peru have been studied by Jorge Basadre (1994, 71–115).

11. Adriana de Verneuil claims that her husband had wanted to visit Europe for several years. Since the public welfare office had purchased a house from the family at about that time, the trip became a possibility; besides, Prada had not been bound to the National Union Party because it had been his intention to form a party of principles, without chiefs (González Prada 1947, 166). Prada, in 1916, explains that he never trusted the members of his party and that one day he noticed that their ambitions were beginning to be exploitative, so he preferred to leave for Europe (*Obras* 7:484). Vargas Llosa claims that Prada

knew or intuited that anyone committing himself to action would be obliged, at least once, to dirty his hands, and was afraid to run that risk (Vargas Llosa 1958, 13, 50). Finally, according to Bruno Podestá, there are reasons to believe that Adriana's pressure on him to travel to Europe was the determining factor (Podestá 1975, 33).

12. The original version appears in *El Ateneo de Lima* 1 (1886): 28–47. The definitive version is in *Pájinas libres,* in *Obras,* 1:35–49.

13. As mentioned in note 8, Kristal claims that at the time he delivered his "Lecture at the Athenaeum of Lima," Prada enjoyed very good relations with Palma, since he praised him in the speech. This is true: don Manuel acknowledges that Palma interprets Heine in bringing "the treasure of other nations into the Spanish language" (Palma had translated Heine's poems from the French version of Gerard de Nerval in his *Enrique Heine* [1886]), but his later criticism in the definitive version of the speech could already be perceived between the lines, as Prada argues that those who imitate and slavishly copy Bécquer are not Germanists or Germanizers but Teutomaniacs (1886, 37). Subsequently Prada left no room for confusion, asserting that those who translate Heine from French do not deserve to be called Germanists or Germanizers but Teutomaniacs, an indictment he later repeats against those who translate Heine from French (*Obras,* 1:46), and he openly criticizes archaism and old-fashioned writing, which is undoubtedly a dig at Palma. Palma must have noticed Prada's malicious intent, but he did not react until after Prada's speech in the Olympus Theater two years later, when he wrote the anonymous article, "The Propaganda of Defamation," which appeared in *El Comercio* (1888, 4).

14. Efraín Kristal denied in "Problemas filológicos" that there was any antagonism between the Club Literario and the Círculo Literario around 1886, since Prada was vice president of both groups at that time. But two years later Ricardo Palma confirmed the existence of this antagonism in the anonymous reply that he published to Prada's speech at the Olympus Theater, indicating that the group of young writers around Prada "constitute a distinct association or circle" (Palma 1888, 4).

The supposed connection between Prada and the Civilists between 1873 and 1888 is belied by several circumstances: (1) Don Manuel removed the honorific *de* from his name in 1871 and signed himself simply "Manuel G. Prada." (2) Between 1871 and 1879 Prada scarcely lived in Lima at all, but rather in Tútume; between 1879 and 1881 he enlisted for obligatory service in the defense of the capital; and between 1881 and 1883 he didn't leave his house, so there was little opportunity for him to interact with the Civilist intellectuals. (3) In the lecture at the Athenaeum of Lima in 1886 Prada declared himself a socialist (1886, 42), a declaration that he eliminated from the definitive version of the speech. (4) In that same speech he championed the young members of the Círculo Literario against the members of the Athenaeum. That Prada agreed in 1873 to participate in the founding of the Club Literario—along with certain intellectuals who belonged to the Civilist party—is of little significance: that connection was not political in nature but cultural, and at the time there was no other important literary center in which to participate.

15. Juan Bustamente Dueñas: "The Peruvian nation is not an association of individuals who live on the Peruvian coast—those aren't the people who make up the republic. The nation has numerous peoples in the interior and these peoples are the Indians. The nation consists of a huge number of Indians who surpass by far the number of Whites who live on the Pacific coast; Indians as well as Whites contribute to conducting the affairs of State" (*Los indios del Perú* [1867]; cited by Tamayo Herrera 1982, 297).

16. González Prada: "The real Peru isn't made up of the groups of *criollos* and foreigners living on the strip of land situated between the Pacific and the Andes; the nation is made up of the masses of Indians living on the eastern slopes of the mountains" ("Speech at the Politeama," in *Obras*, 1:89).

17. The *Baladas Peruanas* were collected and published for the first time in 1935 by Luis Alberto Sánchez—an edition that has been reproduced in *Obras* (Lima: COPE, 1988), 5:387–468. According to Sánchez, Prada succeeded in publishing three of his ballads, with the titles "La cena de Atahualpa," "Las flechas del Inca," and "El mitayo," in *El correo del Perú* (*Obras*, 5:392)—which began to appear in 1871.

18. The reference appears in "Junto a Renán" (*Obras*, 2:378).

19. In *Obras*, 1:191–208.

20. In *Obras*, 2:89–92.

21. Now in *Obras*, 1:376–382.

22. In *Obras*, 2:161.

23. In *Obras*, 1:201.

24. Guyau remarked that the experimental novel of the nineteenth century came about as a consequence of the scientific evolution of the century (Guyau 1943, 175); Prada argues that a book of verse should also reflect the scientific spirit (in *Obras*, 1:342).

25. In *Obras*, 1:225.

26. Belaunde 1991, III.

27. In *Obras*, 1:181–190. Unamuno found such admiration excessive and partial and some of the Prada's opinions on Hugo atrocious to a fault. See his article, "Algunas consideraciones sobre la literatura hispano-americana; A propósito de un libro peruano," in José de la Riva-Agüero 1962; 1:358.

28. In *Obras*, 1:188, 241, 251, 364, 366, 394, among others.

29. In *Obras*, 1:188–189.

30. In *Anarquía* (*Obras*, 3:230); and to his famous dictum, "Property is theft," in *Obras*, 3:240.

31. In *Obras*, 1:468; 3:229, 235, 256.

32. In *Obras*, 1:468; 3:229, 235, 256.

33. In *Obras*, 3:229, 287.

34. In *Obras*, 3:333, 335.

35. Prada assimilates his propositions on the predominance of the social factor over the political and economic, and the importance of the idea of justice in society.

36. He cites Bakunin in *Obras*, 3:230, 235; Kropotkin in *Obras*, 1:468; 3:229, 256, 287, 344.

37. Cappelletti 1990, cix–cx.

38. In *Obras*, 3:347–351.

39. The book was translated into Spanish by Pedro González-Blanco as *El único y su propiedad* [The individual and his property] (Valencia: *Sempere*, n.d.). There we learn that "in France, during that same year (1892), in the *Entretiens politiques et littéraires* and in the *Mercure de France*, two extracts from Stirner's book were published that would be useful for anyone desiring to have a succinct understanding of the ideas of the German thinker" (p. xi).

40. This distinction appears especially in "Socialism and Anarchy" (3:237–290), and I will refer to it in detail below.

41. In *Obras*, 3:289, 337.

42. In *Obras*, 3:337; he paraphrases this in his speech "Los Partidos y la Unión Nacional" [The parties and the National Union] in 3:33.

43. In *Obras*, 3:343–345.

44. Cf. "José Nakens," in *Obras*, 3:307–309. A reference to Mateo Morral appears in *Obras*, 3:317.

45. In *Obras*, 3:343–345.

46. In *Obras*, 3:316.

47. On Valera: *Obras*, 1:209–225; on Castelar: *Obras*, 1:226–231; and on Núñez de Arce: *Obras* 1:235–253.

48. Unamuno thought Prada's attacks against Castelar, Valera, and Núñez de Arce were emotional and harsh, full of partial truths and sectarian feeling (Unamuno 1963, 358).

49. In *Obras*, 1:235.

50. In *Obras*, 1:230–231.

51. On one occasion he cites Nietzsche, transforming the concept of *superman* to "*superwoman* in the Nietzschean mode," with reference to Luisa Michel, in *Obras*, 3:335. Another quote from Nietzsche appears in *Obras*, 3:349.

52. Compare his letter to Francisco Gómez de la Torre, which stands as an appendix to *Horas de Lucha* (in *Obras*, 3:iv–viii).

53. On February 4, 1914, the garrison in Lima, under the command of Colonel Benavides, issued a proclamation against President Guillermo Billinghurst, who subsequently resigned. The Congress authorized the formation of a govern-

mental junta presided over by Benavides, but on February 15 a congressional minority under the sway of Benavides elected him president, ending the governmental junta. On that same day, February 15, Prada resigned as director of the National Library in protest over the coup d'état; his resignation was not accepted, and he was fired from the position on May 23.

54. They were published posthumously by his son in 1933 under the title, *Bajo el oprobio (la dictadura militar de 1914–15)* [Under opprobium: The military dictatorship of 1914–15].

55. Note that González Prada's defense of individual action is far more complex than Oviedo (1997) presents it as being.

56. Unamuno (1962, 357); Blanco-Fombona (1915, lxi–lxvi); Anderson-Imbert (1978, 1:338); Belaunde (1991, 110); Mariátegui (1972, 265).

57. Riva-Agüero (1962, 234–254), García Calderón (1910, 394–396; 1946, 33–42), V. A. Belaunde (1987, 197; 1991, 111).

58. Mariátegui (1972, 254–265); Sánchez (1986, 429–435); Vargas Llosa (1958, no. 122).

59. "Ubicación sociológica de González Prada" [The sociological situation of González Prada], in Basadre 1994, 158–170. Basadre's thesis about González Prada being "resentful" in the Nietzschean and Schelerian sense ("having a chip on his shoulder") has been discredited on solid grounds by Luis Felipe Alarco (1952, 63).

60. Concerning González Prada's influence on these writers, compare Antonio Cornejo Polar (1992, 21–27, 56–58, 61, 85).

61. Undated; Tamayo Vargas n.d., 2:938–939.

62. Piedad Pareja (1978, 8off.).

63. This influence has been explicitly acknowledged by L. A. Sánchez (1986, 411), for example.

64. In González Prada we have to distinguish between anticlericalism and antireligiosity, and in both cases between the level of theoretical argument, which in Prada is strongly influenced by positivism, and the purely demagogic. Karen Sanders oversimplifies matters when she states that "most of his [Prada's] invective against religion and especially against catholicism belongs to a class of crude literature that never rises above the level of insult and slander, having the clear purpose of scandalizing and offending his contemporaries" (Sanders 1997, 235).

65. Prada must have concluded toward the end of his life that this "representation of the intellectual" (the phrase is of course from E. Said) was excessive. In his interview with F. del Valle in 1917, asked whether, if he had it to do over again, he would fight with the same tenacity for the establishment of his political and literary ideas in Peru, he answered that he would not, adding, "I'm now convinced that it's futile to struggle for ideas in our environment" (*Obras*, 7:489).

66. In my view, Karen Sanders is also mistaken in her criticism of Prada for having "an essentially nihilist and therefore destructive attitude" with regard to the national tradition (Sanders 1997, 240). If Prada the anarchist preferred internationalism to patriotism, his attitude had to be negative toward nationalism, which does not necessarily imply that he was a nihilist. It's like criticizing a liberal for not preferring equality, when the liberal ideology by its very nature privileges freedom over equality.

Selected Bibliography

This bibliography is not exhaustive and seeks only to offer guidelines for subsequent reading.

I. WORKS BY GONZÁLEZ PRADA

1. Bibliography

There exists a "Bibliografía de y sobre González Prada" [Bibliography of Works by and about González Prada], prepared by Miguel Angel Rodríguez Rea, which goes up to 1985: Manuel González Prada, *Obras* (Lima: COPE, 1989), 7:601–696.

2. Complete Works

The *Obras* have been edited with prologue and notes in three tomes and seven volumes by Luis A. Sánchez (Lima: COPE, 1985–1989). The first tome (vols. 1–2) contains Prada's philosophical prose and essays, the second (vols. 3–4) his poetic and journalistic prose, and the third (vols. 5–7) his study of orthometry, Prada's poems and poetry collections, interviews (compiled and edited by Willy Pinto Gamboa), Prada's chronology (assembled by Marlene Polo Miranda), his bibliography (by M. A. Rodríguez Rea), and an appendix that includes unpublished documents concerning González Prada's family and a photograph album.

The content of the volumes of the *Obras* is as follows (first editions are enclosed in parentheses): Volume 1, *Pájinas libres* (1st ed. 1894; 2d ed. 1915; 3d ed. 1946; 4th ed. 1976); *Nuevas pájinas libres* (1st ed. 1937). Volume 2, *El tonel de Diógenes* (1st ed. 1945); *Figuras y figurones* (1938); *Bajo el oprobio* (1st ed. 1933). Volume 3, *Horas de Lucha* (1st ed. 1908); *Anarquía* (1st ed. 1936); *La polémica de la biblioteca* (1912). Volume 4, *Propaganda y ataque* (1st ed. 1939); *Prosa menuda* (1st ed. 1941). Volume 5, *Ortometría* (1st ed. 1988); *Minúsculas* (1st ed. 1909); *Presbiterianas* (1st ed. 1909; 2d ed. 1928); *Exóticas* (1st ed. 1911); *Trozos de vida* (1st ed. 1948); *Baladas Peruanas* (1st ed. 1935). Volume 6, *Grafitos* (1st ed. 1937); *Libertarias* (1st ed. 1938); *Baladas* (1st ed. 1939); *Adoración* (1st ed. 1949) *Poemas desconocidos* (1st ed. 1973); Volume 7, *Letrillas* (1st ed. 1975); *Cantos de otro siglo* (1st ed. 1979); and "Entrevistas" (1985).

This edition of the *Obras* has its merits, but it leaves much to be desired due to the quantity of errata. Lamentably, there are no critical editions of any of Prada's books, nor have his letters been published. Isabelle Tauzin Castellanos has recently edited M. González Prada, *Textos inéditos* (Lima: Biblioteca Nacional del Peru, 2001). It contains short stories and dramatic compositions by Prada between the year 1870 and the beginning of the twentieth century.

3. Biographies and Remembrances

Sánchez, L. A. 1930. *Don Manuel: Biografía de Manuel González Prada, precursor de la revolución peruana*. Lima: Rosay. This biography has been reedited on different occasions (e.g., the fourth edition appeared in the series Populibros [Lima, n.d.]) and has been translated into French (Paris: Excelsior, 1931).

González Prada, Adriana de. 1947. *Mi Manuel*. Lima: Cultura Antártica.

González Prada, Alfredo. 1945. "Recuerdos de un hijo." In Manuel González Prada, *El tonel de Diógenes*, 11–18. Madrid: Tezontle. Now printed in volume 2 of *Obras*, 17–24.

Sánchez, Luis Alberto. 1986. *Nuestras vidas son los ríos . . . : Historia y leyenda de los González Prada*. 3d ed. Lima: Banco de Comercio.

II. About Gonzalez Prada

1. Books and Pamphlets

Beltroy, Manuel. 1948. *Presencia y ausencia de González Prada*. Lima: Biblioteca Peruana de Bolsillo.

Calcagno, Miguel Angel. 1958. *El pensamiento de González Prada*. Montevideo: Universidad de la República.

Díaz Falconí, Julio. 1960. *La reforma ortográfica de González Prada.* Lima: San Marcos. Appendix 3 of the journal *Sphinx* (Lima) 13 (1960).

Fernández Sessarego, Carlos. 1951. *Manuel González Prada.* San Juan, Costa Rica: José Martí.

García Salvatecci, Hugo. 1972. *El pensamiento de González Prada.* Lima: Arica. The second edition of this book—rewritten but not substantially changed—has been published with the title *Visión de un apóstol: Pensamiento del maestro González Prada.* Lima: Emisa, 1990.

Guerra Martiniere, Luis Felipe. 1964. *González Prada.* Lima: Universitaria.

Lazo, Raimundo, and Vigil Palma. 1943. *González Prada.* La Habana: Publicaciones de la Universidad de La Habana.

Pérez Reynoso, Ramiro. 1920. *Manuel González Prada.* Lima: Lux.

Velazco Aragón, Luis, ed. 1924. *Manuel González Prada por los más notables escritores del Perú y América.* Lima: Rozas.

V.V.A.A. 1938. *González Prada. Vida y obra. Bibliografía. Antología.* New York: Instituto de las Españas en los Estados Unidos.

Ward, Thomas. 1998. *La anarquía inmanentista de Manuel González Prada.* New York: Peter Lang.

2. Articles and Shorter Texts on González Prada

Alarco, Luis Felipe. 1952. "Manuel González Prada." In *Pensadores peruanos,* 51–74. Lima: Sociedad Peruana de Filosofía.

Anderson-Imbert, E. 1978. "González Prada." *Historia de la literatura hispanoamericana,* 1:338–340. Mexico: FCE.

Basadre, Jorge. 1994. "Ubicación sociológica de González Prada." In *Perú: Problema y posibilidad,* 159–170. Lima: Fundación Bustamente de la Fuente.

Belaunde, V. A. [1917] 1987. "La desviación religiosa." In *Meditaciones Peruanas,* 187–199. Vol. 2, *Obras Completas.* Lima: Comisión Nacional del Centenario.

———. "González Prada." [1931] 1991. In *La realidad nacional,* 109–112. Lima: Horizonte.

Blanco-Fombona, Rufino. 1915. "Manuel González Prada: Estudio crítico." In M. G. Prada, *Páginas libres,* vii–lxxxix. Madrid: Sociedad Española de Librería. Also in Manuel González Prada, *Figuras y figurones,* 1938: 15–116. Pris: Bellanand.

Cappelletti, A. J. 1990. "Manuel González Prada." In *El Anarquismo en América Latina*: xciv–cxii. Caracas: Biblioteca Ayacucho.

Chang-Rodríguez, Eugenio. 1957. *La literatura política de González Prada, Mariátegui y Haya de la Torre,* 51–125. Mexico: De Andrea.

———. 1987. "Manuel González Prada." In V.V.A.A., *Historia de la literatura hispanoamericana*, 2:473–485. Madrid: Cátedra.

Franco, Jean. 1975. "Manuel González Prada." In *Historia de la literatura hispanoamericana*, 153–157. Barcelona: Ariel.

Gamarra, Abelardo. 1923. *Una faz de González Prada: Su cariño por los animales. Anécdotas históricas.* Lima: Scheuch.

García Calderón, Ventura. 1910. *Del romanticismo al modernismo: Prosistas y poetas peruanos,* 387–399. Paris: Ollendorff.

———. 1946. *Nosotros,* 33–42. Paris: Garnier.

———. [1914] 1986. "La literatura peruana (1535–1914)." In *Obras Escogidas,* 1–97. Lima: Edubanco. González Prada is discussed on pages 81–87.

Haya de la Torre, V. R. 1977. "El civilismo y la inteligencia" and "Nuestro frente intelectual" [1926]. In *Obras completas,* 1:116–118. Lima: Mejía Baca.

Higgins, James. 1987. "Manuel González Prada." In *A History of Peruvian Literature,* 72–73, 93–97. Liverpool: F. Cairns.

Iberico Rodríguez, Mariano. 1926. "González Prada, pensador." In *El nuevo absoluto,* 43–50. Lima: Minerva.

Kristal, Efraín. 1986. "Problemas filológicos e históricos en *Pájinas libres* de González Prada." *Revista de Crítica Literaria Latinoamericana* 23: 141–150.

Leguía, J. G. 1989. "Manuel González Prada." In *Hombres e ideas en el Perú,* 82–109. Lima: Integración. First published in 1941.

Loayza, Luis. 1977. "González Prada y Riva Agüero, hermanos enemigos." *Diners,* March, 16–17.

Mariátegui, José Carlos. 1972. "González Prada." In *7 ensayos de interpretación de la realidad peruana,* 254–265. Lima: Amauta.

Martinengo, Alessandro. 1962. "González Prada como prosista." *Eco,* April, 601–623.

Mead, Robert G., Jr. 1959. "González Prada, el prosista y el pensador" and "Panorama poético de González Prada." In *Temas hispanoamericanos,* 13–40, 60–75. México: De Andrea.

Mejía Valera, Manuel. 1953. "El pensamiento filosófico de Manuel González Prada." *Cuadernos Americanos* 12, no. 5: 122–135.

Meléndez, Concha. 1948. "La poética de González Prada." *Asomante* 4, no. 4: 72–77.

Neira, Hugo. 1996. "González Prada: El fundador." In *Hacia la tercera mitad. Perú XVI–XX. Ensayos de escritura herética,* 354–363. Lima: Sidea.

Núñez, Estuardo. 1942. "La poesía de González Prada." *Revista Iberoamericana* 2, no. 10: 295–299.

Orrego, Antenor. 1945. "En torno a la figura de M. González Prada." *Renovación* 20–21: 3, 18.

Oviedo, José Miguel. 1997. "Manuel González Prada. Un apocalíptico de fin de siglo." *Debate*, July-August, 44–46.

Podestá, Bruno. 1973. "Manuel González Prada: Apuntes para una sociología de la literatura peruana." *Cuadernos Americanos.* September-October, 96–112.

———. 1975. "[M. González Prada:] Breve noticia sobre su vida y otras coordenadas." In *Pensamiento político de González Prada*, 17–52. Lima: INC.

Rodríguez Peralta, Phyllis. 1980. "González Prada's Social and Political Thought." *Revista Iberoamericana de Bibliografía* 30: 148–156.

Salazar Bondy, Augusto. 1967. "El pensamiento de González Prada." In *Historia de las ideas en el Perú contemporáneo*, 1:10–37. Lima: Moncloa.

Sanders, Karen. 1997. "Manuel González Prada: La tradición antiautoritaria." In *Nación y tradición: Cinco discursos en torno a la nación peruana 1885–1930*, 197–242. Lima: FCE/BUC.

Unamuno, Miguel de. [1906] 1962. "Manuel González Prada." In "Algunas consideraciones sobre la literatura hispano-americana: A propósito de un libro peruano [de José de la Riva-Agüero]". In J. de la Riva-Agüero, *Obras Completas*, 357–362. Lima: PUC.

Vargas Llosa, Mario. 1958. "Manuel González Prada." *Cultura Peruana* 122 (August): 13, 50; 123 (September): 10, 50; 124 (October): 11, 50; 125 (November): 11, 50.

Zum Felde, Alberto. 1959. "González Prada y el movimiento indigenista en el Perú." In *Índice crítico de la literatura hispanoamericana*, 1:211–288. México: Guaranía.

About the Editor and Translator

David Sobrevilla is professor at the University of Lima. His principal publications include *Las ideas en el Perú contemporáneo* (1980), *Repensando la tradición nacional,* 2 vols. (1988–1989), *César Vallejo* (1994), and *La filosofía contemporánea en el Perú* (1996). He has published *Jorge Basadre* (1992) and *Augusto Salazar Bondy* (1995).

Frederick Fornoff is professor at the University of Pittsburgh at Johnstown, Pennsylvania, and former president of the American Literary Translators Association (ALTA). Translator of works by Laureano Albán, Mariano Azuela, Tirso de Molina, Simón Bolívar, and Jotabeche.

FREE PAGES AND OTHER ESSAYS
Anarchist Musings

Contents

I   Free Pages

Lecture at the Atheneum in Lima   9

Speech at the Olympus Theater   30

Grau   40

Speech at the Politeama Theater   46

Peru and Chile   52

Vijil   61

Catholic Education   73

Propaganda and Attack   93

Renan   105

Notes on Language   119

Death and Life   131

II   Times of Struggle

The Parties and the National Union   143

The Intellectual and the Worker   165

Our Judges   173

Our Indians   181

III   New Free Pages

Poetry   197

A Moment of Philosophy   208

IV   Diogenes' Cask

Our Mother   217

V   Anarchy

Anarchy   223

The Universal Holiday   227

The Responsibility of the Anarchist   230

The State   239

Authority   241

The Beginning   243

The Sword   245

Socialism and Anarchy   248

Strikes   251

The Soldiers Rebellion   253

The First of May (1907)   255

Antipoliticians   258

Revolution   260

The First of May (1908a)   263

The Police   266

The Two Nations   270

The First of May (1908b)   273

The Individual   275

The Paris Commune   279

Force   282

VI   Under Opprobrium

Caporalismo   289

The Good Revolution   293

The Rotten Core   296

Tyrannicide   301

I

Free Pages

Lecture at the Atheneum in Lima[1]

(1886)

I

Gentlemen:

If men of genius are snow-covered mountain ranges, their imitators are little more than rivulets fed by the snow melting from the peak.

Not only do we have geniuses who invent and geniuses who renew and apply what's invented, but we're overrun by the mediocrity that apes and copies. How many third-rate epic poems were inspired by the *Iliad* and the *Odyssey!* How many lame tragedies inspired by the works of Sophocles and Euripides! How many vacuous songs by the odes of Pindar and Horace! How many rancid eclogues by the pastorals of Theocritus and Virgil! Everything good, everything grand, everything beautiful, was perverted, diminished, and made ugly by unskilled imitators.

For centuries there was an obsession with composing variations on Greco-Latin topics, and there was in literature a falsified Rome and a doubly bewitched Greece because everyone looked at the Greeks through a Roman lens. Many tried to follow faithfully the tracks of

---

[1] The lecture in the Atheneum was M.G.P.'s first public presentation, and it corresponds to the period when the Literary Circle was being formed in 1885, an event that took place in the year immediately preceding this lecture. M.G.P. had been a member of the Literary Club in which the previous generation had held meetings—L.A.S., 1976.

Latins and Greeks, as if a strong, healthy man could be followed by a cripple wobbling on crutches or a paralytic stumbling over his own feet! Imitation, which serves as an exercise in the practice or technique of the arts, should be considered neither an art in itself nor art's primary object. Imitation is the same as moving and wearing oneself out pushing a railroad coach: we think we're accomplishing much and all we're doing is following the impulse of the engine.

In literature, as in everything, Peru always lived on imitation. Yesterday we imitated Quintana, Espronceda, Zorrilla, Campoamor, Trueba, and today we continue the series of imitations with Heine and Bécquer in verse, with Catalina and Selgas in prose. Since Bécquer wrote miniature poetic compositions and Selgas wrote rather short articles in short, almost biblical, sentences, in Peru now there's a vogue for poetry consisting of two quatrains with vowel rhyme only, as well as a fondness for very short essays bristling with antitheses, verbal conceits, and puns; in other words, we've given ourselves up entirely to frivolous literature.

II

Stern Catalina had an exquisite poetic sensibility, obvious talent, and vast erudition. A student of Hebrew with a blind faith in the dogmas of Catholicism, he set out to refute the *Life of Jesus*, when it had become fashionable to break lances with Renan. Once the fad was over, the refuters as well as their refutations sank into oblivion, but Catalina remains afloat today, not because of his *Response* to Renan, but for his book *Woman*, which he published when he was very young, with a prologue by Campoamor.

In *Woman*, Catalina takes a perspective opposed to Balzac, but he lacks the good judgment of Aimé-Martin and the generous spirit of Michelet. The book exalts the fair sex to such an extent, and emanates such a pronounced flavor of mysticism, that it seems to have been written with rose dust dissolved in holy water. Works like this are entertaining when you're eighteen years old, make you smile when you're twenty-five, but put you to sleep when you're thirty. They shouldn't be taken seriously, like a dithyramb by a seminarist who hasn't yet lost his virginal grace.

Here the asthmatic rhythms of Saavedra Fajardo alternate with the perfervid rhythms of Quevedo at his worst, a Quevedo wielding his pen in a moment of frustration. Now and then there's a glimmer like the mind of a Lamennais who has been chastized and censored by the Sacred Congregation of the Index.

In works written subsequent to *Woman,* Catalina changes style but not substance. He abandons the closed style and begins to use the endless, languid sentences of Mateo Alemán. He continues to bow down before the yoke of faith, never experiencing the torment of doubt, never rising to the summits of reason.

If he never manages to convince the disbeliever or support the waverer with any of his writings, neither does he inflame hatred or induce revulsion; in all of his work we can discern a sincere believer and a man of loyal heart. In his works he emits melancholy, that vague presentiment or sadness of men destined to die young.

*   *   *

CATALINA WAS FOLLOWED by José Selgas y Carrasco. After publishing two collections of verse, *Spring* and *Summer,* Selgas abandoned poetry and devoted himself energetically to prose.

With a superficial and secondhand erudition, with passages copied from French polemicists, he undertakes a crusade against modern science and civilization. He comes across as aggressive, caustic, sarcastic, and bloody, and like all men quick to attack, he doesn't know how to defend himself or resist when he is attacked. Using weapons that he doesn't handle well, he tries to land mortal blows and leaves his whole body vulnerable to the enemy. Although now and then he stuns, he never disables because his arguments are like loud but harmless blows with an airbag. Pressing hard, suddenly he draws back like Voltaire, firing off a joke.

Forgoing wornout and stale ideas, it would be unfair to deny that Selgas has a quick, subtle, and penetrating wit: there may be no more paradoxical man in Spain. However, in straining for sharp effects, he often fails to make himself understood. Because he overuses antiphrasis, we never know if he's speaking seriously or joking with us.

In Selgas, there is no logical succession of conclusions but rather associated generally unconnected ideas. You can take your scissors to entire sections of anything written by Selgas, put the cuttings into a lottery wheel, take them out and read them, and in all likelihood come up with a new article. He lacks concision, the gift of saying much with few words. Far from dispensing gold dust, he buries you in sand. Selgas is like a Castelar sifted and dyed with Carlist hues.

In his style, asthmatic amid asthmatics, he wears you out with puns, bores you with his antitheses, befuddles you with his preciosity. To use a phrase from Voltaire: "he weighs ant eggs on spider-web scales." He shouldn't be regarded as a tamer of phrases but as a punisher of words. He plays with words the way Japanese prestidigitators play with knives. He wrenches from the inkwell line after line of short, motley phrases, the way carnival sword-swallowers pull from their stomachs yards and yards of narrow, multicolored ribbons.

His primary weakness is not ambiguity but affectedness, revealing in each flourish a writer eager to produce some startling effect. He even tries to display his wit in the way he places his orthographic signs. It's impossible to read him for more than a few minutes at a time. Reading Selgas is like a tiresome ascent up an endless, dark, solomonic stairway. We expect gusts of light, moments of respite, but respite and light never come.

He never proceeds in a direct line toward the subject, but always in curves and angles, twisting and convoluting; so that when we think he's far away from us, he takes great pleasure turning somersaults right behind us. Like a character from a magic show, he hides in the clouds, then suddenly appears through a trap door. Selgas, finally, climbs onto the tightrope, executes mortal leaps, achieves prodigious feats of agility, then finally loses his balance, drops his cane, and falls on the spectators.

*   *   *

THAT'S WHAT CATALINA and Selgas are like in brief: prose writers with no real originality, since they are right out of the Parisian tabloids. Pour any article by Catalina and Selgas into French (if Selgas can be translated at all), publish them in any newspaper sold along the Seine, and they'll be indistinguishable from the thousands and thousands of articles produced by innumerable French writers.

III

Who is Heine, who is that man who founds his school in Germany, becomes popularized in France, penetrates England, invades Russia, gets translated in Japan, and ends up having an irresistible influence in America and Spain? No one has succeeded in characterizing Heinrich Heine with more precision than Heine himself, when he refers to himself as "a German nightingale nesting in Voltaire's wig," for he combines the Germanic sentiment of a Schiller with the French spark of a Rabelais.

Despite being a consumate artist, he doesn't produce with the firm serenity and rhythm of a painter doing illuminations, but with the pangs of a woman giving birth to a child. His poetry, a glass of bitter gall with sugared brim, as he describes it in *Atta Troll,* is "frenzy guided by prudence, prudence gone crazy, death rattles turning suddenly to belly laughs."

Since he thinks with the mind of Mephistopheles and feels with the heart of Faust, his irony approaches the satanic and his sensibility tends toward the paradisal. Woman instills in him the tenderness of a mother and the lasciviousness of a satyr; his love isn't like the blue lake where the sky is reflected, but like the torrential river hurtling toward the sea, gathering streams from the mountains and sewers from the cities.

We shouldn't believe him when he tells us that "he only truly loved statues and the dead." To the contrary, let's believe instead that he should have repeated with the old *minnesänger:* "I fed on love, the soul's marrow."[2] He was born with an astonishing precocity of sentiments. As a child, he was reciting the Buzo by Schiller in a lyceum festival, when suddenly he grew mute and stood as if petrified: his eyes had fixed on the blue eyes of a beautiful girl. He loved his cousin Molly Heine to the point of delirium and always felt a deep affection for his mother. True, neither of them escape the darts of his irony, nor did he himself escape them, because it was Heine's nature to conceal his passions with mockery, to hide his sorrows with laughter. Like the heroine in the story, he dances with a dagger in his chest; like Voltaire, he has one foot in the grave and does pirouettes with the other.

He hated with all his soul. Almost dying, having to prop open his eyelids to see, he was writing his memoirs when he cried out in feverish joy: "I caught them. Neither the dead nor the living will escape me now. Woe unto him who reads these lines, if he ever dared attack me!

[2] Ulrich von Lichtenstein (author's note, in ink, unpublished)—L.A.S.

Heine doesn't die as others die, and the tiger's claws will outlive the tiger."[3]

Heine's audacity seems unbelievable to anyone unfamiliar with the childish simplicity of German authors. He respects no one: he censures Schlegel, Hegel, and Boerne, blasts Goethe, is merciless with all the Swabian poets, laughs sarcastically at Madame de Staël, ridicules Ballanche, calls Villemain "an ignorant Latin teacher," Chateaubriand "a gloomy madman," and Victor Hugo "a moral humpback."

A Prussian, he flays Prussia and mocks the old Germany and the good old order glorified by Uhland. Not long after Arndt had written hymns to the formation of the German fatherland, when Koerner's ashes were still warm, Heine has the audacity to celebrate in his *Dos Granaderos* the apotheosis of Napoleon Bonaparte, the conqueror of the Prussian cities of Jena and Tilsit. He never pretended to be a patriot, and he loved only one country unconditionally—France—where he lived much of his life, where he married, where he drew his last breath. In a letter addressed to his friend Christian Sethe around 1822, he had already reached the point of writing: "Everything German is hateful to me, and you, unfortunately, are German. Everything German makes me feel like vomiting. The German language hurts my ears."

He believes in nothing, except the perfidy and beauty of his beloved. "I do not believe in the devil, or in hell, or in infernal torments; I only believe in your eyes and in your diabolical heart." He calls the Christian gods "foxes in sheep's clothing," Catholicism "humanity's morbid period." For all religions he reserved Voltaire's belly laugh. Although he was a Jew by birth and a Lutheran by convenience or whim, he only paid literary homage to the Greek divinities. Sick, already immobilized by paralysis, he wandered through the galleries of the Louvre and never turned his eyes toward the madonnas of the Italian painters. Instead, shedding tears like a fourth-century pagan, he falls on his knees before the Venus de Milo.

Heine's originality is based on his serio-comic way of feeling, his independence of thought, and his frankness of expression; his form is in no way superior to Goethe or Schiller, though he's less harmonious than Tieck, more concise than Rückert, more plastic than Uhland. He

---

[3] Camile Selden, *"Les derniers jours de H. Heine."* (Note in ink in the original we used.)—L.A.S.

himself confessed that in his *Lyric Intermezzo* he had imitated the cadences of the *lieder* composed by Wilhelm Müller, that prior to learning from Wilhelm Schlegel's works the secrets of prosody he had already surrendered to the influence of popular German songs. And he was right: before Wilhelm Müller, before Goethe, the *lied* existed in all its freshness, in all its simplicity, in all its flexibility. Looking all the way back to the *Greek Anthology*, we can see that many Greek epigrams have all the characteristics of the Germanic *lied*. Some of the compositions of the *Lyric Intermezzo*, of his *Return*, and of the *New Springtime*, could stand without embarrassment beside the epigrams of Meleager, Rufinus, and Paul the Silent.

However, nothing would be further from the truth than to characterize Heine as essentially Greek; he is more like a Greek from Alexandria who has traveled through Asia, read Lucian, and leafed through Meleager's *Anthology*. Hellenic good taste isn't common in Germany; if works by the Greeks resemble a well-ordered English garden, works by Germans are more like an American virgin forest, where you dare not enter without a compass and a machete. Heine, gifted with a nomadic and cosmopolitan spirit, picks up his material wherever he can find it; he moves from the Bible to the Shah-nameh, from the Shah-nameh to the Ramayana, from the Ramayana to the Scandinavian Edda, and from the Edda to the Spanish Romans, to Scottish ballads, or French fabliaux.

A poet and a German, he succumbs to Goethe's influence, just as no German philosopher can resist the influence of Kant. Heine follows the singer of Faust the way Schopenhauer follows the philosopher of the *Critique of Pure Reason*. When men like Kant and Goethe shake the earth with their footsteps, the ground trembles for such a long time that whole generations surrender to the movement out of trepidation.

However, amid the swarm of poets springing up in Germany at the turn of the century, Heinrich Heine stands out as a personality. He is different from everyone and can't be confused with anyone else. The acridity of his character and the bitter gall of his verse have to be attributed not to inherent malice, but to the hardship of his life, his unfortunate love, his constant illnesses, and the paralysis that kept him confined to his bed for years at a time until it finally finished him off in 1856. Famous for his poems, he is even more famous for his afflictions.

*   *   *

To move from Heine to Bécquer is like moving from the master to one of his disciples setting up a school. The Sevillian painter and poet Gustavo Adolfo Bécquer died in the fullness of life, never having succeeded in putting down on canvas or in books all the fantastic creations spinning around in his head.

He's enjoying a well-deserved popularity today in Spain and America, and his literary influence is growing at the speed of an electric current. Whereas many writers never emerge from obscurity despite publishing long poems and voluminous novels, he, with just a few poems and some legends, occupies a place among the elite and is acquiring a universal reputation.

Bécquer is germanizing Castilian poetry the way Meléndez, Valdés, Cienfuegos, and Quintana frenchified it, the way Boscán and Garcilaso italianized it. With his simple ideas, his sincere sentiments, and particularly his spare and even economical expression, he stands as a revolutionary resisting the verbose intemperance of the Spanish poets.

He imitates without losing his originality; his work consists not in translating the verse of Germanic poets with faithless mastery, but in bringing simplicity, ingenuity, transparency, and a delicate irony to style, in a word, all the effects of the German *lied*. None of his compositions remind us of *The Pilgrimmage of Kevlaär*, *The Poet's Curse*, or *The Bride of Corinth*; but Heine, Uhland, and Goethe never wrote a *lied* like his last quatrain:

> In the vast nave
> of the Byzantine temple
> I saw the gothic sepulcher by the dim light
> trembling in the stained glass windows.

In some of his ideas he is like a legitimate German, he is steeped in the Germanic spirit, he looks at women as the Germans do, and if certain vestiges of mysticism distinguish him from Heine, his idealism moves him close to the Swabian poets.

When he writes:

> She's an inanimate statue . . . but . . .
> She's so lovely!

he shows himself to be a true disciple of Heine, the lover from the *Lyric Intermezzo;* and wheh he exclaims:

> And then I understood why we cry!
> And then I understood why we kill!

the true Spaniard shines through, the man who carries in his veins the blood of *García del Castañar* and *El alcalde de Zalamea.* From his ideal journey through the land of Hermann and Thusnelda he returns full of melancholy, that flower growing in northern snows, and he contrives a pleasant but strange fusion of Andalusian with German.

Thanks, perhaps, to the good taste of his editor and biographer, Bécquer appears before us with light but rich literary baggage and succeeds in avoiding the defect that Heine acknowledged in his own works: monotony. It's tiresome to read the *Intermezzo*, the *Return*, and the *New Springtime* straight through because of the repetition of the same matter in different words, whereas you can read and reread with endless delight the tiny collection of *Rimas*. Is there any poet or lover of poetry who doesn't know them by heart?

Less ironic and bitter than Heine, but equally melancholy and passionate, the Spanish poet differs from the German by a touch of resignation and goodheartedness. Bécquer, wounded to the heart by the hand of a woman, tries to heal himself with some kind of balm, covers himself with bandages, and puts his hope in the mercy of something higher than man. It's just the opposite with Heine, who scratches at the stitches in his wound, pours corrosive water onto the irritated flesh, and raises his fists to threaten heaven and earth. The works of both poets have "traces of tears and love."[4] In the *Rimas*, however, we don't have that abuse of epigrammatic plunges nor those constant sardonic belly laughs that degenerate into a kind of tic in the author of the *Intermezzo*. Somewhat attenuated, then, warmed over perhaps, and if we may, more appealing to Spanish eyes, Heine's influence shows through only after being passed through Bécquer's sensibility.

A studied casualness of language, the rhyming of vowels only for the most part, and the smooth but somewhat careless rhythm make Bécquer a poet sui generis. He introduces no innovations in stanza or verse, the

---

[4] Edmond Schérer (manuscript note by the author, unpublished).—L.A.S.

way Iriarte, Espronceda, Zorrilla, Avellaneda, and other lesser poets do; but in his very ancientness he has marked the seal of his individuality. The vowel-rhymed quatrain, the seven- and eleven-syllable verse, these will say: Bécquer passed this way.

At times he has all the tenderness of Lamartine, and he recalls the sculpted, figural form of Théophile Gautier. Some of his essentially graphic compositions seem like marble forms or like colored cloths. And he does much effortlessly, a few hammer blows or brush strokes sufficing to make the statue emerge from the block or the figure from the canvas.

In prose he imitates the *Reisebilder* or *Travelscapes* of Heine himself. Although at times he overwhelms us with architecture, as Victor Hugo does in *Notre Dame de Paris*, he suggests the idea of a Jean-Paul without the nebulous mists of the Black Forest, or a Hoffmann without the pipe smoke or beer foam. His legends stand comparison with Nodier's *Trilby*.

In verse as in prose, he skillfully conceals his art without bringing the man in contradiction with the writer; in his works we touch life, we feel the trembling of the muscles and the tingling of the nerves. He possesses, like no other, the rare and enviable gift of making his readers love him.

Heine and Bécquer, then, seem like master and populizer of the German style in Spain. Populizer, not initiator, is what we should call the poet of *Rimas*, because already Barrantes in his *Baladas Españolas* (1853), Augusto Ferrán in *Soledad* (1860), and Ventura Ruiz Aguilera in the *Dolor de los Dolores* (1862), had preceded him in their tendency toward imitation of the German style. But these germanists came too early, whereas Bécquer appeared at the most propitious moment, when all eyes were turned toward Prussia haloed in the prestige of her victories, when the German empire had just been proclaimed by the palace of Versailles.

*   *   *

THOSE WHO INTERPRET the Germans most precisely situate the Spanish cradle in the gold of the Rhine. But those who translate Heine from French translations or imitate or copy Bécquer, do they immerse themselves in the Germanic spirit? They walk groping in the dark, they imitate and copy just to be imitating and copying; they don't deserve the label of Germanists or Germanizers, but of Teutomaniacs. They replace bad with bad: they trade lachrymose intimism, the decadence of Espronceda and Zorrilla, with a nebulous individualism, the decadence of Schiller and Heine.

Besides the subjective poetry of the *Lyric Intermezzo,* Germany abounds in the objective poetry of the ballads. Why don't our Spanish Germanists assimilate German objectivism into their language? Why don't they assimilate the dramatic element prevailing in the ballads of Bürger, Schiller, Uhland, and in many of Heine's? Since our poetry lacks perspective, depth, chiaroscuro, and rhythm, why don't our poets study the architectonic, sculptural, pictoral, musical form of Goethe? Yes, Goethe, despite his marmoreal coldness (a coldness explainable by the dominion of genius over inspiration), possesses an overwhelming rhythmic power, and in his verses he seems to pull off the impossible, like architecture in motion, or petrified music, or a painting with words.

We have to say it again: poets imitate without knowing how or to what purpose. Out of this extravagant habit of imitating thoughtlessly, countless hybrid compositions come about. The cloudburst of poetic lamentations, the flood of sonnets, is followed today by a drizzle of homeopathic, lilliputian poems. Is there any literary period in America or Spain that doesn't offer up two vowel-rhymed quatrains, with the indispensable title of *Rima,* or *Imitation of a lied,* or *Becquerism?*[5]

What nausea and boredom we feel when we come upon one of those embryonic abortions or two-headed monstrosities, after savoring the lyric outpouring of a Lamartine or the epic exuberance of a Victor Hugo! If Castilian poetry has to reduce itself to such vacuous ineptitudes handed out in infinitessimal doses, let's renounce once and for all both poets and poetry.

IV

If refrains and popular songs mark the birth of literatures, euphuistic and diminutive compositions of this sort are signs of exhaustion and senility. Man walks with tiny steps in infancy and in old age. Decadence

---

[5] An obvious swipe at the Becquerian style and at translating Heine out of French, an allusion perhaps to Ricardo Palma, who had recently published a volume of "Translations."—L.A.S.

is betrayed in the taste for bagatelles, not in the naturalism of a prose master like Zola or the atheism of a poet like Richepin.

There are texts in which the sent. sententious, epigrammatic phrase works well, and no one finds fault with the *Maximes* of a Vauvenargues or the *Pensées* of a Joubert. Is there anyone who doesn't like the biblical tone and Hebrew parallelism of a Lamennais? Violent passions, delicate thoughts, bird's-eye vistas, require a poetry of concision; that's why in Greece all writers include works in the *Anthology*, from Homer to Plato. Lope de Vega has written thousands of sonnets, Gutierre de Cetina is rescued from oblivion by a single madrigal, and eight-verse epigrams keep the name of Iglesias alive. But the fleeting compositions of true poets are dazzling flashes or friezes of pentilic marble, while the vowel-rhymed quatrains of the Bécquerists are a mere fragment of opaque and amorphous matter. The *Rhymes* are a step away from acrostics, charades, riddles, logogriphs, mazes, and other products of minds whose primary activity is the yawn.

In the physical world, things that are very small are immune to cataclysms, thanks to their tenacious and relatively perfect organization, and in literature, that which is short and good endures. Whereas a history or a poem may perish, the short story and the ode survive. Diminutive productions require original thought and a style in harmony with the subject: the form provides the merit; let's not forget that, based on form alone, carbon is sometimes called coal, at other times diamond.

If the thought doesn't rise above the ordinary, if the style lacks plasticity, what is it that those Gallic-Germanic authors writers offer us with their asthmatic prose and their microscopic verse? Does smallness of productivity denote economy of energy or impotence? Rocks produce lichen because they haven't the substance to nourish a cedar. If those of us who enjoy the prose and verse of masters can feed on lion's marrow, why should we subject ourselves to the diet of dispeptics in measured doses? If the nations of Europe figure among the grand pachyderms of the intellectual realm, we Peruvians should avoid being represented by literary microbes.

Improvisation is proper to the rostrum or the daily paper. We tolerate confusion of ideas, unevenness of style, and even grammatical carelessness in orators and journalists. It's true that in what we improvise we often crystallize the best and most original of our wit, something like the spontaneous secretion of sap in the tree; but once we get used to work that is incorrect and rushed we become incapable of composing works destined to survive. What costs little, lasts little. The books that delight and amaze humanity were conceived and written in long hours of solitude and concentration, and they cost their authors the iron from their blood and the phosphorous from their brains.

It's true that the world just keeps progressing. In the vortex of modern societies we feel compelled to live lightly, to move along the surface of things; however, we still have time enough to read a novel by Galdós or attend the performance of a play by García Gutiérrez. Happily, the time has not yet arrived when poetry is reduced to refrains and prose to raw telegrams. We still know that the difference between a hundred pseudo-Germanic rhymes and a poem by Quintana or Núñez de Arce is the same as that between a sand dune and a block of marble. We know that there's no similarity between fragmented, arrythmic, antiphonal prose and the prose of a real writer: a succession of disconnected, incoherent, motley paragraphs doesn't constitute a discourse, just as a row of unstrung rings placed one after another doesn't form a chain.

Don't imagine, gentlemen, that I'm recommending the kind of anemic, unconscious, heteroclite prose that mistakes fiction for nature, emphasis for magnificence, obesity for robustness; the prose of violent inversions, archaic exhumations, and senile purisms; the prose of clauses embedded in clauses, of accidents clarifying earlier accidents, of endless, incomplete sentences; the prose invented by Spanish academics seeking to resuscitate the volapuk or esperanto of the Mesozoic period; the prose imitated by American corresponding members of the Spanish Academy who in Venezuela and Colombia are corrupting the rich, progressive Castilian language.

Somewhere between the shower of phrases flitting about dizzily like the flapping of a bat's wings and the pileup of sentences plodding along with the unbearable slowness of a drowsy serpent, there exists a natural prose, a Greek prose, which comes forth naturally when we refuse to follow blindly what we learned in school or to adopt a conventional style. Sainte-Beuve advises us to "do everything possible to write the way we talk," and hardly anyone communicates in elephantine or ponderous sentences. If we consider it in a mature manner, good prose is like a conversation between cultured people. In it there's no affectation, squeamishness, or inflated rhetoric; everything flows and slips along plainly, unemphatically, easily. Energetic flights of imagination serve as a model of simplicity or naturalness and have the air of something that could occur to anyone who happened to pick up a pen.

The so-called majestic effect of the Castilian language often consists of the garish dress of a village woman with pretensions of nobility, of pure phraseology in direct conflict with the character of the period. The public always prefers writing that nourishes over writing that stuffs, and it prefers the concision and lucidity of a Condillac to the diffusion and obscurity of a Byzantine. If you write today and want it to survive tomorrow, you should belong to the day, to the hour, to the instant in which you are wielding the pen. If an author steps outside his time, it should only be to anticipate future events, not to dig up dead ideas and words.

Archaism implies regression: archaic style, reactionary thinker. No author with an antiquated language, however youthful his thoughts, will ever win the favor of the public because contemporary ideas injected into a wornout style remind us of balsamic essences injected into the arteries of a corpse. They postpone the fermentation of the cadaver, but they don't communicate vigor, warmth, or life. The reasons that Cervantes and Garcilaso had for not expressing themselves like Juan de Mena or Alfonso el Sabio help keep us today from expressing ourselves like writers of the sixteenth and seventeenth centuries.

Languages aren't renewed by reverting to an earlier form, nor do old men get rid of wrinkles by wrapping themselves in a baby's swaddling clothes or returning to the breast of the wet nurse. Plato said that "when it comes to language the people need an excellent teacher." Languages are invigorated and tempered in the fountain of popular speech, not in the dead rules of grammarians or in the prehistoric exhumations of scholars. Original words, graphic phrases, and bold constructions—all these sprout from songs, refrains, and sayings of the common people. The masses transform languages the way infusoria modify continents.

Purism is little more than an affectation, and as Balmes so aptly puts it, "affectation is intolerable, and worst of all is the affectation of naturalness." In the style of our modern purists, nothing ever folds or bends with the smoothness of a joint; rather, everything creaks and shudders like a rusty hinge that is never oiled. In their art their artifice leaps out at you. It's not unusual to see authors using the entire gamut of seventeenth-century grammar in one clause and then changing style in the next and committing unpardonable Gallic constructions. They remind us of young beggars who disguise themselves as crippled old men until all of a sudden they throw away their crutches and walk freely and with great agility.

Purists also sin through obscurity, and where there's no clarity in elocution conceptual clarity is also lacking. When your thoughts are jumbled in your mind like serpents coiled inside a jar, words crash against words like one file rasping against another. In the prose writer of stately rhythm, ideas parade beneath the vault of the cranium like a row of white doves beneath the cupola of a temple, and simple sentences alternate with natural sentences, like vibrations of bronze sheeting shaken by the hands of a colossus.

Writers ought to write the way we all speak, not like an Apollo uttering dubious prophecies or a sphinx posing indecipherable enigmas. Why flaunt a rarified and extravagant vocabulary? Why that excessive indulgence in idiomatic expressions that make translation impossible or difficult? Why use a natural language in life and an artificial language in books? Mannerism and bombast constitute risky territory: anyone who vacillates like Solís may well slip like the Count of Toreno and fall like Friar Jerundio de Campazas.

Not even the best poetry can tolerate a puerile fastidiousness, a schoolboy's rhetoric, a convoluted style, or a violent transposition. A poet who becomes entangled in a strained hyperbaton is like a traveler wandering up and down stream looking for a bridge because he can't find a ford and is afraid of the river. Any sort of license in poetry betrays the poet's impotence. Molière is rightfully called *the* comic poet of modern times, and what is it about Molière's poetry that is so different? Fray Luis de León shines among among the greatest lyric poets of Spain, and what is it about Fray Luis de León's poetry that is so different. "I repeat," exclaims Hermosilla, "that in the best verses of Garcilaso, Herrera, who was even bolder, the Argensolas, Rioja, and others, there are no archaisms, there is no license, nor do they need them to be surpassingly beautiful, as indeed they are."

There's an enormous difference between a versifier and a poet: the versifier grinds, strains, and pulverizes words; the poet forges rhythms the way the Cyclops pounded iron and tosses grand ideas about the way the Titans smashed huge boulders. The masters also have their weak moments: Victor Hugo and Quevedo are unlikeable; Goethe and Dante, dry and obscure; Lamartine, too luxuriant of branch and leaf;

Lope de Vega, imprecise; Calderón, overly influenced by Góngora; Quintana, puffed up; Campoamor, prosaic; but none of them ever lapses into effeminacy: at times they fall like a weary gladiator, but they never swoon like an effete courtier.

V

Góngora, Cienfuegos, and Zorrilla, three impenitent sinners of Castilian literature, but at the same time three true poets, exemplify innovation, even revolution. Something similar is achieved in the national sagas by the authors of the *Romancero,* by Cervantes in the novel, by Lope de Vega, Calderón, and Echegaray in the theater. It could be said that Spanish geniuses carry all the heat and rebelliousness of the African sirocco in their guts. They're savages perhaps, but free-spirited savages. That's why the classicism of Racine and Boileau never took root in Spain, which displayed its romanticism as early as Lope de Vega and Calderón, even before Germany with Tieck and Schlegel, before France with Madame de Staël and Chateaubriand. Spain had a law: orthodox in religion, heterodox in literature.

Based, then, on the tradition of literary independence, which may go back as far as Iberian-Latin poets like Seneca and Lucan, let's leave behind the habits of childhood and seek new elements and new impulses in other literatures. We prefer the free and democratic spirit of the present day to the spirit of Catholic monarchies.

So let's turn our eyes to the Castilian authors, study their masterpieces, grow rich on their harmonious language; but let us constantly remember that the intellectual dependency of Spain would signify for us an indefinite prolongation of childhood. We are separated from the Spaniard by the influences of climate, by ethnic mixing, by intimate contact with the Europeans, by a frenchified education, and by sixty-four years of stormy republican life. The immigration of foreigners doesn't reach Peru like a sudden gust, but like a stable atmosphere gradually displacing the air from Spain and penetrating into our lungs and changing us physically and morally. We are gradually losing our alienation from life, an alienation so marked in Spaniards of old, and we are becoming infected with the keening melancholy that characterizes the native of Peru.

Today we don't talk the way the conquistadores did. The American languages provide us with neologisms that we use with every justification, since there are no equivalents in Castilian for expressing ideas that are exclusively ours and for naming things intimately connected with our lives. Even in pronunciation, how we have changed! We tend to leave out the *n* in the particle *trans*, and to replace the *x* of the Latin preposition *ex* with *s* before a consonant at the beginning of a word. Gentlemen, the person speaking to you at this moment, what would they make of him in a Spanish Academy? Almost a savage, a person who pronounces the *ll* as a *y*, who confuses the *b* with the *v* and can't distinguish between the *s* and the *z* or the soft *c*.

A hundred factors act on us to distinguish us from our parents: let's keep pushing, let's march to where the century pushes us. The literati of Hindustan were Hindustani, the literati of Greece were Greeks, the literati of America and of the nineteenth century should be nineteenth-century Americans. And let's not accept as an Americanism the lengthy enumeration of our flora and fauna, or the meticulous description of our meteorological phenomena, in a language saturated with gratuitous and recherché provincialisms. The nationality of the writer is based not so much on a photographic copy of the scenery (almost the same everywhere) as on the sincere expression of the self and in the precise presentation of the social environment. Valmiki and Homer are valued not because they described sunrise over the Ganges or moonlit nights in Piraeus, but because they bring to life two dead civilizations.[6]

Political emancipation would be worthless if we limited ourselves in form to the exaggerated purism of Madrid, if we subjected ourselves in matters of substance to the *Syllabus* of Rome. Exorcising the tendency that leads us to prefer the foliage of words to the fruit of ideas, and the chattering of consonants to the music of rhythm, let's learn to think with Germanic independence and to express ourselves in prose like the French or in verse like the English. Let's look to other peoples and other epochs, other governments, other religions, other literatures.

Let's be done with the millenary journey through realms of flighty idealism and return to the bosom of reality, remembering that outside nature there is nothing but illusory symbols, mythological fantasies,

---

[6] He is alluding to the so-called romantic Americanism, based on descriptive lists, which made many believe (among them the Spanish critic Rubió y Lluch) that "Americanism" and picturesqueness were synonymous—L.A.S.

metaphysical vapors.[7] Because we are so accustomed to frequenting rarified summits, we have become vaporous, as formless as air. Let's solidify ourselves! Better iron than clouds.

Mathematics, the natural sciences, and industry have no cause to look with envy on earlier centuries. Only literature and art cry out for a gust of air from the old Hellenic world to freshen the ambrosia of the universe, to evaporate the mystical hallucinations of Catholic fanaticism and rehabilitate things unfairly reviled by the hypocrisies of Tartuffe.

Coming to terms with neologisms, foreign influence, or provincialism, all of which can rejuvenate and enrich language, breaking the conventional mold of form when ideas demand it, and professing no other literary religion than a respect for logic, let's leave behind the crossroads of an elitist system and head down the broad, luminous road of liberated art. Let's stop regarding as oracles the judgments of authorities, no matter who they are, and let's not be afraid of attacking error that has been deified by unconscious masses. Only science is infallible; only truth is inviolable.[8]

These ideas are far removed from the theoreticians and dreamers who would draw boundaries between citizens and the poet. A convenient recourse for saving energy and lives while the good, simple folk work and struggle and die for us! Against an Archilochus and a Horace, who throw down their shields and flee from combat, we can offer a Garcilaso in Frejus and a Cervantes in Lepanto. A genius in poetry, a genius in action. Ercilla writes at night what he does on the battlefield by day, Byron envies the victories of Bonaparte and rushes off to die at Mesolonghi. Espronceda climbs over the barricades in Paris. When Ugo Fóscolo speaks to us of the "warrior spirit roaring in his gut," he reveals himself to be a man of inspiration who doesn't make the mistake of identifying himself as a mere manipulator of consonants. The legitimate poet is like the tree born on a mountain peak. By virtue of his branches, which constitute the imagination, he is a creature of the clouds; by virtue of his roots, which make up his sensations, he is connected to the soil.

If yesterday's writers worked on our behalf, those of us writing today

---

[7] A clear example of Prada's positivism in 1886—L.A.S.

[8] Prada rejected the possibility of belonging to the Academy of the Language. The continuation of this speech is connected to "Propaganda and Attack" in this same volume—L.A.S.

have an obligation to work on behalf of those to come. We are indebted to a creditor—the future. Instead of drifting by like an endless procession of wailing zombies heading for the *danse macabre*, our poets ought to be marching past us like legions of men with the fire of a fecund passion in their hearts, predictions of victory on their lips, and the color of blood in their cheeks—the sunrise hue of youth, love, and roses! And our prose writers, instead of emasculating themselves through a feeble, courtly prose, ought to be writing wholesome, faithful prose, choosing the cloudless day of reason over some sectarian twilight, looking beyond the narrow circle of family and country to the horizon of humanity.

Let's not wait for the Octavian peace. In America, and especially in Peru, we are capable of wasting years thinking we are living in utopia just because we are waiting for a golden age. We are likely to die in the desert without ever glimpsing the promised land. Of all the generations ever born in this country, we are the saddest, most conflicted, most long-suffering.[9] The earthquake demolishes our cities, the sea flattens our ports, frost and cryptogamous spores destroy our crops, yellow fever decimates our towns, foreign invasion lays waste, burns, and kills, and civil war finishes what the invasion began. An abyss opens up beneath our feet, two bronze walls are raised up on either side; but let's not be dismayed! Let's imitate Gunnar of the Scandinavian sagas, the hero who chants bravely as serpents coil themselves around him and vipers feed on him.

If there is pleasure in conquering with the sword, it is also sweet to light the way with a torch. Glory for glory, it's better to leave sparks of light than pools of blood. Alexander in India, Caesar in the capitol of Jupiter in Rome, Napoleon in Austerlitz, these will never eclipse Homer wandering from city to city singing the rhapsodies of the *Iliad*, or Bernardo de Palissy burning his furniture to feed his porcelain kiln, or Galileo locked in a prison and calculating the movement of the earth. If the warrior whose iron sword incarnates justice is worthy of golden pages, how much more enviable the writer who stays clear of sects and bandwagons and follows noble causes, only to be accused like Béranger at the end of his life of a single flaw: "That he fawned on misfortune!"

Nowhere more than in the nations of South America is it fitting to

---

[9] A reference to the 1876 bankruptcy, the war of 1879, and the wars preceding those of 1879, 1883, and 1885.

exalt the brilliance of arts and sciences above the dazzle of military victories. We Americans live between the Paleozoic and Mesozoic periods, in the kingdom of gigantic reptiles and colossal mammals. Let pen and word serve the purpose they were designed for: away with fawning mendacity. There's no reason for intelligence to give way before force; on the contrary, the voice of the reasonable, learned man should be a corrective to the pernicious work of rudimentary minds.

Our country, which gives us water from its rivers and fruits from its fields, has the right to savor the use of our arms and the consecration of our intelligence. What would we respond if the hour of accounting had arrived? Let's get rid of the daily paper, since journalists don't figure among the literati, and concentrate on true literature. Those meaningless articles, plagued with antitheses, equivocations, and trifles; those vowel-rhymed quatrains devoid of originality, inspiration, or sound rhythms—are these the sum total of nourishment we have to offer a people wounded and mutilated by a foreign enemy? Such literature doesn't break forth like a rain of fireflies on a gloomy night, but like the flicker of jack-o-lanterns on tombstones in a cemetery.

Let's insist on the need for work and study. Novels, poems, and plays don't sprout from the mind like islands from volcanic eruptions. They're born in fragments, from successive spurts. We are like fountains that spring forth intermittently, that bubble forth; good or bad taste depends on whether we channel the water through marble aqueducts or earthen ditches.

Diderot practices a hundred trades for more than twenty years and goes from workshop to workshop copying materials for the *Encyclopedia,* Rousseau meditates for six or seven hours looking for the precise word, Goethe mingles among German students to listen to the lessons of the anatomist, Wilhelm Loder, Wilhelm Schlegel devotes himself for fifty years to the study of Sanskrit, Balzac dies worn from fatigue, Bello learns Greek in his old age and recopies his manuscripts as many as eight times. But there's one example even more worthy of remembering: Buffon, the man who called genius "prolonged patience," writes *The Ages of Nature* at age seventy and transcribes it with his own hand eighteen times.

Baudelaire maintains that "Spaniards born in America generally lack originality in their literary works and power in their ideas and expression, like feminine souls created only for contemplation and pleasure."

Yet in America, and even in Peru, there are men who display a singular aptitude for sciences, arts, and literature; many, giving up contemplation and pleasure, persevere in fecund and serious works.

Despite what certain distinguished mediocrities and malcontents may say, our public read everything that was worth reading, and our governments supported and provided our writers with benefits.[10] With very few and voluntary exclusions, what Peruvian of clear intelligence never got to be a university professor, deputy, minister, magistrate, financial agent in Europe, consul, or an ambassador? It may well be that we suffered two calamities: excessive official protection for hollow, fossilized books, and the appointment of literary mediocrities to public office.

To accuse one's country of ingratitude is a tactic of inept or careless writers. Let's hide our light beneath our cranium because intelligence, with the ascendent power of a hydrogen balloon, always rises to the summit, leaving the aristocracy of blood and the aristocracy of money trailing behind in the foothills. Today the road is clear for everyone. Today publication is accessible to everyone, and everyone can speak and demonstrate what they are. If there are hidden sages, let them show us their wisdom; if there are eminent writers, let them show us their works; if there are politicians of broad horizons, let them unveil their plans; it there are invincible warriors, let them teach us their tactics and strategies; if there are brilliant industrialists, let them patent their inventions or applications. Let's put no faith in mute geniuses or in superhuman modesty: if you don't raise your voice in the arena of the world, it's because you have nothing to say. Don't complain about insurmountable obstacles; the man of solid talent, like the Caesar of pure stock, can cross the Rubicon.

In summation, gentlemen: the philosopher and economist Saint-Simon had a servant who always woke him at daybreak, saying: "Get up, my lord Count, you have great things to accomplish." If only our scientific, literary, and artistic societies would come together to tell Peru constantly: "Open your eyes, leave behind the horrific nightmare of blood, because the world is passing by with giant steps, and there's a long way to go, many wounds to stanch, and much ruin to rebuild!"

---

[10] In fact, most Peruvian writers of the period held, for short or long periods, intermittently or continuously, one or more public offices—L.A.S.

Speech at the Olympus Theater[1]

(1888)

Gentlemen:

"I'm about to be dragged down the good road," I said in 1887 when I assumed the presidency of the Literary Circle, and today I'm obliged to say that during the past year I was not the captain at the head of his company, but the recruit enlisted in the ranks of men with smooth brows and strong hearts.

Happily, far from futilely marching around a pole like the character from popular legend, we marched toward the realms of light and glimpsed the land where storms are born.

The Literary Circle, that peaceful society of poets and dreamers, is being transformed into a militant center for social change.[2] Where do

---

[1] I The speech at the Teatro Politeama was read by the young student Urvina (or Urbina) on July 29, 1888. The organizer of the conference at which it was read was the professor of music José Benigno Ugarte, director of the Colegio de Lima and its representative for the private schools in the Peruvian capital. The object of the conference was to initiate the national campaign to raise a million soles, which Peru was to pay Chile if the vote to determine the definitive fate of the provinces of Tacna and Arica favored Peru. This had been agreed in the Treaty of Ancón on October 20, 1883. The conference was attended by the president of the republic and his ministers. M.G.P. attended incognito—L.A.S., 1976.

[2] After 1891 the Literary Circle was the nucleus of the National Union Party, a kind of Peruvian "Radical Party."—L.A.S.

the impulses toward radicalism come from in literature? Here we're experiencing strong winds from the hurricanes pounding the European capitals, according to reports from a disbelieving and republican France. Here we have a youth who struggle openly to destroy the bonds linking them to the past; youth who want to kill off violently what seems destined to succumb and die over an inordinantly long period; youth, in short, who are growing impatient to push aside obstacles and open a path to hoist the red banner over the crumbling towers of national literature.

Their propositions could not be more audacious: they have begun to open the trail, but setting out isn't the same as arriving. At the point where we now stand, we need to orient ourselves, assess our strength, and determine who will guide us and how much resistance we'll have to overcome.

I

How strong are we?

We can't assess our strength with precision. Each day there are more of us, our number growing hour by hour. Yesterday we were a group, today we're a legion, tomorrow we'll be many batallions. It seems that in response to the voice of encouragement emanating from the Literary Circle in Lima, all the enlightened youth of Peru are awakening and becoming infected with the healthy fever of marching ahead.

Because provincialism and the petty concern with nationality do not reign here, many young people from our provinces and from abroad are collaborating with us.[3] Men of different nationalities but with the same sentiments and aspirations are like forests with gigantic trees; their trunks are separate, but their roots and highest branches are intertwined. They are conjoined at their deepest and highest points.

We are in our formative period: we have barely begun to write or speak. What we have accomplished is of little value, nothing compared to what we can and must do.

This is far removed from the ludicrous and boastful notion of thinking we know it all or the puerile vanity of believing ourselves to be

---

[3] This is the source of the federalist tendency, whose primary centers were Cuzco, Arequipa, Trujillo, Piura.—L.A.S.

privileged talents; our power comes from unity: all the rays of the sun, spread over the surface of the earth, are insufficient to ignite a single grain of powder, but solar light reflected and concentrated in a concave mirror can set fire to a mine and blow up a granite mountain.

When the time comes, when the clarion call sounds and our guerrillas come down from the humblest provinces of the republic, Peru will witness a crusade against the decrepit spirit of the past, a war against everything reactionary in science, art, and literature.

II

Who should guide us?

No Peruvian or Spanish writer.

Here no one has to claim the title of teacher because we are all disciples and devotees. We can offer some lovely compositions in verse, but we can't name a great poet; we have some charming and even good prose articles, but we lack a great prose writer. Where do we find the work, in prose or verse, that stands out for its superior qualities? Just try to name a novel, a play, a poem . . . born only yesterday into independence, our intellectual accomplishments are like a grain of salt on beaches just abandoned by the sea.

We practice a literature of transition, hesitations, gropings, and crepuscular lights. The pale imitations of Bécquer are gradually disappearing from our poetry, but in our prose the bad *tradition*[4] still reigns, that monster engendered by bittersweet falsifications of history and microscopic caricatures of the novel.

Peru can't put forward today a single literary figure who for the richness and boldness of his ideas reaches the level of the European writers, nor whose style has been liberated from pseudopurist imitation or embryonic romanticism. There is a parade of archaisms, a wealth of proverbs, and even the crash of grandiloquent words; but where do we find the ideas? We hear the sound of many wings but can't see the soaring of the eagle.

In our blood all the vices and virtues of our ancestors are in ferment: we'll learn nothing new from monarchist, Catholic Spain. In the old

---

[4] An allusion to the *Tradiciones* of Ricardo Palma and his imitators. The reference to Bécquer seems also to be an allusion to Palma.—L.A.S.

metropolis a republican, freethinking youth now exist who are working to diffuse germs of life into the Dead Sea of the Spanish monarchy, but we don't know their writings and barely know the names of those young writers. We are beneath their consideration; they disdain us, then forget us. The Spain that looks toward Peru, that calls us and wants to dazzle us with academic titles, is the Spain of Nocedal in religion, Cánovas in politics, the Spain of war and empire in literature.[5]

To return to Spain in order to reinject its blood into our veins and its seeds into our literature is sheer regression. A sick man who wants to transfuse someone else's blood into his veins will choose the blood of a strong, young friend, not that of a decrepit and exhausted grandfather. The renewal of seed should also be taken as a literary precept: the same seed repeatedly planted in the same ground brings about the degeneration of the species.

Saint-Beuve offers good advice: "We don't choose our masters in our own language without coming too close to them and being absorbed by them; it's like marriages within the family, never productive of vigorous offspring. And we should stay even farther away when forming religions or alliances."

Those leveling old forests to plant new seeds aren't from Spain. Hegel and Schopenhauer were born in Germany, Darwin and Spencer in England, Fourier and Auguste Comte in France. So why drink from a small stream when we can go directly to the source? The water from the stream (Madrid) comes from the source: Paris. Today, with few exceptions, there is no Spanish literature, only French literature written in Castilian.

Biot's words to the teaching orders can be applied to the official representatives of Spanish literature: "They're like old statues who served to guide travelers, and even today, thousands of years later, they still point with motionless fingers to roads that no longer exist." We should seek direction, then, in the study of the great foreign writers, in the imitation of no one. To study in organized fashion is a way of assimilating the juice segregated by others; to imitate in a servile fashion is a way of becoming petrified in a mold.

---

[5] Note that here as well as in the lecture at the Atheneum, Prada distinguishes two Spains, one liberal and heterodox, the other Catholic and Orthodox, which he combats.— L.A.S.

III

What resistance will we have to overcome?

Here's what we have in European nations: a wealthy nobility with powerful influence and deeply rooted traditions; a clergy respected both for its knowledge and for its austerity of conduct; a mercantile bourgeoisie seeking to convert bank notes into honors; and masses of peasants fanatical out of ignorance and monarchists by habit. That nobility and that clergy, that bourgeoisie and those peasants, offer tenacious resistance to the democratic, rationalist spirit.

Nothing like that occurs in Peru.

Here we have no noble class. The notion of pure lineage provokes a malicious smile in those who know how the noble families of Peru lived during the colonial period, especially in the seventeenth century.

Here the clergy lacks all knowledge, intelligence, or virtue, and they do not make up a united or homogeneous body: priest, friar, and cleric find each other repugnant, live divorced by hereditary hostility.

Here we know nothing of the European bourgeoisie; there is, of course, a kind of middle class, intelligent, sound of judgment, hardworking, Catholic but indifferent to religious conflicts, patriotic but tired of a politics offering only prejudice, disillusionment, and dishonor.

Here, the people of the mountains, an inert mass, obey the first push; the people of the coast, adrift, succumb to every breeze and every wave. Today the people, who can't be called Christians but fetishists, listen to the priest and follow him; but the day when the law of total freedom arrives, they will listen to the philosopher and follow him.

Thus there are no elements in our country to make up a reactionary party capable of offering insurmountable resistance.[6]

A party without a leader can't be called a party. Is there anyone here named Francia, García Moreno, or even Núñez? The so-called parties of Peru are organic fragments agitating and clamoring for a mind, pieces of serpent writhing, flopping about, trying to merge with a head that doesn't exist. There are craniums but no brain. None of our public figures stands out sufficiently to sway or command us; they're all moving away from us, stooped and burdened down beneath a mountain of ignorance.

---

[6] Time has gradually justified this profound observation by the author.—L.A.S.

With the exception of our war for independence and May 2, a single drop of blood has never been shed in Peru for an idea, nor has a revolution ever been based on principle; the causes have always been partisan; the parties, underground struggles for personal ambition. The newest groups of conservatives or clergy being formed today confirm the rule: they appear as amorphous bodies, sedimentary, formed from the detritus of our worst parties. All the sinners from the political arena, all the prodigal sons of democracy, all the men whose flesh has already begun to stink of grave dust, are coming forth to ask for pardon and amnesty of those willing to forget and forgive, and are taking refuge in those alms houses we call reactionary parties.

The influence of the secular clergy in Lima, Cajamarca, and Arequipa cannot be denied. If a few men are breathing the healthy air of the nineteenth century, almost all the women are asphyxiating in the atmosphere of the Middle Ages. Woman, the sensitive part of humankind, doesn't belong to the thinking part. She is in our arms, not in our minds; she feels, but she doesn't think with us because she lives in mystical betrothal with the Catholic priest, because she has entered into a dark wedding with those men of error, obscurity, and death.

To save woman and with woman, the child, we'll have to take on the secular clergy, scattered in small groups, shielded behind the Law of What's Printable and armed with theology.

Let the religious press slander and lie: the sower of ideas doesn't do battle with those who thunder reproaches or those who knead mud. The peasant plowing the fields to plant wheat doesn't pause to trample the worms dug up by the point of the plow and left to dry in the sun.

Let's not be afraid of theology with its phantasmagoric, otherworldly creatures. When Europe invaded Asia, the sons of the Orient tried to stop the sons of the North with huge idols made of wood, cardboard, and rags. When the men of today invade the land of darkness, up pop the men of yesterday, thinking they can intimidate us with superstitious fantasies and simulacra.

The philosopher doesn't retreat but pushes forward; he enters the temple and pulls aside the veil because he knows that inside the sanctuary there is only a priest with all his human foibles and an idol with no lips to respond to the threats of our lips or arms to ward off the formidable blows of our arms.

IV

Whatever the program of the Literary Circle turns out to be, there are three things we shouldn't forget: honesty in the writer, truth in style, and truth in ideas. Gentlemen, let's always remember this: if there's anything stronger than iron, more lasting than granite, and more destructive than fire, it's the word of an honest man.

Unfortunately, nothing was ever more egregiously prostituted in Peru than the word. It was meant to unite but it divided; it was meant to civilize but it brutalized; it was meant to censure but it flattered and fawned. In our general unhinging, the pen is as much to blame as the sword.

The daily paper lacks prestige. It doesn't represent the intelligent power of reason, but the blind stampede of evil passions. From the bombastic, mile-long editorial to the frivolous, scurrilous chronicle, you can hear the sordid diatribe, the subtle envy, and something like the ripping of live flesh on the teeth of a hyena. Those wornout phrases and trivial thoughts emptying themselves onto those endless, vicious newspaper columns remind us of a roiling river of mud and stone hurtling down the deep ravines of a valley.

If the moral level of the country has been in constant decline since the war with Chile, no one has contributed more to that decline than the fawning lies of our writers or the dishonesty and bad faith of our journalists. Both, who ought to have transformed themselves into crusaders for justice and accusers of political criminals in high office, became instead their accomplices in the cover-up. Our legal correspondents heaped sympathy on the looters of the national treasury, and our poets lavished verses on military leaders whose hands were covered in blood from the civil wars. Sedition by praetorians, low-empire dictatorships, persecutions and forced exiles, assassinations on barracks grounds, the sacking of the public treasury—all of this was possible because tyrants and thieves knew they could count on the silence and applause of a cowardly, venal, or courtly press.

In Edgar Quinet's *Ahasverus* women who have risen from the grave, their hearts still bearing the wound of incurable love, pass before the eyes of the poet; so tomorrow, in the eyes of posterity, our writers will steal by, trying to hide in their breasts the leprosy of venality.

The thing is, gentlemen, that there's a literature of eternally prostrated writers, like the stone sphinxes in the Egypt of the slaves, and a literature of men eternally upright, like the marble Apollo in free Greece.

By distancing ourselves from schools and systems, we acquire truth in style and ideas. Classicism and romanticism, idealism and realism, merely a question of names, pure logomachy. There are only good or bad works: good work means truth in clear, concise form; bad work, mendacity in ideas and form.

Truth in style and language is as important as truth in substance. To speak today with the idiosyncrasies and vocabulary of other centuries is to lie, to falsify language. Because words express ideas, they have their own environment in which they're born and live; injecting an antiquated phrase into a modern text is like affixing the glass eye of a mummy no onto the forehead of a living person.

In all literatures there abound archaic writers, applauded by the academies and disdained by the public; but there's no example in history of a reactionary movement of an entire people toward the primitive forms of their language.

Language is to words as geological periods are to species; once the species disappears, it never reappears. Cuvier was able to reassemble the skeletons of fossilized animals, but it never occurred to him to try to reestablish the physiological functions, to restore living muscle to the dead skeleton. Thus the antiquated writer can compose works that have the rigidity of wire and the coldness of marble, but not the plasticity of flesh or the warmth of blood.

Style, if it is to crown truth, must be adapted to our character and to our epoch. Men of ardent imaginations and wills inclined to accede, we need a style that will seduce with brilliant images and impose itself with compelling bursts of energy. Here we amuse ourselves with a style sprinkled with images and we burst out with phrases as cold and hard as the blade of a sword.[7]

The word that is addressed to our people today has to awaken them all, make them rise to their feet, and stir them to action the way a fire alarm does late at night. After San Juan and Miraflores,[8] in the cowardly

[7] A key concept for attaining a clear understanding of the author.—L.A.S.

[8] Battles that took place on January 13 and 15, 1881, between Peruvians and Chileans. The author took part in the second.—L.A.S.

depression that corrupts and overwhelms us, no one can afford to wail in puerile misery; we're obliged to speak in ways that will uplift our spirits and fortify our hearts.

Something is dying, but something is also being born. Falsehood, with its ponderous metaphysical and theological pretensions, is dying; truth is being born with positivist science.[9] An old Atlantis is gradually sinking beneath the waters of the ocean, but a new and beautiful continent is rising from the sea, brandishing its thornless flora and its tigerless fauna.

Let the reign of science begin now in our literature. People are no longer interested in being entertained with the music of insipid, over-polished stanzas or empty, high-sounding sentence. Everyone, from the child to the old man, is thirsty for truths. Yes, even if they're humdrum truths. It's better to strap on wax wings and soar for a few yards and fall, than to have powerful feet shod in triple layers of bronze and trample triumphantly over the earth's thorns and pebbles.

Courtiers, politicians, and diplomatics don't see it this way. They call fear prudence, collusion they call holding their tongues, and they lie without words. True, the path to sincerity isn't covered with roses: every truth we speak incites implacable hatred, each footstep straight ahead means one less friend. The truth isolates, but that doesn't matter. There is nothing as solitary as summits, nothing more luminous than the rays of the sun.

Let's break the infamous and unspoken pact of speaking softly. Let's abandon the crossroad for the high road, ambiguity for the precise word. When we attack error and move boldly against its followers, let's not mete out spankings with swords still sheathed in their scabbards. Let's stab deeply with blades bare and bright and shining in the sun.

Let truth come, then, in its pure, beautiful nakedness, without the veil of satire or the vestments of apology. The fragile child and the meticulous woman sweeten the lips of the goblet holding the heroic but bitter balm; man will quaff in a single swallow the most pungent potion, as long as it proffers life and health.

Finally, gentlemen, let's be truthful, even if the truth brings our mis-

[9] We have to remember the time in which the author of this lecture was speaking: 1888.—L.A.S.

fortune. As long as the torch is bright, it's not important if it burns the hand that lights and holds it aloft.

Let's be truthful, even if the truth unhinges an entire nation. The tears and sorrows and sacrifices of a single generation are not important if those tears and sorrows and sacrifices redound to the benefit of a hundred generations.

Let's be truthful, even if the truth turns the globe to rubble and ashes. The desolation of the earth isn't important, as long as the echo of truth rings endlessly down the silent, empty solitudes![10]

---

[10] A paraphrase of one of Schopenhauer's thoughts.—L.A.S.

Grau[1]

(1885)

I

There are epochs in which an entire country is personified in a single individual: Greece in Alexander, Rome in Caesar, Spain in Carlos V, England in Cromwell, France in Napoleon, America in Bolívar. In Peru in 1879 it wasn't Prado, La Puerta, or Piérola; it was Grau.

When the *Huáscar* set sail from some port in search of adventures, always full of risk, although at times fruitless, all eyes followed the captain of the ship, the wings of all hearts followed him, everyone was with him. No one was unaware that victory was next to impossible, given the superiority of the Chilean navy. But our national pride rejoiced to see in the *Huáscar* a knight errant of the sea, an image of the famous knight who did not bother to count his enemies prior to the battle because he was waiting to count the defeated and dead.

We, the legitimate heirs of Spanish chivalry, became intoxicated with the perfume of heroic deeds, while others, less deluded than we and

---

[1] This article can be considered M.G.P.'s first foray into polemics. It appeared in 1885 in a collective pamphlet of homage to the famous Peruvian sea captain. We have not been able to locate the issue of *El Comercio* in which it also appeared. The version inserted here is the fourth, having been edited for the pamphlet, for the first edition of *Pájinas libres* and, to a lesser extent, for the posthumous edition.—L.A.S. 1976.

more imbued in the values of the age, scorned the smoke of glory and grew fat on the booty from cheap, easy victories.

And we deserved to be forgiven!

The *Huáscar* broke through blockades, chased down transport ships, surprised squadrons, bombed ports, escaped intact from ambushes and pursuits, and seemed not so much a ship as a living creature, lynx-eyed, sly as a fox, soaring like an eagle. Thanks to the *Huáscar*, the world, which always follows the cause of the victors, forgot our disasters and burns incense to us; thanks to the *Huáscar*, hearts least open to hope gathered enthusiasm and felt the generous stimulus of sacrifice. Thanks to the *Huáscar*, in short, the enemy became disoriented, suffered discouraging hesitations, and had to swallow the bitter taste of vanity humbled because the ironclad vessel, guarding the southern coasts, appearing out of nowhere when least expected, seemed to be saying to Chile's ambitions: "Beyond here you will not pass." All this we owed to the *Huáscar*, and Grau was the soul of that ironclad vessel.

II

Miguel Grau was born in Piura in 1834. Nothing extraordinary happens during his childhood, and the only thing worth noting is that, after receiving his primary education in the Nautical School of Paita, he transferred to Lima to continue his education in the school of the poet Fernando Velarde.

On the death of his disciple, the teacher consecrated to him an enthusiastic composition in verse. Setting aside the exaggerations, natural to a sentimental and romantic poet, we can conclude from Velarde's eleven-syllable verses that Grau was a peaceful, quiet child, even taciturn.[2]

He must have wearied early of his studies and even earlier of the regimen at the school, because at the start of his adolescence, he joins the crew of a merchant ship. For six or seven years he sailed around

---

[2] *Nunca fuiste risueño ni elocuente*
Y tu faz pocas veces sonreía,
Pero inspirabas entusiasmo ardiente,
Cariñosa y profunda simpatía.

You never joked or spoke with grace
a smile never danced on your face
but you inspired an ardent zeal,
a sympathy deep and fond and real.
(Fernando Velarde)

America, Europe, and Asia, preferring to be an experienced pilot rather than a maritime theoretician, preferring to skirt the coasts of continents and ride storms rather than sail the endless, steady waves of the Pacific.

He regarded the merchant marine as temporary schooling, not as a permanent profession, so as soon as he thought he was ready to command a ship he enlisted in the Peruvian navy. We won't bother following step by step the career of the man who was a coast guard marine in 1857, the captain of a ship in 1873, and a rear admiral in 1879. Such a reconstruction superimposes a mathematical plan onto the existence of a person, grants intentionality to the most insignificant of his actions, reads predictions of prowess into a child's innocent games: the stuff of legend, not biography. In the ordinary course of a life, a man walks along prosaically, at ground level, and only discovers he's superior to others at intermittent moments, the supreme moments.

In 1865 there was a moment when Grau attracted the attention of the whole nation, when he held the fortunes of the country in his hands. He was commanding a warship from the English shipyards at the very moment when the republic rose up to repudiate the Vivanco-Pareja treaty. Yielding to the revolutionaries, conceding control of the seas to them, Grau contributed effectively to the overthrow of Pezet.[3]

Grau's popularity begins with the outbreak of the war against Chile. Prior to that he might have been confused with his emulators and companions in arms or sketched in among the more notable figures of the painting; but in those days of crisis, he was sketched in full body, stood out above everyone, eclipsed everyone. He was compared with Noel and Gálvez, and like Washington he enjoyed being "first in the hearts of his countrymen." All of Peru praised him as Napoleon did Goethe: "You are a man."

III

And so he was, both for his courage and for other moral qualities. In his life, his person, and the least significant of his actions, he fit the legendary profile of the seaman.

---

[3] The Vivanco-Pareja treaty was a transaction between the governments of Pezet (Peru) and Isabell II (Spain), which Peru rejected by overthrowing Pezet and continuing the war against Spain until she was defeated (1866).—L.A.S.

Human to excess, he practiced acts of generosity that in the clamor of war ended up arousing our wrath. Even today, when we recall the implacable fury of the Chilean conquerors, we deplore Grau's excessive clemency on the night of Iquique. To understand and forgive him, we have to make an effort, to muffle the pangs of the half-open wound, to see matters from a higher perspective. Then we admit that it isn't the tigers who kill just to be killing or wound just to be wounding who deserve to be called great, but men who even in the vertigo of battle know how to spare lives and limit casualties.

A simple man, rooted in the religious traditions, unaffected by the doubts of the philosopher, he was proud of being a Christian and requested a priest's absolution before setting out with the blessing of all hearts. Being sincerely religious, he knew nothing of covetousness (which motivates cowards), violent rage (that momentary courage of cowards), or pride (an accursed heat that only spawns vipers in the breast). So humble was his character that, harrassed one day by the praises of the fools who swarm around men of merit, he exclaimed, "Come on, I'm just a poor sailor trying to serve his country."

Because of his quietness in danger, he seemed to be the child of other climes, for he never showed signs of the noisy giddiness that marks the people of the south. If he had ever wanted to harangue his crew, he would have said in Spartan manner, like Nelson in Trafalgar: "The country assumes that everyone will do his duty." Even in his relations with his family he proved sober in his words: far from him the verbosity that fakes eloquence and copies talent. He spoke as if he could read the minds of those he spoke with, as if he were afraid of annoying them with the least contradiction. His mind discerned slowly, his speech flowed with long intervals of silence, and his voice with its feminine timbre contrasted sharply with his viril, rough features.

This sailor forged on the anvil of strong minds, inflexible in applying to the guilty all the rigor of the law, was endowed with an exquisite sensibility, loved his children tenderly, and had a marked fondness for all children. However, his moral energy was not enervated with sentiment, as he proved in 1865 when he joined the revolution: rejecting promotions and demeaning offers of gold, ignoring the suggestions or advice of his closest friends, resisting the pleas and intimations of his own father, he did what he thought best, he fulfilled his duty.

As immaculate in his private as in his public life, as honorable in his drawing room as in his ship's stateroom, he contrasted sharply with our politicians and our soldiers, and he existed as a living anachronism.

As the flower of his virtues, he transcended resignation; no one knew more about danger, and he marched forward with his eyes open, his face calm. In him, nothing comical or affected: he personified naturalness. When you looked at his loyal, open face, when you grasped his hard, calloused hand, you felt that the blood was flowing from a noble, generous heart.

Such was the man who in a poorly outfitted ship, with a crew of inexperienced sailors, found himself surrounded and assaulted by the entire Chilean navy on October 8, 1879.

IV

In the Homeric battle of one against seven, Grau could have surrendered to the enemy, but he realized that he was doomed to die for the sake of his nation's will, that his countrymen would never have forgiven him for begging for his life on the ladder of the conquering ships. In effect, if you had asked Grau's admirers what they demanded of the captain of the *Huáscar* on October 8, they would have all responded with Corneille's Horace: "Let him die!"

He could have endured anything with stoic resignation, except the *Huáscar* adrift with its captain still alive. We needed the sacrifice of the good and the humble to erase the opprobrium of the wicked and the proud. Without Grau on the Point of Angamos, without Bolognesi on the Morro of Arica, could we really call ourselves a nation? Is there any shameful behavior that we haven't displayed before the world, from ridiculous skirmishes to inexplicable mass desertions, from treasonous retreats by our leaders to byzantine acts of sedition, from underhanded machinations by ambitious lowbrows to sad acts of folly by clown heroes?

In the war with Chile, we not only shed our blood, we displayed our moral leprosy. We can forgive the scuttling of a frigate with an inexperienced crew and a confused captain, we can excuse the defeat of an untrained army with inept or cowardly officers, we can accept the demoralization of a people due to constant disaster on land and sea. But we can't forgive, excuse, or accept the corruption of the moral order, the complete chaos in public life, the *danse macabre* of puppet figures disguised as Alexanders and Caesars.

However, in the grotesque and gloomy drama of the defeat, now and then there emerged a luminous and admirable figure. War, with all its ills, did us the favor of proving that we are still capable of engendering men of virile character. Let us take heart, then: the rose doesn't bloom in a swamp, and a country where men like Grau and Bolognesi are born isn't utterly dead or completely degenerate. Let us take heart, if we can. The sadness of people unfairly conquered can be brightened by moments of sincere happiness, just as the sleep of implacable conquerors can be marred by bitter awakenings, terrible nightmares.[4]

The rostral column erected to commemorate May 2 is crowned with the figure of Victory climbing toward heaven—toward that impassible region oblivious to both the cries of the victim and the curses of the executioner. The future monument to Grau will display at its highest point a colossus standing with his right arm stretched out toward the southern seas.

On a street leading south from St. Petersburg, Catharine of Russia set up a sign that read: "The road to Constantinople starts here." When the Slavic race feels the urge to set out for the "green lands," will it not remember Catharine's words? If Grau rose from the grave today, he would tell us . . . but it's useless to repeat his words. We all know where our duty lies and what road we should take tomorrow.

---

[4] This paragraph and many others belie those who have insisted in presenting the author as a stubborn professional pessimist, and even as being anti-Peruvian: a gross, or even deliberate, misrepresentation.—L.A.S.

Speech at the Politeama Theater[1]

(1888)

I

Gentlemen:

Those who have barely stepped across life's threshold come together today to teach a lesson to those who are approaching death's doorway. The celebration we are attending is replete with patriotism but also touched with irony: the child wants to ransom with gold what the man could not defend with iron.

Old men ought to tremble before children because the rising generation always accuses and judges the declining generation. From these happy, boisterous groups we'll witness the emergence of the austere and taciturn thinker, the poet who gives voice in stanzas of tempered steel, the historian who marks the forehead of the guilty with a seal of indelible ignominy.

[1] The reader needs to keep in mind the epoch and the circumstances in which the lecture at the Politeama was presented. A great national fund-raising campaign was under way to ransom the provinces of Tacna and Arica, which had been surrendered to Chile ten years earlier with the signing of the Treaty of Ancón. The scholars of Lima organized an evening gala at the old Politeama Theater. González Prada, a symbol of the politics of retribution, was invited to speak. He prepared the speech that is reproduced here and had a child read it. All the expressions of patriotic oratory mentioned in it refer to the epoch and the circumstances of 1888. The editor wants to emphasize that fifty-eight years have passed since then, and the international situation has changed radically.—L.A.S.

Children, be men, rise early to life, because no generation ever inherited a more dismal legacy, no generation ever had more sacred duties to perform, more serious errors to make right, or a more righteous vengeance to carry out.

In the orgy of the independence epoch, your ancestors drank down the rich wine and left the dregs. Since you are better than your fathers, you have the right to compose the shameful epitaph of a departing generation stigmatized by a civil war half a century long, a fraudulent bankruptcy, and the mutilation of the national territory.

If it were appropriate at such a moment to recall our shame and renew our sorrows, we would not accuse one group or excuse another. Who can throw the first stone?

The brutal hand of Chile tore our flesh and crushed our bones, but the true victors, the enemy's true weapons, were our ignorance and our spirit of servility.

II

Without specialists, or rather with amateurs who presume omniscience, we live from effort to effort: the efforts of amateurs in diplomacy, amateurs in political economy, amateurs in legislation, and even amateurs in tactics and strategies. Peru was a living body laid out on the marble stage of an amphitheater to suffer amputations by surgeons with senile cataracts in their eyes, their hands trembling with paralysis. We saw lawyers directing the public treasury, doctors supervising engineering projects, theologians fantasizing about domestic politics, naval officers running the department of justice, businessmen commanding army batallions . . . What didn't we see in that tumultuous ferment of all mediocrities, in those dizzying apparitions and vanishings of figures with no human solidity, in that constant changing of roles, in that Babel, finally, where vain, prattling ignorance always prevailed over quiet, humble knowledge!

With the free but undisciplined masses of the revolution, France marched to victory; with its armies of undisciplined, unfree Indians, Peru will always march to defeat. If we turned the Indian into a slave, what country should he serve? Like the medieval serf, he will fight only for his feudal lord.

Though it may be harsh and even cruel to repeat it here, don't imagine, gentlemen, that the spirit of servility is peculiar only to the Indian of the high mountains. We coastal mestizos also remember that the blood of Phillip II's subjects runs in our veins, mixed with the blood of Huayna-Capac's subjects. Our vertebral column tends naturally to sag.

The Spanish nobility left us their degenerate, spendthrift legacy: the winner of independence bequeathed his progeny of soldiers and bureaucrats. Rather than sow wheat and extract metal, the youth of the past generation preferred to atrophy their brains on the parade grounds of military barracks and let their skin grow brittle and yellowed in government offices. Men capable of doing hard work in the fields and mines preferred to dine on the leftovers from the government banquet. They drained the public treasury dry with their insatiable thirst and placed the strongman who offered bread and honors above the country that demanded gold and sacrifices. For that reason, though there have always been liberals and conservatives in Peru, there has never been a true liberal party or a true conservative party, merely three grand divisions: those in government, those conspiring against the government, and those rendered indifferent by selfishness, imbecility, or disillusionment. For that reason, in the supreme moment of the struggle, we weren't a bronze colossus against the enemy but a pile of lead filings; we weren't a strong, united country but a series of individuals drawn by particular interests and repelled one from another by partisan spirit. Although the most obscure soldier of the invading army had no name but Chile on his lips, we, from the commanding general on down to the lowest recruit, were repeating the name of a strongman,[2] like medieval serfs invoking the feudal lord.

Indians of the uninhabitable peaks and mountain ranges, mestizos from the coast, all of us were ignorant and servile. We didn't win and we couldn't win.

III

If the ignorance of those governing and the servility of the governed were our true conquerors, let's turn to science, that redeemer who

[2] A reference to General Andrés Avelino Cáceres, leader of the resistance in the Peruvian mountains.—L.A.S.

teaches us to gentle nature's tyranny; let us adore freedom, that mother who engenders strong men.

I'm not speaking, gentlemen, of the mummified science turning to dust in our backward universities, but science fortified with the blood of this century, science with ideas of vast scope, science that radiates youth and tastes like honey from Greek honeycombs, the positivist science that in a single century of industrial application has produced more benefits for humanity than entire milleniums of theology and metaphysics.

I'm speaking, gentlemen, of freedom for everyone, and especially for the most destitute. The real Peru isn't made up of the groups of American-born Spaniards and foreigners living on the strip of land situated between the Pacific and the Andes; the nation is made up of the masses of Indians living on the eastern slopes of the mountains. For three hundred years the Indian has been relegated to the lowest strata of civilization, a hybrid with all the vices of the savage and none of the virtues of the European. Just teach him to read and write, and in a quarter of a century you'll see whether he's capable of achieving human dignity, or not. It's up to you, schoolteachers, to galvanize a race fallen to sleep under the tyranny of the justice of the peace, the governor, and the priest, that unholy trinity responsible for brutalizing the Indian.[3]

When we have a people no longer afflicted by the spirit of servility, and military and political leaders capable of staying abreast with the century, we'll get Arica and Tacna back, and then and only then will we march on Iquique and Tarapacà and strike the first, the last, the decisive blow.

Until that great day, which will arrive at last because the future owes us a victory, let us put our trust only in the light of our minds and the strength of our arms. Gone are the days when valor alone decided the outcome of battle: today war is a problem, and science will provide the solution. Let us abandon international romanticism and our faith in superhuman aid: the earth mocks the vanquished, and heaven has no thunderbolts for the executioner.

In this work of reconstitution and vengeance let us not count on the

---

[3] González Prada has persisted in this motif throughout his work, and especially in the article, "Nuestros indios" from *Horas de lucha*.—L.A.S.

men of the past: those decrepit, worm-eaten trunks already produced their flowers of unwholesome aroma and their bitter fruit. It's time for new trees to proffer new blossoms, new fruits. Old men to the grave, and young men to the task at hand!

IV

Why despair? We haven't come here to shed tears over the ruins of a second Jerusalem but to fortify ourselves with hope. Let Boabdil weep like a woman, and let us be hopeful like men.

Never less than today can we afford the discouragement of cowardly minds or effeminate whining. Today when Tacna is breaking its silence and reminding the free brother of the captive brother, let's lift ourselves a few inches above the swamp of personal ambition and respond with words of encouragement and brotherhood to their words of love and hope.

Why be discouraged? Our climate, our soil, are they the last in the universe? There isn't enough gold on earth to acquire the wealth Peru can produce in a single springtime. Are our minds perchance as rudimentary as those of the Hottentots? Was our flesh molded from the clay of Sodom? The people of our mountains are men heavy with sleep, not petrified statues.

Our race doesn't lack electricity in the nerves or phosphorous in the brain; what we do lack is consistency of muscle and iron in the blood. Anemic and nervous, we don't know how to love or hate with constancy. Versatile in politics, today we love a leader to the point of sacrificing our rights on the altar of dictatorship, and tomorrow we'll hate him enough to overthrow him and trample him beneath a torrent of mud and blood. Lacking the patience to await the good, we insist on improvising what should be the product of slow incubation and expect a man to repair in a single day the faults of four generations. You can encapsule the history of many of our Peruvian administrations in three words—imbecility in action—but the entire life of the people can be summed up in these three—inconstancy in motion.

If we're inconstant in love, we're no less so in hatred. The dagger can still be sticking out of our gut, and already we're pardoning the murderer. Someone has carved up our fields, burned our cities, mutilated our territory, made an assault on our wealth, and converted our whole country into cemetery ruins; well, gentlemen, that someone against whom we vowed eternal rancor and implacable vengeance has now begun to figure among our friends, is no longer abhorred by us with all the fire of our blood, with all the rage of our hearts.

Now that hypocrisy and lies constitute the two poles of diplomacy, let our governments lie hypocritically, swearing friendship and amnesty. Let us, free men gathered here to listen to words of loyalty and honesty, fearing no explanations and respecting no susceptibilities, raise our voices to straighten the spines of these stooped masses, do what we can to provide oxygen to this atmosphere corrupted by the respiration of so many infected bodies, and strike the spark to ignite in the hearts of the people the flame to love steadily what we should love, and also to hate steadily what we should hate.

Gentlemen, may the lesson offered today by the Free Schools of Lima take root in the humblest shacks of the republic! May the phrases repeated on occasions like this not be mere mellifluous utterances destined to die inside the walls of a theater, but rude hammer blows that will echo throughout the country! May each of my words become a thunderclap beating in the hearts of all Peruvians and awakening the only two sentiments capable of regenerating and saving us: love of country and hatred of Chile! Let's place our hands on our chests, our hearts will tell us who we should hate . . .

If an unjust hatred can destroy an individual, a just hatred can always save a nation. For hatred of Prussia, France today is powerful as never before. When a defeated Paris stirs, a victorious Berlin is startled to its feet. Every day, at each moment, we admire the prowess of the men who triumphed on the plains of Marathon or went to their deaths in the ranks of the Thermophilae; and truly, "the moral grandeur of the ancient Greeks consisted in their constant love of their friends and their immutable hatred for their enemies."[4] let's not cultivate the anodyne sentiments of the eunuch in a seraglio, but the formidable passions of the man born to engender future avengers. Don't let the world say that the memory of the injury was erased from our memory even before the welt raised by the Chilean lash disappeared.

True, we can do nothing today, we're impotent, but let's nurse our rancor and wallow in our indignation like a wild beast in thorns. If we have no claws to scratch or teeth to bite, at least let the unmuffled roars of our virile wrath disturb the sleep of the proud conqueror from time to time.

---

[4] Lessing, "Laokoon," VI (handwritten quotation added by the author).—L.A.S.

Peru and Chile[1]

(1888)

I

Peru has suffered no calamity more disastrous than the war with Chile. The campaigns for independence and the second war with Spain cost us precious lives and great sacrifices; but they gave us our own life and identity and uplifted the national spirit. We were born on December 9 and grew into a giant on May 2.

The difference is that in 1824 and 1866 we did not suffer the humiliation of defeat. The blood shed on the fields of battle, the capitals destroyed by fire, the wealth lost in the sacking of the villages and towns pale by comparison with the evils infecting the body of a defeated nation. The harm caused by our conqueror does not consist in the killings, the devastation, or the plunder; it lies in what it leaves us and in what it teaches us.

Chile takes away the guano, the saltpeter, and long strips of territory; it leaves us dejection, humiliation of spirit, resignation to defeat, and the tedium of living modestly and frugally. We can see in people's spirit a rise of apathy, an infuriating indolence, and a nauseating debasement.

[1] It's important to remember that this article was written during the war with Chile, from 1879 to 1883, which explains the violence of its tone.—L.A.S.

Chile teaches us its Araucanian ferocity. In the last civil strife[2] our cruelty to one another reached the point of barbarism, and we demonstrated that contact with a bloody and implacable enemy had hardened our hearts. Enraged souls, wild beasts never before encountered in the Peruvian fauna, appeared as if from nowhere. The inborn mildness of the national character suffered a regression to primitive savagery. In the magnanimous nation (where always before civil discord ended in forgiveness of common errors and pity for the fallen brother) all that's left today, after the conflict, is hatred of our Basque[3] enemies and a bitterness of tiger against tiger. Rancor and hatred that we ought to reserve for our common enemy we direct instead against ourselves. We awaken from our cataleptic dream only to strike out with our fists and curse each other with death.

In our private dealings with one another, in our long-term relationships and in secular conquest, we see at work a fusion of races with a mixture of vices and virtues. But in the destructive and violent invasion, vanquished and victor forget their own virtues and take on the vices of the foreigner. The most civilized peoples hide their savage and bestial underside: in war we experience the collision of man against man precisely in his bestial, savage side.

If Peru became infected by Araucanian ferocity, Chile contracted the Peruvian virus. The contact between the two nations reminds us of Almanzor's embrace, a way of transmitting the plague. No one is unaware that our conqueror of yesterday finds itself afflicted now by the cancer of the most sordid public corruption; the presses of Santiago and Valparaiso make this clear at every hour and in every nuance. Chile is today imitating the Peru of the *consolidation* and of the *Dreyfus contract*: it is heading down the path we followed, and it will be what we were. The beggar who a short while ago felt happy with a slice of watermelon and a handful of pinto beans tomorrow will be stuffing himself in the sumptuous feasts of the improvised magnate. The gambler who walks into a casino poor and comes out rich through a stroke of luck turns effortlessly into a wastrel.[4]

But let's not seek compensation for our calamities in the political

---

[2] This is a reference to the struggle between Iglesias and Cáceres.—L.A.S.

[3] Allusion to the Basque origin attributed to the majority of Chileans.—L.A.S.

[4] Allusion to the Treaty of Ancón.—L.A.S.

corruption of our enemy, nor even think of abandoning our wealth and our territory to him like a Trojan horse, nor imagine that we have just injected his body with the germ of premature death.

Chile, with all its miseries, will defeat us tomorrow and always if we continue to be what we were and what we are now. Garbed in the prestige of its victories, it has credit; thus in any war it will have money, and with money, soldiers and ships, rifles and cannons, friends and spies.

A people would have to be mad to place all its hopes for growing strong in the weakness of neighboring peoples. When our neighbor grows stooped, does that make us taller? When we see an enemy bleeding, does that add a drop of blood to our veins? The decline of Chile ought to make us rejoice, but only if our own decline were ending or becoming mitigated, if we were growing strong as Chile grew weak; but it happens that as Chile declines in arithmetic progression, we're doing so in geometric progression. The strength of nations is concealed within, and it comes from moral elevation. The gaslight that dazzles our eyes radiates sunbeams stored deep inside the earth; the man who dazzles us with his generosity or heroism, discovers virtues incubated slowly in the warmth of a good education.

II

For twenty years now, since the victories of Prussia, the European world has been converting its men into soldiers and its towns into barracks. Alcohol, the plague of individuals, has its counterpart in the plague of nations, militarism. No one asks if there will be a universal conflagration, but only who will be the first to draw a sword, where will the battlefield be, which nations will be overrun, trampled, pulverized. Everyone awaits the supreme crisis, knowing that those who drink blood suffer their own kind of delirium tremens.

Chile, with its instinct for imitation, natural to juvenile peoples, imitates the warrior spirit of Germany and hoists the banner of conquest high in America. The German empire hooked its eagle talons into Alsace and Loraine; Chile dug its vulture claws into Iquique and Tarapacá, and, in order to be greater than Germany, intends to seize Arica, Tacna, and perhaps all of Peru.

Meanwhile, what are we doing? Living in the realm of theories, we forget that states aren't governed by romantic humanitarianism, don't turn the left cheek when they're slapped on the right; we forget that when faced with the immolation of a people everyone observes a selfish prudence, when they don't cover the victor with flowers and oppress the defeated with ignominy. We forget, finally, that in individual relationships the least civilized men harbor a vestige of social modesty and give the appearance of being guided by philanthropy, whereas in international life the most cultured nations strip off their veneer of civilization and proceed like savages in the jungle.

We didn't fall because the civil wars had weakened us or left us exhausted. Far more brutal and tenacious wars than ours were endured by Argentina, Venezuela, Colombia, and particularly Mexico. We fell because Chile, which watches while Peru sleeps, caught us poor and without credit, unprepared and poorly armed, without an army or a navy.

If only we had gone through a few of those radical revolutions that turn society up side down and divide it into two bands that leave no room for neutral or selfish individuals. Unfortunately, like storms at sea, all our barracks uprisings slid along the surface without shaking the depths.

If uprisings by praetorians betray decadence, constant popular uprisings manifest a superabundance of life. Young nations have an excess of strength that they direct against themselves when they aren't employing it in agriculture, industry, the arts, or in conquest. Countries become agitated for their own good, the way children run and jump to lubricate their joints and develop their muscles. Civil wars serve as an apprenticeship for foreign wars: they are the gymnasium of the nation. Joseph de Maistre called them holy, and Chateaubriand maintained that they tempered and regenerated peoples.

Our enemy surpassed us in practicality and even in the humility that made them seek enlightenment everywhere and accept help no matter where it came from. Foreigners reformed their universities, foreigners drew up their laws, foreigners restored their public treasury, foreigners trained them to aim their Krupp cannons at us.

We did just the opposite. Under the illusion that our semitheological and semischolastic empiricism was the height of knowledge, we blocked the way to anything that wasn't exclusively national and surrendered ourselves blindly to the initiative of our leaders. What was the result?

The same as always: splendid scholars who turned public education into chaos; splendid treasury secretaries who never balanced a budget, splendid diplomats who drew up disastrous pacts, splendid sailors who ran our ships aground, and splendid soldiers who lost the battles.

Even today, after the tremendous cataclysm, we're sleeping soundly, forgetting that Chile would gladly give us a thousand lives for the sheer pleasure of taking them away one by one, and we continue to educate our young, not as men who will have to fight on battlefields but as passive bureaucrats whose joints will grow stiff between the four walls of an office. We continue with all our preoccupations about caste and sect, with all our batty pettiness. If a foreigner comes to offer us light or to try to inoculate us against the ferment of modern life, we rise up en masse, feel that our national pride has been offended, and call wounded dignity what everywhere else is called presumptuous and shameless ignorance. When a foreign pen censures our social vices or reveals the wretchedness of our public figures, we burst into a rage and proclaim to the world that only Peruvians should meddle in Peruvian affairs, that our public figures are not under the jurisdiction of the court of Humankind, but the private jurisdiction of their compatriots . . . affirmations of the mole that conceives of nothing beyond the molehill, the exclusivism of the infusorian that limits its visual radius to the drop of water.

III

There is nothing as beautiful as knocking down borders and destroying the egotistic sentiment of nationalism in order to make the earth a single people and humanity a single family. All elevated and generous minds are moving toward cosmopolitanism today and repeating with Schopenhauer that "patriotism is the passion of fools and the most foolish of passions." But until the hour of universal peace arrives, as long as we are living in a land of sheep and wolves, we have to be prepared to behave like lambs toward the lamb and like wolves toward the wolf.

We have to block the way to conquest and defend our territory inch by inch because the country isn't just a piece of land that drinks our tears today and will drink our blood tomorrow, but also the special mold into which our being is poured or, more precisely, the intellectual and moral atmosphere we breathe. Man owes as much to the country he is born in as the tree to the ground in which it's rooted. To conquer us is the same as suddenly changing our way of living, or submerging us in another environment in order to condemn us to asphyxiation.

And not everything can be reduced to wretched personal interest. We should enjoy our national heritage the way one enjoys free use of some benefit. If we inherit a large, unencumbered piece of land from our parents, we should leave our descendants a large, unencumbered piece of land, sparing them the affront of being born in a defeated and mutilated country, sparing them the sacrifice of recovering at the cost of their blood the goods and rights that we failed to defend at the cost of ours. There's nothing as cowardly as a generation that pays its debts by passing them on to future generations.

More noble ideas also oblige us to repel any attack and to avenge any invasion. "To suffer an injury is to give wings to violence and contribute in a cowardly manner to the triumph of injustice. If an abused right were given up without resistance, the world would very soon fall into the clutches of iniquity." [Louis Ménard, *La moral avant les philosophes*].

The men of yesterday, who forgot all this, file before our eyes stifling in their hearts the voice of remorse and longing to erase from their foreheads the indelible stains of mud and blood; we men of today will be abhorred by the generation of tomorrow, if we don't demonstrate the strength to strike and the wisdom to know where to strike.

We need to evolve to adapt ourselves to the international environment in which we live. By nature, and because of the mildness of our climate, the wealth of the land, and the boon of being able to live effortlessly and well, we are peaceful, little inclined to conquest, fond of repose, and averse to emigration. But because of our geographical position, surrounded by Ecuador, Brazil, Bolivia, and Chile, we are doomed to be the battleground where the destinies of South America are played out, and so must transform ourselves into a bellicose nation. The future summons us to a defensive war. We must be combatants or slaves.

True, capricious desire isn't enough to create national instincts or to improvise events; but the will, firm and guided by science, can modify the external world, can slowly change the moral condition of societies, and can convert man into the true providence of humanity. There is an underwater animal that, for lack of eyes, acquires antennas to move by feel through the dark vastness, yet a people sunken in the opprobrium of defeat can't stir up sufficient passion to hate or the strength to avenge itself!

The redeeming evolution will come about by the spontaneous movement of the social body, not by simple initiative of the leaders. Why wait for everything to come from above? The lack of confidence in ourselves, the pernicious system of centralizing everything in the hands of the government, and the mania for surrendering humbly to the impulse from the capital have had a disastrous effect on the fortunes of the country. Like a species of blind men accustomed to waiting for the boy who guides us, we stop dead in our tracks when we feel that we're alone. When we lost Lima in the war, we were without eyes, without minds, as if we had been decapitated. In a well-organized nation the people don't behave like a passenger drowsing restfully in his cabin who only opens his eyes from time to time to satisfy his curiosity as to the number of miles traveled. On the contrary, all rule, all work, all keep watch because they play simultaneously the part of captain, crew, and passengers.

IV

There is a quality that leads us to make sacrifices in times of great crisis, and another quality that drives us to fulfill ordinary obligations in our daily life. In the present crisis, we don't need that poetic quality, which is perhaps less demanding because it takes only a moment of resolve; we do need that more prosaic virtue, which is perhaps more demanding because it requires consistency of effort and a willingness to submit to a dreary routine. To die violently, in full sunlight, amid the cheers of our countrymen, is less bitter than dying slowly in the darkness and silence of a mine.

We are fallen but not pinned against a rock; mutilated but not impotent; bloody but not dead. A few years of sanity, of building up our strength, and we'll be ready to act effectively. Let's be a constant threat, since we can't be more than that. With our rancor always alive, with our stern attitude of men, we'll keep the enemy in a state of constant anxiety, force him to spend vast sums building up armaments, and drain him dry. One day of tranquility in Peru is a night of nightmares in Chile.

To speak of imminent armed retaliation borders on delirium; the safe, sane course consists in preparing for tomorrow's action. Let's work with the patience of the ant, then attack with the sureness of the hawk. Let Chile glut itself on guano and saltpeter; the time will come when its flesh eats lead and iron.

Let others dream of redress without combat or revolutions without victims, and let us remember that the bad thing is not to spill blood, but to spill it in vain. Countries have no rights other than those they defend or win with force; freedom is born on the barricades or on the battlefields, not in diplomatic protocols or legalistic jargon from Salamanca. Let sentimental fools say what they wish, whoever wins, wins. The victor, although he pulverizes the defeated and commits crimes against humanity, nonetheless dazzles and seduces the world. In the charade of history, every crime haloed by success is a victory in the name of virtue. If you want to know whether it hurts to be defeated, just ask the inhabitants of Iquique and Tarapacá, condemned to live as guests in their own house; ask those from Arica and Tacna, doomed to await some dubious indemnification, like seamen captured by pirates from Algiers.

We, who are able to see the sun directly without the intervention of the invader's shadow, can't even imagine the repressed rage of those Peruvians subjected to Chilean domination. They put their trust and hope in us. They say nothing, but they extend their arms toward us silently, turn their eyes toward us silently, listen silently, with bated breath, for the sound of our footsteps. Like Victor Hugo's Poland, the towns in the south wait and wait, but no one comes.

And who could possibly come? Before we go to their aid, someone will attack us again. Chile hasn't forgotten the road to Peru, and will return. And their coming is something to fear because they're like the invasions of the Huns and swarming insects through trees. The swarm destroys everything that doesn't move from its path, from the house of the rich landowner to the hut of the poor Indian; anything that isn't nailed down, it takes to Santiago, from the school laboratory to the public urinal. Anyone who builds a dwelling, works a mine, or sows a field should assume he is building, or working, or sowing it for Chile.

The mother rejoicing in her firstborn son should assume she'll eventually see him riddled by Chilean bullets; the father preening over his favorite daughter should assume she'll be raped by a Chilean soldier.

While the second invasion speeds toward us, let's watch for Chile's cunning hand, or worse, its brazen meddling and undermining, in all of our financial affairs. Once the problem of Arica and Tacna is resolved, new complications will arise to keep us constantly off balance; and on the day it seems to have forgotten us or pretends to be regarding us with benevolence, that will be the day when it will be thinking about us most intently and plotting the greatest treachery to harm us. Not satisfied with having wounded and despoiled us or with forcing us to feel unrelenting humiliation over the defeat, Chile will look for petty excuses to denigrate and persecute us, because it is pursuing a systematic and brutal course to brand and shame and stigmatize us, to bury a dagger in our heart.[5]

---

[5] This article corresponds to the typically retaliatory stage of the author's work, growing out of the war of 1879–1883.—L.A.S.

Vijil[1]

(1885)

I

Francisco de Paula González Vijil was born in Tacna on September 13, 1792. In the *Notes about My Life*, a short, unpublished autobiography that he composed in December 1867, he says:

> My parents were don Joaquín González Vijil and doña Micaela Yáñez. I was the first born of my brothers, and for this reason my parents decided I should devote my life to study.
>
> I received a scholarship in the council seminary in Arequipa on July 16, 1803, when Mr. Chávez de la Roza, a distinguished protector and priest of the seminary, was serving as bishop. I studied grammar, philosophy, mathematics, and theology.
>
> On September 12, 1812, I graduated with a doctorate in theology from the University of San Antonio del Cuzco. I returned by way of Arequipa to Tacna, where I studied natural law with the priest and doctor don Juan José de la Fuente y Bustamante.

[1] The article on Vijil, a true autobiographical page, was written by M.G.P. on the tenth anniversary of the death of the great Peruvian heresiarch. It is one of the few carefully documented articles that he produced. Its final lines are prophetic: they portray the end of Prada himself and spell out his ethical concept of politics and history.—L.A.S. 1976.

In 1815 Bishop la Encina offered me the vicerectorship and chair of theology at the seminary, provided I was willing to be ordained. I set out for Arequipa, began ordination exercises in the house of the bishop himself; but terrified by the step I was about to take, I disappeared on the eve of my ordination. After a few days, I presented myself before the bishop, who received me with open arms. He appointed me to the chair of philosophy and mathematics in the school.

In 1817 I became seriously ill, and once again entertained the idea of taking orders, a step encouraged by my spiritual director, the venerable friar Father Mateo Campló. I was ordained as subdeacon in December 1818, as deacon in March 1819, and as priest in September of that same year, by Mr. Goyeneche, who had previously appointed me vice rector and professor of theology. I went to Tacna to say my first mass.

In 1822 I declared my candidacy for the teaching chair of the Arequipa choir. In 1823 I cut ties completely with the Seminary and returned to Tacna. . . ."

The *Notes* do not shed much additional light on what is known about the years from 1823 to 1826. Perhaps those three years were a period of violent crises in the Jouffroy mode or of endless conflicts as in the career of Lamenais. Why this sudden and mysterious departure from the seminary? Why did it only occur to him again to become ordained when he fell seriously ill, and perhaps when his mind and free will were not functioning at full capacity? That flight or escape in 1815, on the eve of his ordination: are we to interpret that as an exaggerated scruple on the part of the true believer, or as an instinctive repugnance of a man without faith to allow himself to be invested with religious office? Who knows whether Vijil consecrated himself to an ecclesiastical career, not by spontaneous inclination but by one of those artificial vocations fomented in the bosom of Catholic families. Perhaps the phrase, "my parents decided I should devote my life to study" should read "my parents decided I should devote my life to an ecclesiastical career."

Vijil prudently says nothing about the circumstances surrounding his ordination and limits his explanation to say that he was ordained in good faith; but in another section of his *Notes* he confesses that from the time of his first trip to Lima, in 1826, he found himself being gradually transformed in that new theater due to the influence of new ideas. And that is conceivable, though it's also arguable that for an individual to undergo a total moral transformation the environmental factor is not in itself sufficient without a favorable inclination of the will.

With the entry of the army of liberation into Lima, a gust of modern spirit swept through the decrepit palace of the viceroys, and the city that had been born, according to the expression of d'Edgard Quinet, "with all the wrinkles of Byzantium already in place," suddenly displayed on its countenance the beauty and healthy exuberance of youth. There was a general impulse to move forward, an impulse that could easily have turned into stagnation or regression if the Spanish had won the battle of Ayacucho. Men who, as if committing a crime, had stealthily devoured a truncated section of a book by Voltaire or Rousseau, began to express freely their loss of faith and their liberalism. Died-in-the-wool royalists were suddenly posing as republicans of long standing, priests filed into the masonic lodges, and the poets who had been courtiers to viceroys and cantors for mothers superior suddenly took up the lyre of Apollo to sing hymns to Bolívar and Sucre. It's not surprising that, in such an atmosphere, a man like Vijil could lose his faith or finish losing it.

The philosopher succeeds the believer; but in his first writings, the politician restrains his propagandistic bent. Judging it inconvenient and even counterproductive to reveal suddenly a whole new way of thinking, he doesn't attack any dogma, and in his canonical and priestly disquisitions he limits himself to merely preparing the ground for more radical work. However, with his actions he reveals what his words do not say: from that point on, though he continues to wear the priestly habit, he does not perform any ecclesiastical function and renounces any honors the governments offer him within the Church. Despite his difficult pecuniary circumstance, he does not accept a canonship in the choir of Lima or the deaconate in the Trujillo diocese. "I ceased to be," he says, "a clergyman subject to theologians and canons with their questions, and became a man and a citizen."

II

As the context for his activities, or rather, as a substitute for religious and teaching duties, he chose politics, and he entered the ring with all the enthusiasm of youth. It was only a short while since independence, and the hour of illusions was still shining bright. Imagining that South

America would soon establish republics equal or superior to the United States, all men of good will wanted to lend their support and regarded abstention as a crime. Bolívar had not yet pronounced his dispiriting words: "America is ungovernable. Those who have served the revolution have plowed the sea. The only thing that can be done in America is to emigrate."

Vijil's public life begins in 1826 when he is elected deputy by Tacna. From that point on he leads a varied and active existence. He spends the years between 1826 and 1830 in Chile for reasons of health, in 1831 he graduates with a doctorate in law, from 1831 until 1834 he occupies, with some interruptions, the rectorship of the School of Independence in Arequipa, and from the end of 1836 until the beginning of 1838, holds the position of librarian in Lima. He also publishes articles in some newspapers, composes some lengthy books, attends sessions of the houses of congress, and makes several trips to Lima, Tacna, Arequipa, and so on.

In his *Notes*, he writes:

> In 1826 I came to Lima as deputy for the province of my birth; I attended the preliminary meetings, and did not sign the petition signed by fifty-two deputies asking that the installation of the Congress be suspended, as did happen . . .
>
> In 1827 I was elected deputy again and, though my health was not good, I participated in the sessions that ended in 1828. I wrote some articles in the *Eco de la Opinión*. When Congress recessed, I sailed to Chile for my health, using the money I had saved from my salary as a deputy, and I returned to Tacna in 1830.
>
> Elected deputy in 1831 for the 1832 Congress, I went to Arequipa, as the supreme government council had named me rector of the School of Independence. I received the title of doctor in law from the University of San Agustín in Arequipa, for having been one of the founding members of the Lauretana Academy. From Arequipa I came to Lima for the second time, as a member of the chamber of deputies, and at that time I and twenty-one other deputies faced impeachment (1832).
>
> In 1833 I was elected deputy to the convention by my province and by the province of Arequipa. I published pieces in the *Constitutional* of that period; I confess now, repentent and ashamed, that I let myself get carried away by partisan exaltation, as I have mentioned in the issue in the library and in another issue of my own, no. 20 (February 15, 1834) . . .
>
> In Tacna I took part in a debate on March 14, 1836, in a public meeting

concerning various subjects, arguing that the province should separate from the capital of the republic and from the district capital and put itself under the protection of General Santa Cruz, president of Bolivia, who was in Peru as an administrative adviser.

In 1839, after the victory of Yungay and the fall of the confederation, I contradicted an agent of the prefect of Arequipa who had been commissioned to try to bring the new district back under the control of its former state, reincorporating its provinces into the district of Arequipa . . . Shortly thereafter, with the approval of President Gamarra, I was conducted into exile by soldiers under the command of the general, who at the time exercised absolute power in the South: they thought I was acting in complicity with the confederation . . . On July 28 the ship carrying us into exile set sail for Valparaíso.

I returned to Tacna from Chile in January of 1840.

Vijil's activity in public life ended in 1845 when for the second time he accepted the position as librarian in Lima. He had already completed his work, *Defense of the Authority of Governments against the Pretensions of the Roman Curia*, and thereafter he dedicated himself exclusively to his chosen studies and to the publication of his writings.

He no longer wants to be involved in militant politics and even avoids intervening in parliamentiary debates, alleging as an excuse the poor state of his health. Thus, in 1851, he attends very few sessions of Congress, and in 1866 he refuses to accept senate office. Who knows whether this was because he felt the premature weariness of age or whether he was disillusioned with public life. Several years had passed since independence, and Bolívar's prediction had been fulfilled: "These countries will inevitably fall into the hands of uncontrolled mobs and then pass almost imperceptibly into the hands of petty tyrants, of all colors and races, consumed by every crime and extinguished by ferocity."

Although he was elected deputy eight times and senator once, although he fought with determination and energy both inside and outside the houses of congress, Vijil never occupied a place of power or managed to have a decisive or significant influence on the great events of the country. With his career as lay priest he had put himself in a delicate position. In countries like France, a Lakanal can be a member of the Academy of Science, a Daunou can be a peer, a Sieyès can be a director as well as a consul. But in nations like Peru, the priest who breaks with the Church is doomed to isolation, a kind of social quarantine. He's fortunate if they let him die in peace. Vijil as minister of justice, Vijil as officer of the court, Vijil as president of the republic, would have aroused general opposition. Although priests publicly known to be libertines or simonists could serve as ministers and bishops as long as they were orthodox, he, publicly impeccable, but heterodox, died a mere librarian.

His political ideas provoked less scandal than his religious ideas. He always came across as a moderate republican, liberal in the style of the French revolutionaries of 1848. He defended freedom of conscience, tolerance of cults, civil matrimony, and divorce; but he always held the Roman concept of the omnipotent state. Thus, in striving to take from the Church its privileges and its absolute authority over the conscience of the individual, he did so less to bring about the complete emancipation of the individual than to consolidate and broaden the power of the state.

Because he always maintained the same convictions, because he remained firm and loyal while his correligionists gave ground and prevaricated, he was surrounded by immense prestige, but not by many disciples or imitators. Thousands applauded his attitude and conceded that he was right; no one imitated or followed him. Confined to his library, he played the role of honorary leader of a liberal party without liberals, as they say, general of an army without soldiers.

III

When he fled the political arena, Vijil did not enter a more tranquil terrain. The troubles of the public man were followed by the penury of the writer, the painstaking task of entire years scraping together resources to pay for the printing of his books. His first work, begun in 1836 and finished in 1845, wasn't published until 1848 and 1849. He writes in his *Notes:*

> In 1845, I came for the fourth time to Lima to seek subscriptions to print the first part of the work, interrupted in exile and finished in Tacna after my return.
> I have suffered dearly for lack of the necessary funds to pay the cost of printing my writings. I've endured many humiliations. I wrote to people

both inside and outside the capital asking them to please round up subscriptions; and because the subscriptions did not cover the costs incurred, I ended up in debt and had to borrow from the family my part of the inheritance I was to share with my brothers, to pay my creditors . . .

When the work was published in 1848 and 1849, Pope Pius IX condemned it in a special brief at the request of the gentleman who was archbishop at the time. In response to that condemnation I wrote a letter to the pope and analyzed his brief. The letter as well as my analysis were condemned by the Index Congregation with full approval of the pontiff.

Two condemnations in a row: that's all it took for Vijil to become an object of admiration for some and the target of scandal for others. A heretic, who instead of humbling himself in the face of the anathemas, held his head high and confronted the Supreme Pontiff was unheard of in Peru. Olavide had been merely an unpublished heretic, a salon sinner, a pseudophilosopher who ended up striking his colors and publicly acknowledging the error of his ways.

Enduring the insults and slander of the pious folk, with no governmental protection, relying solely on his own resources, Vijil continued for more than twenty-five years his work as propagandist and defender of the state against the Church. The *Notes* contain the enumeration of his principal works:

In 1852 I published the *Abstract* of the work ordered chronologically and a notebook of *Additions to the Defense of the Authority of Governments against the Pretensions of the Roman Curia,* followed by the papal condemnation.

In 1856 I published the second part, *Defense of the Authority of the Bishops,* and in 1857 its *Abstract,* as well as the *Quick Look at the Balance of Power,* an expanded second edition of the one I wrote in 1853 . . .

In 1858 I had a volume published in Brussels attacking the papal bull of December 8, 1854.

In 1859 I composed and published the *Patriotic Catechism.* In 1861 the *Compendium on the Jesuits.* In 1862 the first volume of the *Social and Political Treatises;* others were published separately or in newspapers, and most were never published. I wrote for the *Constitutional* in 1858; for *America* and *Democracy* in 1862. In 1863 I published the work on the *Jesuits.* Also published in 1863 were five treatises on tolerance and civil liberty for religious cults and another in defense of these: these fill a single volume.

Also in 1863 I published the *Manual on Ecclesiastical Public Law for the*

Use of American Youth and some *Dialogues on the Existence of God and the Hereafter*. Both works were condemned by the Index Congregation on April 25, 1864, with the approval of Pope Pius IX on the twenty-ninth of the same month. Concerning the condemnation of the *Dialogues*, in which I defended the existence of God and the afterlife, I've written a second letter to Pius IX, which I decided not to send to him.

In 1867 I worked on the refutation of a pamphlet entitled *Comparative Examination of the Monarchy and the Republic*. Also, a *Historical Profile of Bartolomé de las Casas*, a *Defense of Bossuet and Fenelón*, and several treatises on various events that occurred that year.

As we have seen, Vijil wrote the *Notes* in December 1867. Several years later, he added this bibliographical note: "Subsequently, a volume was published in 1871 containing my three letters to Pius IX, the first concerning the condemnation of the Defense of the Authority of Governments, the second concerning the condemnation of the *Dialogues*, and the third concerning the doctrine of Infallibility. It contains several relevant documents."

He leaves unpublished an important work in which, setting aside canonical and curial matters, he takes a frankly rationalist approach and refutes one by one all the Catholic dogmas, from original sin to the divinity of Jesus Christ. A book burdensome in style and hardly original in substance, it will never make us forget works in a similar vein written by Peyrat, Larroque, and especially Strauss. Published today, twenty or twenty-five years after its composition, after the profound works produced by the Germans, the English, and the French, the book would provoke among European scholars and critics the same effect as the resurrection of a corpse in the sixteenth century.

But if the unpublished work lacks the merit of originality, it does have great documentary value concerning the psychological evolution of the author and for laying out his method of procedure in his work as a propagandist.

He writes in the prologue:

> In a cleared, level field, all it takes is irrigation and the plow and a few other operations to sow the seed of the crop one wants to harvest; but when there are trees, plants, and undergrowth, it's necessary to clear the land, and do other kinds of work, often difficult and prolonged, until the goal is reached.

These principles, based on prudence, have served me as a guide in my studies and in the works I have undertaken in the service of my country and all of America. In Catholic countries, where there is a deeply rooted belief system and the Catholic religion occupies a place in the fundamental laws of the state, it is neither possible nor convenient, and could even be extremely prejudicial, to express every latest idea one has in mind, and to express it abruptly; to do so would not only provoke scandal and great perturbation in people's conscience but would produce an effect contrary to that intended and would delay rather than bring about its realization.

Therefore I chose to proceed gradually.

Vijil, in his religious evolution, stripped himself of his Catholic beliefs, to live confined in a kind of liberal Christianity or a vague Christian deism. When he wrote that he "ceased to be a clergyman subject to theologians and became a man," he felt obliged to add: "though I'm still a Christian, because the Gospel, as it existed in the head and heart of Jesus Christ, is the religion of every man of good will." This notion of Christianity is somewhat vague and vast in scope, since no one knows for certain and with precision what was in the head of Jesus Christ: if we knew that, there wouldn't be a thousand Christian sects, all of them based on the authority of the Gospels. (In his *Dialogues,* more worthy of Father Almeida than of Plato, he defends with such zeal the existence of God and the immortality of the soul, expresses so much confidence in the power of his arguments, that even the least malicious reader enjoys the pleasure of a smile, if not the joy of being persuaded.)

Compared with the formidable assaults of modern revolutionaries against the social and religious order, the attacks by this heterodox Peruvian seem like musket shots as opposed to shots from a Krupp cannon. Still, in this land of Spanish secular fanaticism, the writings of Vijil seem even today daringly original, like trails blazed through the heart of a primal forest.

IV

Unlike Olavide, who lived sadly during his last years, scorned by the orthodox as an old apostate and by the heterodox as a new prevaricator, Vijil lived an honorable old age and won for himself the supreme glory longed for by an old man: seeing himself respected and believed.

Because he knew even in his early years how to surround himself with sympathy, because he managed to win hearts with his austerity and good faith, he suffered no persecutions and was able to practice freely his propaganda or solitary apostleship.

He died in Lima on June 9, 1875. Priests hovered over his dying hours, trying to force from him a last minute retraction or find a way to invent one; but he rejected all such efforts and died a lay death, "in the arms of the good Jesus," as he said in his last moments.

Afraid at one time that his cadaver would become an object of profanations, he had designated as sepulcher the island of San Lorenzo until his remains were moved to Tacna. But his fears were not realized; Lima in 1875 was no longer the Lima that a few years earlier had poured into the streets to stone the deputies who defended freedom of religious cults in the convention. Just as some provinces of the republic, unintimidated by the anathemas of Pope Pius IX, had elected the excommunicate to the national Congress, so now the people of the capital, ignoring clerical imprecations, carried the body of the impenitent on their shoulders.

The people were right: there have been few lives as pure, as full, as worthy of being imitated, as that of Vijil. You might attack the form and substance of his writings, you might characterize his books today as being outdated or insufficient, you might, in short, demolish the entire structure forged by his intelligence; but one thing will remain standing and invulnerable—the man.

Vijil spent the last years of his existence immersed in study, kept himself apart from the wretchedness of an atmosphere steeped in all the worst passions, and emerged uncorrupted from the shameful epochs of corruption in which the strongest fell and even the most innocent were besmirched. When it came time for him to depart for the Unknown, he sank down into his sepulcher without issuing a cowardly retraction or being intimidated by hallucinations or mirages from beyond the grave. In a word, he succeeded in living and dying as a philosopher.

Selling his inheritance to pay for the publication of his books, burying himself for more than thirty years in the parchments of a library, fighting without fear or boast to carry out the grand enterprise of secularizing life, working constantly to bring light to people with myopic minds and vigor to those whose wills were sick, responding courteously or with light irony to the brutal attacks of superstition and ignorance, he stands as an example and also as an accusation. Luther, when he broke with the Church, experienced an endless rage, interrupted by cries of remorse that made him envy the dead; Vijil, after losing his beliefs in his early years, maintained an inborn mildness of character. One look at his physiognomy was enough to convince us that he had killed hatred in his heart. But we shouldn't attribute his imperturbable mildness to timidity or cowardice: beneath the peaceful facade, he concealed the fortitude of the gentle man. He was capable of taking on Santa Cruz, Gamarra, and Castilla when many held their tongues and trembled. As a writer, he figures among the audacious and the brave. To attack fanaticism in a society of fanatics, isn't that equivalent to manning the barricades or stepping onto the field of battle?

Among his many qualities "the moral energy of the will" stands out. He never gave in. In his periods of most intense cerebral productivity he had to contend with his own weak and sickly constitution. Prostrate in bed, afflicted with constant hemorrhaging, hounded by intense neuralgic pains, he thought and produced without having the strength to edit his ideas. Obliged to remain immobile and on his back for hours at a time, he wasn't even able to read. During those times an ignorant, paralytic boy with barbaric handwriting and an atrocious French or Latin pronunciation served as his scribe and reader.

When referring to Vijil, his adversaries pronounced as their deepest condemnation the same word that Luther and Calvin heard yesterday and that Renan and Father Jacinto hear today: apostasy. An infantile accusation: if mature men hadn't put aside the errors they acquired in childhood or the illusions forged in their youth, humanity would never have emerged from caves and forests. The fanatic, forgetting that there is nothing definitive in human thought, becomes locked into a sect or party, while the true thinker evolves constantly, considering every political or religious belief as a provisional hypothesis.

Let them condemn Vijil for exaggerating his good qualities, but never for excess of bad ones. He was an altruist with the flush of optimism. He possessed a childish simplicity that kept him from seeing the ridiculous aspect of certain actions or words. Only through some ineffable naïveté could he have written at the end of his *Notes:* "If my works are appreciated or worthy of some consideration, I ask in recompense that the governors of my country serve faithfully and bring happiness to a people who deserve to be be happy on many accounts."

Governors and governed won't find their *vademecum* in Vijil's works because in general they are indigestible, lack the magic of style: instead of being read and studied, they'll be debated and quoted secondhand. But whether they're read or not, their author deserves to be remembered with pleasure: the men in Peru who fight for reason and science against faith and ignorance should be deeply grateful to their true precursor, the old soldier who blazed the trail, who fought in the vanguard, who gave and received the first blows.

In summary, for his strength of character, the sincerity of his convictions, and the purity of his life, Vijil redeems the faults of an entire generation. He had no rivals and leaves no successors, and he stands out in Peru like a solitary marble column on the banks of a muddy river.

Catholic Education[1]

(1892)

Je ne veux pas que les prêtres se mêlent de l'éducation publique.

NAPOLEON

I

Let's get a map of Lima and mark in red the buildings occupied by religious orders, the way doctors mark on the world map the places infected by an epidemic. We'll see that we are threatened by an irresistible inundation of priests. Fathers of the Sacred Hearts, Redeemers, Salesians, Jesuits, and Barefoot Brothers, all of them are setting up or preparing to set up schools. Even our ancient, moribund convents are trying to get face-lifts and come back to life to incorporate themselves as teaching institutions.

From the capital, the congregations radiate throughout the republic: they rule in Arequipa, dominate in Cajamarca, invade Huánuco, threaten Puno, and will end up controlling the most remote settlements and villages. All with the tolerance of our congresses, the consent of governments, and the approval of municipalities and houses of charity. Our bishops, whose minds never emerged from the Middle Ages, have no notion of the effectiveness of proselytizing in a tolerant manner and

---

[1] Originally entitled "Secular Education." Changed by the author—L.A.S.

render themselves odious with their sectarian intransigence, while the priest from abroad, who comes schooled with the experience of more sophisticated countries and follows the methods of well-run corporations, proceeds softly and carefully, slowly, and cautiously. He takes two steps forward and one step back; he avoids confrontation, never attacks directly, and never grows impatient because he trusts in the assistance of time: *patiens quia aeterna.*

All the foreign priests go toward the same goal and avail themselves of the same methods, from the Dominican inspector to the apostolic delegate, from the saccharine French priest who represents the masculine metamorphosis of Madame Pompadour, to the grotesque Catalan friar who personifies the mystical evolution of the bullfighter.

They work like termites on the foundation of a house or like coral in seawater; we notice the immensity of their labor when the beams start falling on our head or the coral reef rips open the keel of our ship.

Repeating with Leibniz that "the one who controls education controls the world," they try to take control of the child, and in Lima they've begun by nearly monopolizing the education of upper-class women.

The schools run by secular institutions eke out a precarious existence because the mothers of families prefer to educate their daughters in Sacred Heart, Sacred Hearts, or Good Shepherd, even when the directors of those renowned seminaries turn their daughters into anything at all, queens or courtesans, but never into good wives and good mothers. The result: the ethic of a nun is reduced to the cultivation of vanity; religion, to the unconscious practice of superstitious ceremonies; science, to nothing at all, or to something no different from ethics and religion. A young lady with a third-grade diploma knows enough geography to wonder whether you get to Calcutta by land or by sea, and she knows all you need to know about languages in order to speak Gascogne gibberish and call it French, or babble in Cajun English. Those most accomplished in fine arts can plink from the piano a little singsong tune, or paint (only during their stay at the school) pictures that are copies of religious images and Virgins from Quito. On the other hand, all the young girls educated by nuns turn out to be gifted embroiderers in silver: they embroider slippers for papa who never wears them, clock cases for their brothers who have no clocks.

It's even worse: all of those schools, founded with the pretext of educating women, have no other purpose than the spread of fanaticism. Agents of male corporations headquartered in Paris or Rome, all the female orders in the style of Good Shepherd, Sacred Hearts, or Sacred Heart, play the role of cogs moved by visible or concealed gears. What is the rationale for all those spiritual directors, chaplains, and inspectors? The clergy rarely comes around, but it always makes its presence felt. The clergy in society are like opaque bodies in the firmament: although they never make themselves visible, they manifest their presence in the disturbances they cause in nearby stars.

And it gets worse: the nuns stop at nothing to satisfy their voracity for acquiring money. They suffer from gold fever and even show signs of kleptomania. Since they aren't driven by personal desire for lucre, since they aren't hoarding money for themselves, their shamelessness in rapacity seems somewhat mitigated. They parody Saint Martin, since not having a cloak of their own, they take another's to divide it, though not always with those in need. Not only do they collect an exorbitant room and board, not only do they include in it so-called personal improvement courses, augment to a fabulous degree the list of extraordinary expenses, present mind-boggling charges for endless pious works, not only do they speculate in the sale of books, writing, and drawing supplies, lacework, and religious doodads, but their parsimony leads them to impose homeopathic nutritional diets on their charges.

Undernourished during the most critical stage of their organic development, the women fail to develop sufficiently or to store up strength for later, so that when they complete their education, when they return to the bosom of their families after six or seven years of abstinence in cloistered circumstances, they have the decrepit and aged body of a person in the final stages of a sorrowful life.

Such women, what kind of offspring can they hope to conceive? An anemic, rickety progeny, doomed to lifelong supplements of iron and cod-liver oil just to survive. In well-to-do families, it's not unusual to see children today with loose, flabby stomachs, bowed legs, sunken chests, stooped spines, and, what most betrays the deterioration of a race, faces as senile as those of old people. We are threatened, then, by an inverse evolution, a regression to the ancestral type. A calamity of this nature does not sadden the *good mothers* or the *good fathers* because the good Catholic does not measure human perfection according to the dictum of the ancient philosopher: "a sound mind in a sound body."

Good, perfect, the nun is an incomplete woman and consequently a poor instructress who turns school into a copy of the convent instead of transforming it into a moral institution where women can receive instruction for practicing the two most elevated functions of life: love and maternity. What can they know about love, these hearts that are open to God but closed to man? What can these wombs, which never experienced the joy of conception or the pain of childbirth, possibly know about motherhood? Good, perfect, stepping out of character and straining to be like the mother, the nun confuses sweetness with tenderness, inclemency with justice, hypocrisy with modesty, and only manages to offer a frigid maternity, sticky-sweet, perfunctory, in a word, counterfeit, stale goods marketed as new year after year.

It is generally accepted that if men make laws, women establish customs. Here, where the man is distinguished by his weakness of character, where strength of mind seems concentrated in the feminine sex, society would experience a wholesome evolution if the woman didn't use sexual attraction as her sole instrument of domination. Unfortunately, the Peruvian woman's control over the man is a double domination of harem and sacristy: the priest oppresses the woman through fanaticism, the woman oppresses the man through sex.

*   *   *

THE EDUCATION OF young men is no less flawed than that of young women. Boys, contaminated by the example of a perverted and fanatic home, enter religious schools where the corrupting process is perfected or secular schools that fail to set them straight.

In the upper classes (just as with young women), the number of boys handed over to religious schools is even greater. A man from one of our villages doesn't check to see whether the primary school is called free or national, whether it is run by priests or secular administrators; he is happy as long as it is free, no matter the source of instruction; but our semibourgeois citizen, our pseudoaristocrat, whether through conviction, style, spirit of imitation, or sheer vanity, almost always prefers a religious school, in particular one run by Jesuits (which in Lima passes for an aristocratic center). A deputy, magistrate, general, minister, representative of the court, in short, any one of those half- or quarter-breeds who has accumulated his wealth through fraud or brutality or attained his high office through favor and intrigue, is not inclined to let his sons rub elbows with the son of a craftsman or field worker in some municipal school.

Even individuals who boast of being agnostics give in to the influence of their families and entrust their sons to the clergy, imagining that the mature man will easily rid himself of the errors acquired in childhood. True, the harmful effects of a poor primary education can be remedied through a good middle school or high school education; but where do we find those in Peru? Here, children aren't educated, are scarcely even instructed. The Peruvian who has finished his education has two tasks to perform if he wants to live an intellectual life corresponding to this day and age: forget everything he has learned and start over. He has to be an autodidact.

What goes on in official education? Since normal schools don't exist, the directors of lyceums spring up spontaneously or are appointed by government decree; since the professors can't live on an insecure, wretched, deficient salary, the professoriate, instead of being an exclusive occupation or a public career, becomes a supplementary, auxiliary, or luxury profession.

What goes on in independent education? Free universities don't exist, lyceums or gymnasiums strive desperately not to be overwhelmed by competition from the religious schools of the same level. We have teachers who are gifted, enlightened, and so morally elevated that they carry selflessness to the point of self-sacrifice. But those good workers labor silently and obscurely like the sap inside a tree: merit is regarded with suspicion, self-promotion is the rule, the true pedagogue is eclipsed, the pedant shines. There are men who choose teaching as a career the way you might choose manual labor, who open a lyceum as you might open an agency for domestic servants, and who turn themselves into pedagogues overnight the way Don Quixote had himself dubbed a knight.

Whether they're connected to universities or lyceums, are paid by the nation or by families, the teachers go along with the routine: a purely scientific program of instruction without theological contamination is inconceivable, inadmissible. With personal initiative forbidden and all stimulation stifled, there are great numbers of professors whose lectures are little more than exerpts from dissertations framed in *ergos* and *distingos*, or worse, the straightforward reading of excerpts copied from perverse, inaccessible books.

To sum it all up: if official education is almost always disease through inoculation, independent education usually degenerates into plagiarism or fraudulent commerce in stolen ideas.

* * *

IN THE MEANTIME, who's going to remedy this evil? The pompously titled Superior Council of Higher Education? This is nothing but a pale copy of the conseil supérieur de l'instruction publique, a conclave of dunces, a chamber run by deceit and chicanery. The ministers of education? More concerned with politics than with social issues, they continually sail overhead like dry clouds, leaving not even a good memory in their wake. The houses of congress? They have more than enough to do approving contracts, debating projects in clear violation of the law, and setting budgets no one observes. The municipalities and public charities? Municipal mayors and directors of public charities have the same lovely vision: hand over all primary schools to the Christian brotherhoods. Since time immemorial, there has been a committee for instructional supervision on the provincial council of Lima. However, not a single initiative for useful reform has ever emerged from that long line of supervisors, and even if it had, it wouldn't have made the least impression in the minds of the council members.

The government neglects vocational and professional education. The school of arts and crafts was converted into a military barracks, the agriculture institute into a wheat farm. The school of civil engineering and mining, which seemed ideally suited to satisfy an urgent need, now constitutes the exclusive domain of a few professors, the privileged legacy of a few students, and a direct assault on the interests of the majority. Is it right to invest prodigious sums of money to graduate a dozen engineers annually, while thousands of men lack schools where they can learn the most indispensable rudiments?

The push for scientific or higher education at the expense of vocational and primary education further widens the abyss separating the different social classes. On one side are those who have some knowledge and think they know everything; on the other side, those who know nothing and have no hope of learning. What good does it do to improve education without making it accessible? Does the education of a people consist in merely providing a few privileged individuals a more or less pure font of transcendental knowledge? If the privileged few turned out to be deeply, and therefore humanely, knowledgeable, they could serve as civilizing and benevolent mentors. But it's not like that: they end up semieducated, with just enough wit to sharpen their malice, without the moral sense required to restrain their evil instincts. Balloons half inflated, they fly at ground level, using their anchor to pull the roofs off houses and the plants from our fields.

Look at our universities. What good did they do, what light did they shed, all those men who spent their lives embedding into their brains Justinian's *Corpus Juris Civilis*, the civil code, and the canon law? A university education served only to puff up the pride of the mediocre, to instill exaggerated ambitions into incompetents, and to glut the nation with tireless pretenders to public office. Tolstoy says that "the Russian universities prepare, not the minds needed by the human race, but the minds needed by a corrupt society" [*la liberté dans l'école*]. Our universities spawn legions of lawyers who hurl themselves into politics the way the black pavillions hurl themselves into the China Sea. For our doctors of civil and canon law, there are no experimental or laboratory sciences, only petitions and appeals. Beyond their codes and their forensics, they know nothing; yet they constitute the prime material from which our financiers, diplomats, pedagogues, literati, and even our colonels are derived. When a man in Peru gets his law degree, he obtains his certificate of omniscience and his license to kill. With a moral sense based on an elastic interpretation of the law, without scruples or remorse (since the ambiguities and casuistry of the code exempt him from all obligations and sanctions), these shysters sail through society perfectly equipped for the fight for survival. Our military officers deserve no panegyrics and have some horrific crimes on their conscience; but to be fair, you should remember that beside every satrap with gold braids, you'll find a lawyer with a Hebrew soul and a Carthaginian heart buzzing in his ear.

If the Peruvian forum can forge the weapons to hold back this black horde, we'll be shining. All our doctors belong to the Catholic Union, to the Order of Perpetual Adoration, and to the Ancient Brotherhood of Our Lady of the Rosary, and the few who manage to break free of the religious yoke conceal their emancipation as they would a veneral disease: they let the priest alone as long as the priest lets them live and prosper.

II

To teach engineering, medicine, or philosophy, we look for engineers, doctors, or philosophers, but to educate people destined to establish families and live in society, we choose individuals who break all connection with humanity and have no idea what's in the heart of a woman or a child. Education can be regarded as a kind of psychic engendering: defective minds are born of crippled minds. How, then, can the benighted soul who boasts of severing ties with everything human, of belonging not to the earth but to heaven, hope to educate men who will be useful to their fellow men? What does the solitary individual who has never had to work to support himself know about the struggle for the basic necessities of life? What does this fortunate creature who neither reaps nor sows know about sweat or fatigue? What does this cripple of love know about human passions, about the most generous and fecund sentiment? Viewed from whichever perspective you choose, the priest lacks the qualifications for teaching.

There's something rigid, marmorean, and unappealing about a person who lives segregated from his fellow men and passes through the world with his gaze fixed on some unknown goal and his hopes fixed on something that never comes. His emptiness of heart without the love of a woman and his bitterness at not being a father or having to be one secretly turn the bad priest into an angry soul, the good priest into a bottomless well of melancholy. There's nothing quite so unbearable as the hysterical geniality or the mewling sweetness of priests, who have all the defects of old maids and none of the good qualities of women. A species of androgynes or hermaphrodites, they combine the vices of both sexes.

The judicial records of the teaching orders prove in a most nauseating way the danger of putting a child into intimate contact with the priest. The greater the mysticism and asceticism of the latter, the greater the risk for the former. Religiosity and voluptuousness are so inseparably conjoined that the mystic often ends up entering a harem, just as the libertine frequently ends up vanishing in the clouds. Women's preference for Jesus and men's preference for Mary: is that not an indication that sensuality and sexuality are crucial to devotion? Penitence and prayer, which seem to serve as shields against temptation, act as mechanisms of sensual arousal. Saints, when they emerged from their fits of ecstasy, would writhe like serpents in fire and give voice to sounds like orgasmic moans; hermit saints, after keeping vigil for entire nights on their knees and in a state of mortification, would suffer pangs of lust in their flesh and roar like lions at the memory of Roman prostitutes.

In their behavior and gestures, and even in their way of dressing or disguising themselves, priests are repellent, like the emblematic image of their doctrine. Covered in black from head to toe, encased in a cassock, they don't look like men moving about like other men, but like coffins marching off alone. When they're clean, they're all narrow collar, embroidered wristband, silver buckles, rice powder, perfume of a public woman, and all the frivolities that mark the feminization of their sex. When they're dirty, they're all three-day-old beard, face dripping with the grease from first communion, snowfall of dandruff on their shoulders, fingernail with an implacable fillet of grime, and the smell of filth mixed with sour sweat.

Despite all this, priests and monks imagine they tower over the human race, as if they had fallen from an incorruptible star and enjoyed some divine sanction. Walled within their own egos, thinking themselves superior to other men, they personify pride; and when they try to act humble, their humility, like the rags of Diogenes, lets their pride show through. And what could be more natural: a class that imagines it possesses the only truth, which claims to be invested with sacred character, which tries to redeem the sins of both king and beggar, which has deliriums of transporting God down from heaven can't help bursting with pride, can't help regarding profane and secular human beings as an inferior species. The first among all women, the immaculate Virgin, the Queen of Heaven, the mother of God himself—Mary—humbly presses her lips where the latest priest leaves the mark of his foot. Pride and vanity produce the strangest aberrations in priests and monks: not content with simply considering themselves superior to the human race, they think they are coworkers with the Divinity and even imagine that God lives in a state of eternal gratitude to them for the services they provide in his name on earth.

As a last resort to extol religious education, let's not allege good faith on the part of the teachers: good faith is what the Muslim shows when he dies chanting verses from the Koran; good faith the Congolese black who kills his mother in order to transform her into a benevolent and powerful spirit; good faith the Hindu who throws himself in front of

Vishnu's chariot to be crushed to death; good faith the savage who paints his body with the blood of his enemy to win the goodwill of some fetish; good faith the fakir who remains seated on a bed of nails for twenty years, imagining that the putrefaction of his wounds will serve him as balm in the other world. No, good faith is not enough; and just as we don't look for engineers of good faith, but competent doctors, to cure us of a sickness, we shouldn't resort to theologians of good faith to educate our children, but to professional educators who know what a woman and a child really are.

Religious pedagogy relies on boarding school, seqestration: far from the family in order to stifle the child's natural instincts, seqestration far from society in order to turn the child into a citizen of Rome and not of the universe, far from life in order to guide the child through tradition or the voice of the dead.

The monasterial and military regime flourishes in boarding school, so it shouldn't surprise us to find analogous methods for sustaining that regime between the Church that wants to turn each man into a sectarian and Napoleon who dreamed of converting every Frenchman into a soldier. For the despot, the school is a barracks where everything marches double-time; for the fanatic, it's a monastery where everything is controlled by the ringing of a bell. The mind, one's temperament, in a word, the self of the individual, is seen as something insignificant. Given the infallibility of the catechism and the inviolability of the order, the student is limited to silence regarding any personal initiative, blind respect for his superior, and passive obedience. He is forced to profess doctrines rejected by our reason, to accept feelings contrary to the nature of our being, to live away from our center, to give up will and consciousness for automatism to the point of taking action without desire, eating when he's not hungry, and sleeping when he's not sleepy.

One must never have had to endure the constant pressure of a puerile and absurd system of rules, never been driven to despair by the spying of superiors and the tale-bearing of classmates, never had one's character impeached in the inevitable gossip of a dull, ill-willed mob, never have known the piggish promiscuity of a refectory or have breathed the fetid and dank atmosphere of a common dormitory, to wax eloquent about the excellence of the boarding school.

It's not surprising that such a regimen should have its effect. The student, deliberately isolated from the opposite sex, raised in a spirit of hostility toward women that is encouraged by the Church, becomes involved in social life and starts a family, being more inclined to behave as a libertine and domestic tyrant than as a man, a husband, and a father. Steeped in false ideas, with absolutely no knowledge of the feminine character, what can he do? The priests and all those who run the boarding school forget a man isn't civilized in a campaign tent, in the barracks, in the cloister, or in school, but in the home, under the gentle influence of a woman. They also forget that nothing so influences the acquisition of narrow, wretched ideas, nothing so corrupts the character of a man as the exclusive company of persons of his own sex. Encased in every good student with a sacerdotal education we find, if not a misogynist, then a Prudhonian who acknowledges only two classes of woman: courtesan or keeper of keys.

Clerical education is subject to dogma. As the ancients made the planets, sun, and stars revolve around the earth, the priest make all human activities revolve around the Bible. Everything is adjusted, reduced, enlarged, turned, revolved, disfigured, or deformed to conform with the subtle and sophistic interpretations of dubious and obscure texts. They have an orthodox philosophy, an orthodox history, an orthodox astronomy, and even an orthodox medicine. Accustomed to living in theological shadows, they collect darkness, like the old miner from Germinal who, from breathing coal dust, ended up spitting black saliva. And that darkness favors them because "religions, like fireflies, need darkness in order to shine."

With the subjection of the sciences to dogma there comes the scornful rejection of any rationalist concept and, more than anything, of any philosophy, particularly the Greek, which keeps echoing through the world like the triumphal hymn of reason. For many (not only the tonsured are profane), the quintessence of Hellenic knowledge lives on and is condensed in mythology; as if an Anaxagoras or a Parmenides, an Empedocles or an Epicurus, actually believed in the poetic divinities of Homer and Hesiod! They include in a common anathema all the sages of Greece, even though Thales and Pythagoras shed more light on humanity with their theorems and problems than all the theologians with their nebulous controversies and all the councils with their dogmatic proclamations. Modern science isn't a leap but a continuation of Greek science; those most deeply learned are proud of drinking from the fountains of antiquity, even when they have to rely on mutilated or corrupted texts. Despite this, the most venerable doctors of the Church agree with Bellarmine that there is "more science in the head of a child instructed in the Catechism than in the heads of all the pagan philosophers or all the prophets of Israel."

What is the result of an education based on the catechism? The child abandons the real world at an early age to dwell in a phantasmagoric realm. Adapting himself to a miraculous environment ruled not by immutable laws, but by inconstant, irregular, arbitrary wills, he ends up taking seriously the myths and legends of the sacred books, just as a peasant believes the novels of Dumas are true or the figures in a magic lantern are alive. Those serpents who can speak as convincingly as a doctor of jurisprudence; those angels who delight in seducing the daughters of men, using the wiles of a don Juan Tenorio; those warriors who can immobilize the sun in the heat of battle the way a clockmaker stops the pendulum of a chronometer; that God who today creates and tomorrow repents of having created and who makes and unmakes his creation, like a capricious and fickle artist who amuses himself shaping and destroying clay figures—that universe, finally, eternally fraught with illogic and the supernatural—these have a pernicious effect on the child, habituate him to the false and the marvelous, make him think the absurd is possible, kill in embryo every sane and positive conception of nature, and transform him into a passive receptacle of all errors. The priests convert the man into a kind of palimpsest; they obliterate reason from the mind in order to engrave faith, just as the copyists of the Middle Ages erased a speech by Cicero from the parchment in order to write the chronicle of a convent.

Thus there is nothing more resistant to the mind of science than minds deformed by an orthodox education. Convinced the absurd is true, they continue to believe "precisely because it is absurd." It's easier to make a thousand Jews or Muslims listen to reason than a single Catholic. True believers, really rancid Catholics, are like those glass bottles that have a ball inside larger than the neck of the bottle: you have to break the bottle to get the ball out.

Is the antiscientific nature of religious education compensated by its morality? We should start by saying that there is no difference between science and morality, since the rules of morality are derived from the principles established by science. With good reason Auguste Comte positioned true morality (i.e., morality without theology or metaphysics) on the highest summit of knowledge, like the shining beacon at the top of the lighthouse. Since there is no definitive or perfect science, each century has its own. The sectarians of the most absurd and puerile superstition set up their hypotheses as the only rational solutions, regard their liturgy as the most worthy form of rendering homage to the gods, and consider themselves as the only men capable of attaining moral perfection. No one professes the doctrine of exclusive perfection as shamelessly as the Catholics. The final, incontestable word of morality has already been enunciated by the Rabbi of Nazareth; the nations that don't follow the voice of Christ, corrected and improved by the voice of Rome, are like herds of wild beasts busily procreating and devouring each other.

Happily, the time has passed when perfection could not be acknowledged outside a sect, and today we attribute as much moral beauty to the good Jew as to the good Protestant, to the good Buddhist as to the good Muslim, to the good deist as to the good atheist. The morality of the latter, perhaps, displays the greatest selflessness and nobility: one who does good for a posthumous reward isn't that different from the usurer who lends one coin today so he can pocket ten tomorrow. If we compare the just from the lay diocese to the just from the Catholic Church, it will be easy to determine which are superior.

Does Catholicism, or even Christianity as a whole, have the right to boast at having introduced a new morality on earth? Which precept of those so-called divines had not already been implicitly or explicitly formulated by the philosophers of India, China, Persia, Judea, Greece, and Rome? If not even the chief maxim "to love your neighbor as yourself" belongs to it, how can we maintain that the Christian religion has a morality different from that professed by the great philosophers of antiquity? Christianity has been reduced to little more than the reaction of Jewish and Oriental fanaticism against the sane and lovely Hellenistic civilization; but a reaction sui generis in which the presumptuous conqueror, in spite of having proclaimed itself rich and powerful, did no more than deck itself out in the spoils of the defeated. The same men who raised a basilica on the columns of a Greek temple or transformed a statue of Apollo into an image of Christ converted the maxims of the pagan philosophers into divine precepts.

As for Catholicism, which boasts of keeping in its doctrine the most exquisite essence of the Christian religion, it can be characterized by the words Rossini used to judge an opera: *It has something good and something new, with the qualification that the good isn't new and the new isn't good.* In effect, Catholicism situates its morality in the accumulation of incongruent and ambiguous precepts that the child studies without understanding and that the man forgets or remembers without practicing. Viewed clearly, the Catholic sect embodies the negation of all morality, when Saint Paul says: "by grace we are saved, by faith; and this not from us, for it is a gift of God: not through works, so that none glorify himself"; our will is gratuitous.

A religion that insists that the earth is a passage and the future life a definitive dwelling ends up surrendering the world to the strong and the bold. If the vale of tears offers us little and eternity promises us much, let's surrender the least to others and keep the most for ourselves. Living spiritually without worrying about the material, let's allow our soul to blossom inside our sick, repugnant body as a rose perfumes a cemetery. A Catholic, to be logical, should give himself up entirely to the Church, converting himself, first into a child as Jesus Christ says, and then into a cadaver as Ignacio de Loyola prescribes.

And we can touch all the evils of Catholic education here and now. For more than seventy years (worse, for more than three centuries) our people have nourished themselves on milk sterilized against all impious microbes, have known no nurse but the priest and the Catholic preceptor, and what have they learned? "A few religious ceremonies, a few Catholic rites; in other words, they have been transformed on the outside without a single spark of the Christian spirit penetrating their souls" (Bakunin). If we turn from the common people to consider the upper classes, we see that religion did not serve as a corrective to personal immorality nor to public sensuality. Those who distinguished themselves by the depravity of their customs or by their Gypsy politics received an essentially Catholic education, and they lived and died in the bosom of the Church.

If we leave Peru, we observe the same phenomenon all around us. The brutal and grotesque dictatorships of Spanish America are a genuine product of Catholicism and of clerical education. In Protestant nations, where man acquires the notion of his own dignity from childhood, where self-respect inspires respect for others, where everyone rejects the belief in infallible authorities and passive obedience, a Francia, a Rosas, a García Moreno, or a Melgarejo are inconceivable. But

Catholicism with its two moralities, one for the authority and the other for the subject, is a true sect of tyrant slaves.

III

The nation guarantees the existence and diffusion of free primary education.

CONSTITUTION OF 1860

First-grade primary education is obligatory for all the inhabitants of Peru.

LAW OF EDUCATION

Peruvian legislators mandated free primary education for all levels, obligatory only in the first grade; and they did not stipulate that it should be Catholic, probably to avoid redundancy, since Article 4 of the Constitution says: "The nation professes the catholic, apostolic, Roman religion: the state protects it . . ."

In the schools maintained by municipalities and charities, the children receive education that is Catholic in essence and by mandate. In the *Law of Education*, references to Christian doctrine, sacred history, the life of Our Lord Jesus Christ, and ecclesiastical history are repeated to the point of obsession.

If legal mandate is binding on every father of a family, what does a man do when he doesn't want his children to receive a Catholic education? The rich avoid the problem by sending their children to be educated outside the country or giving them private lessons in their own houses. Those without the resources to hire special tutors or who aren't in a position to teach them in the home, frequently decide that their children shouldn't attend school and thus condemn them to total ignorance, concluding, perhaps rightly, that it's as useful to fill their heads with air as with smoke.

Since the state subvents the schools with money from contributors, or through the collection of charitable donations from everyone, Catholic education privileges a single sect. No one is excluded in the national community or exempted from fulfilling their political duties by not believing in Catholicism: atheists and freethinkers pay their taxes and fill up the knapsack. If there are obligations, why aren't there any rights?

The law, with its obligatory and free education, is no more than a mockery, as outrageous as arousing a man's thirst and holding up to his lips a liqueur saturated with saltpeter.

Should we resort to the explanation that in Peru Catholics are in the majority and the majorities have the power to impose their laws on minorities? Then Catholics in Turkey or England, who are in the minority, would find themselves obliged to educate their children in Muslim or Protestant schools. However, no one takes more advantage of free education than Catholics when they establish their schools in the East, where they demand and obtain from the pagans privileges they deny to civilized people in the West.

The conduct of the Church is worth remembering. In Protestant nations, Holland for example, a figure as eminent as the archpriest of the Frisian Islands calls for neutrality or lay education in the schools, writing that "in order to instill concord, friendship, and charity among the different religions, it was necessary that the teachers abstain from teaching dogmas from the different communions."[2] In Catholic countries, France for example, the clergy openly opposes the secularization of primary education and regards lay schools as "an abominable official factory of atheists and enemies of Jesus Christ." "We only ask the freedom to set up our teaching orders," says any Catholic bishop in a dissident or pagan country, and the entire congregation of the faithful feels that the bishop is perfectly within his rights. But if a group of Protestant clergymen wants to set up a school in some Catholic country, all Catholics protest that the Protestants are entirely unreasonable and in violation of law.

The Peruvian clergy are so confident of their right to monitor the orthodoxy of primary education that the question is never even discussed, and they leap resolutely into action when they fear this right is being threatened. Thus, when Pardo tried to hire a few German pedagogues, not to secularize the national schools, our priests and monks turned society upside down, provoking mob demonstrations and mutinies. More recently, in 189 [ ], we saw them flex their muscles once again when some English priests tried to establish a school in Cuzco. The clergy will never agree to the coexistence of a Catholic school and

---

[2] Paul Bert, *Education in a Democracy* (conference held in the Havre [Cercle Franklin] on March 21, 1880).

a Protestant school, for good reason: they fear the competition. Who wouldn't choose a clergyman who is sociable, humane, and a good father to his family over the antisocial, churlish *philophobe*.

It's laughably simpleminded to argue that because Catholicism is the only true religion, the state has an inescapable obligation to support it and to block the public teaching of other doctrines. Civilized countries are teaching us that when it comes to religions, you don't legislate; we all know now that the truth or falsity of religions is no longer a matter for debate. Religions are now regarded as the infantile science of humanity. Every religion resolves physical and moral problems a priori and proffers a fantasy model of the cosmos, not unlike a theory of colors postulated by a blind man. Religious affirmation, with its nonempirical and superhuman character, is flawed in being antiscientific. Dogmas have nothing to do with cosmological laws, and to speak of religious truth makes as little sense as to speak of opaque transparence or solid liquidity.

The state does not need sect inspectors but law abiders: a collectivity of individuals practicing different cults and following the same political interests shouldn't be confused with the community of monks wearing the same habit and professing "a degrading uniformity of opinions" (Channing). Since true statesmen know that progress springs from diversity of opinions and beliefs, they make laws without taking into account any religious superstitions. In almost all civilized nations, the three great events of life—birth, marriage, and death—are today regulated independently of any religion. The law is secular. But the Church is not content with a secondary role and feels it is being deprived of a natural right when it doesn't reign as absolute sovereign of lives and consciences. It raves to anoint the state with the oil from a sacristy in order to reduce it to the status of an acolyte. The civil power is not its intelligent collaborator but its secular arm: not so much like the falcon in the hands of the falconer, but exactly like a tool in the hands of a worker.

Are religion and religiosity so valuable to society that we should bother to maintain and foster them? Religion is gradually losing its social character and becoming little more than a family custom, a secondary aspect of family life or a habit that is intimately individual. If there was a time when simple disagreements concerning sects turned brother against brother and father against son, if a mere divergence in interpretation of a verse would open an unbridgeable abyss between persons doomed to live inseparably united, today individuals with diametrically opposed beliefs sleep under the same roof: the father a Jew, the mother a Protestant, and the children freethinkers. People do business, sign contracts, socialize, live together, and even make love, without bothering to inquire about each other's religion. With the decline of intolerance and fanaticism, the spirit of conciliation and gentleness spreads through the world. In this universal harmony, the Catholic produces the only discordant note: *in cauda venenum*.

Is religiosity truly so innate to the human species that man can be defined as a religious animal, as he is by some? If it were innate to man, its disappearance would cause morbid effects; but the opposite happens: when intelligence shines most brightly in the mind, the religious sensibility becomes most vague in the heart. Religiosity is little more than an accident on the march of humanity, corresponding to an intermediate period in the evolution of the mind and oscillating between absolute ignorance and full enlightenment. The ignorant neither deny nor affirm because they see nothing; the wise doubt and deny because they see much. To demand, then, that intelligence not transcend religiosity is like trying to keep the body from developing beyond childhood or adolescence. According to Guyau, scientific minds are antireligious, as are even moderately sophisticated intelligences, so religion with its inevitable concommitant, superstition, is lodged in the lowest social strata, as the dregs of wine sink to the bottom of the barrel.

Do pontiffs and kings, politicians and warriors, preach the excellence of religious sentiments and work feverishly to instill them in the popular masses out of conviction or convenience? We can look at the tiger in his cage, the despot who on Saint Helena proclaims his religious sentiments and holds beneath contempt the French general who doubts the divinity of Jesus Christ. If Napoleon had been a Catholic, would he have humiliated the leader of the Church and prohibited the priests from taking part in public education? If he had been simply a Christian, would he have repudiated his legitimate wife or committed incest with his own sisters, lied and perjured himself a hundred times, had the duke of Enghieri shot, and turned half the earth into a pool of blood? If few today accept the Catholicism of Pius IX when he hired armies of condottieri and conducted bloody battles in defense of his temporal power, neither does anyone accept the Christianity of a Von Moltke when in 1875 he said: "As a German I demand war with France because Germany is ready for war; as a Christian I also demand it because within ten years both nations will lose another hundred thousand men."

The state and the Church maintain a continuing secular and apparently irreconcilable conflict; but in the war against individual human rights, Church and state become allies, tacitly defend each other, proving that all tyranny is based on fanaticism, just as all fanaticism is supported by tyranny. In the history of nations, every new outbreak of despotism coincides with an exaltation of superstition. Religion serves as a powerful instrument for servitude: with resignation, it chains the spirit of rebellion; with hope of a posthumous reward, it lulls the immediate pain of the disinherited. It is the monotonous lullaby of the wet nurse, and the man who enjoys listening to it hasn't yet emerged from infancy.

Since the Catholic religion is not a source of knowledge, nor a moral code, nor a bond between men, nor even an individual necessity, but is rather an element of domination and tyranny, why base the entire pedagogical structure on it? Reduced to the category of something exclusively personal and for private use, like underwear, religions escape regulation by the law. And just as there is no policy regulation that requires us to wear cotton underpants or linen undershirts, there shouldn't be an article of the Constitution that implicitly obliges us to receive Catholic education.

Since the state lacks the resources to establish in each town as many schools as there are superstitions, the only way to avoid the problem would be to suppress the obligatory character of religious courses or, better, not to teach religion at all in the national schools and lyceums.

Some people carry neutrality to the point of demanding that the teacher instruct without educating, teach without moralizing. "The school," says Tolstoy, "should propose as its only objective the transmission of knowledge or instruction, without trying to meddle in the moral realm of convictions, beliefs, or character" [La Liberté dans l'école]. Such a pedagogy is based on the purely scholastic difference between education and instruction. Positive morality, the morality professed today by the most select part of humanity, comes from science and has more in common with hygiene and physiology than with any of the religions. If we segregated morality from teaching, we would mutilate the scientific edifice by depriving it of its crowning grandeur. Moreover, would such segregation be possible? When we transmit knowledge, we inevitably inculcate the idea of using it to the integral benefit of the individual, as well as society. We certainly don't consult a philosopher's dissertation on human affection for the purpose of learning selfishness; neither do we consult a naturalist's treatise on the common origin of life on the planet for the purpose of learning cruelty to animals. All teaching, thought it might seem to be directed only at the understanding, affects the will. When our intelligence becomes enlightened, it becomes moral: magnanimous feelings come from the mind.

Neutrality in the school can well be considered impossible or very difficult: you would have to be an imbecile or a great philosopher to profess a doctrine, and be convinced of its excellence, and not try to instill it in the minds of your disciples. Can you imagine a wise man of good faith using theology to explain the formation of the universe and demonstrate the possibility of miracles? Only science, in its universality, should be the grand foundation of public instruction: Religion is specific because there's a Jewish religion, a Muslim religion, a Catholic religion, a Protestant religion, in other words, a thousand religions. Science is universal because there's only one astronomy, only one chemistry, only one physics, one mechanics. Nonetheless, if there are many individuals who prefer religion to science, let's leave them to their error, provided they don't impose on the rest of us by legislating an obligation to receive a Catholic education.

Since we are imitating the revolutionaries of 1789, we should crown the project by imitating also the men of the Third French Republic, who incarnate Condorcet's ideal and profess his aphorism: "Science in the school, religious instruction in the temple."

Propaganda and Attack

(1888)

I

The main vice of Peruvian literature: phraseology. Pick up a newspaper and scan the editorial: what do we see? Words. Pick up any weekly magazine and have a look at the compositions in verse: what do we see? Words. It's like Hamlet said: words, words, words!

We suffer from logomania, or logomachy, and we should undertake the project conceived by Sainte-Juste of imitating the Lacedaemonians and establishing a prize for laconism. That's right, laconism, not for the purpose of transforming the language into a kind of telegraphic jargon but for expressing in the least number of words the greatest number of ideas; not for the purpose of reducing matters to a mere five-line ejaculation but to allow for the proper development of a thought and the necessary extension of a sentence: we can be verbose in a line and concise in a volume.

Numbed by the monotonous splash of a hollow, pompous language, we find ourselves immersed waist-high in a flood spreading down a wide, stony stream bed: the noise deafens us, but the stream doesn't move us along.

Among the indecision and vagueness of the multitude, two groups of writers stand out: those who talk like Sancho Panza, with idiotic nonsense, crude sayings, and ill-suited refrains, and those who express themselves like don Quixote, solemnly, in contorted, high-sounding clauses that never end.

We have a judicial jargon, another for academics, another for journalists, an archaizing jargon for nostalgic *criollos*—in short, a rash of jargons that pock the language the way subcutaneous eruptions pock the skin. We have anything you might want, except for the pure, direct style capable of giving clear focus to the physiognomy of the individual, distinguishing one man from others, or conveying the precise manifestation of the speaking self. We have everything, except for a clear, substantial language with the virtue of bread and water, of which we never tire.

We do not see the emergence of an eminent personality who can seduce and influence us, which is both good and bad. It's good because every literary giant leads to imitation and stifles the free initiative of the individual; it's bad because when there are no superior talents, we invent them and then adore those who are ordinary and mediocre.

Old writers repeat themselves or become sterile; the young aren't even capable of establishing stereotypes with clear, definite features. Now that Althaus is dead, Salaverry paralyzed and dying, and Arnaldo Márquez expatriated (perhaps for lack of fresh air and space here), who are we left with? Even countries we despise can boast a Montalvo and a Llona, a prose writer and a poet.

We lack good stylists because we have no good thinkers, because style is nothing but the blood of ideas: when the organism is rickety, the blood is anemic. And how are we supposed to think clearly if we're still breathing air from the Middle Ages, if in our educational system we're revolving around sterile Catholic dogma, if we can't cast off the theological virus we inherited from the Spaniards?

Even in minds with some pretension of sanity a frightening confusion prevails, the most divergent and irreconcilable ideas cohabiting peaceably. Logic seems not to matter: a sonnet that starts out with an apostrophe to reason concludes with declarations of faith; a speech prefaced with praise for Darwin ends up defending Genesis. To get an idea of the extravagant disorder of our rampant verbosity, picture the promiscuity of an army in defeat, or the panic ensuing when a fire breaks out. From the mouth of one of our coastal writers armed with all the edible goods from a grocery store and all the gaudy gems from a jewelry store, we're regaled with the laughable mix of turnips and rubies, chickpeas and diamonds, hog's pudding and pearl necklaces.

Liberal Catholicism or Catholic liberalism holds sway. Journalists and literary hacks pour the pope's *Syllabus* and the Declaration of the Rights of Man into a single mold. Like certain women I know, they worship at two altars, dedicating half the day to prayer and the other half to free love. They seem to have forgotten that Catholic liberalism represents in the moral order the same role the flying lizards of the Mesozoic period represented in the physical order: organisms with bird's wings and reptile bodies, creatures that fly today and crawl tomorrow.

Many of these writers, as if they were about to undertake the thirteenth labor of Hercules, take pen in hand and discourse for hours on end about freedom of cult, secular cemeteries, and in particular about the two treasures in their sacred coffer: the National Patronate and the Exequatur. But when it comes to accepting the principles of positivist science and applying its logic and its tremendous conclusions, when it's time to raise the ax to deliver the mortal blow, then they draw back afraid, and . . . so much for the thirteenth labor of Hercules!

The writings of our most audacious liberals are like orgies beneath the dome of a cathedral. Amid the clatter of glasses, the scent of wine, and the blasphemous cries, every now and then you hear the bellow of an organ, the monotonous chanting of a drowsy monk, and the sputtering of candles sprayed with holy water.

In short, the diagnosis of Peruvian literature can be summed up as congestion of words, anemia in ideas.

We need to speak to the people of their interests. Then it will be easy for them to see that if in the past everything was done by their efforts but on behalf on the privileged few, it's time for them to exert themselves on their own behalf and to their own advantage. It's the writer's job to open the eyes of the masses and instruct them so they aren't caught off guard by the great movement of social liquidation that is now under way in the most civilized nations.

Human beings have heard enough about their obligations, and now it's time for them to remember their rights. Down with the litany of lies about *respect* and *resignation!* All the sacred cows that were so long respected, though not respectable, served as accomplices of religious, political, and social tyranny. We regard the passing of centuries as some kind of sanction, when to the contrary the most ancient errors deserve our fiercest hatred and most implacable opposition because they're the ones that have deceived us the longest and caused the most harm. Let's open our eyes and we'll see things clearly: we'll see that many individuals seem like giants to us because when we measure ourselves against them we kneel down; we'll see that we regard as sacred today the abominations we ourselves consecrated yesterday; we'll see that we're acting like the child who turns his back to the light and is frightened by the gigantic projection of his own shadow.

The word *resignation,* invented by clever men who use it to handcuff the innocent victims of iniquities and atrocities, should vanish from all our lips, because it smacks of outrageous aggression in the oppressor and cowardice in the oppressed. Let's take from the powerful man some of his power and from the rich man some of his wealth, and then we'll see if they recognize and acknowledge the value of *resignation.* The earth still produces enough fruit to feed humankind bountifully, is still the mother of full and fecund breasts for her children. If some suffer hunger and misery while others enjoy wealth and surfeit, this is because the hungry and the miserable, instead of rising up and fighting back, resign themselves with Christian humility to endure their wretched lot.

Enough of heavenly rewards and illusory hopes in divine justice, enough of those narcotics and derivatives that incapacitate us for action, dilute our energy, and turn us into the eternal victims of our fellow man. No one has an obligation to suffer so others can enjoy life, to fast so others can eat, to die so others can live. On the contrary, the disinherited have the right to use every means necessary to extract themselves from their unfortunate plight. Why should they faint with hunger at the banquet door, when all they need to do is break it down to get food and a place at the table for everyone? Social spoils are born of violence, are based on violence dissembled one way or another. To fight such violence is to exercise the right to respond to force with force.

Respect and *resignation* may have populated heaven and Roman martyrology, but only disrespect and rebellion conquered nature and paved humanity's road with roses. A single act of rebellion usually produces more benefits for the human species than all the resignations and respects combined. Wherever a source of light spreads out, wherever a worry or an error is demolished, wherever something emerges to make our thoughts sublime or our hearts larger, we can be sure that the sweat and blood of some rebel or disrespectful person were spilled there.

And who more than the writer should exhibit disrespect for rules and lack of submission? The writer should always march in the vanguard of the unsubmissive and the undisciplined, as far removed from the sycophants of power as courtiers from the masses. The cry for justice need not wait for the propitious moment or the favorable occasion; it should be heard everywhere and at every moment, especially when crying out for it is dangerous and when everyone is silent and afraid. In this the writer should be different from the politician.

Professional politicians, those who stay awake at night wondering when to switch parties, always speak tactfully, strategically, with circumlocutions, while the man who is truly free speaks his mind in all its crude integrity, unconcerned about whether he's trashing the interests of the wealthy classes or arousing the ire of ignorant, fanatical groups.

II

Many countries, in suffering a defeat, are resilient enough to return to the scene of the disaster. We, after being conquered by Chile, remained prostrate on the ground like some viscous substance. It's galling to witness our senile attachment to the beaten path, our unchallenged cult to the goddess Routine, our servile respect for hollow men and moth-eaten institutions, for ethereal myths and metaphysical entities. While our neighbors move ahead at a trot or a headlong charge, we never stop marching in place.

Here we don't live as brothers, in the shade of the same roof, breathing the same air and loving the same things, but spend our time fighting over a ray of sunshine like gypsies at a fair, trying to cheat one another sordidly like gamblers in a backroom, hating one another secretly with the implacable rancor of oppressed and oppressors.

In the opinion of Bolívar, "there's no good faith in America, neither between men nor between nations. Treaties are just papers, constitutions just books, elections mere disputes, freedom nothing but anarchy, and life nothing but torture." In Peru today honesty doesn't exist in private or in public: everything is violated and trampled on cynically, from our word of honor to our signed documents. Our political life is based on fraud, concussion, and lies; our social life is spent in selfish slumber or, worse, in defensive warfare against our neighbor's envy, calumny, and rapacity.

In every civilized country homogeneous groups work together, or at least tentative party platforms are drawn up for men with common beliefs and ideas; we have no concept of alliances of the mind, only meetings of the gut. We have no individual elements that can be fashioned into a solidary and compact body because our useful and honest citizens avoid the fray, refusing to take action and living huddled inside the shell of the self. Bad men prevail and rule, doing and undoing as they please, while good men sum up their philosophy in three words: digestion in tranquility.

What do we have? In government, robots with their hands tied or counterfeits of free movements; in judicial power, venality and prevarication; in Congress, grotesque squabbling without a trace of courage, soporific debates without a spark of eloquence; in the people, a lack of faith because there's no one to believe in any longer, an icy egotism because they love no one, and an Islamic conformity because they hope for nothing. People, the congress, the judiciary, and the government—everything ferments and gives off an enervating stench of mediocrity. Pettiness abounds in all things: pettiness in character, pettiness in hearts, pettiness in vices and crimes.

The writer is not exempt from the general debasement. Where is the free voice that will speak to the multitudes as they should be spoken to? Or a public figure who will break free of the golden muzzle? Where is the poet moved to wrath by hatred of evil? The writer whose palate is eager for the honey of public office either stands mute or applauds; the journalist vainly sniffing for crumbs from the public treasury raises his voice and attacks. With rare exceptions, what we have are cringing sycophants or peevish critics. Those who distribute the crumbs and swagger forward like idols from India surveying the mob of kneeling supplicants at their feet, they know the real meaning of the curtsies in the journalists' editorials, the congratulatory homage in the professor's academic address, or the tears of the poet in the graveside elegy.

Because we profess a skin-deep liberalism, because we have become accustomed to the colonist's shackles, we have no idea how far we have to go, and we can scarcely move our feet without stumbling. Independence overwhelms us, like a mountain of lead. You could almost say we lament our lost slavery, just like a bird accidentally set free by the master's carelessness that comes fluttering and chirping back to its cage. Following the tradition of the fawning writers who chose their Maecenas from among dukes and marquises, we prostitute ourselves for governmental, congressional, and municipal appointments and salaries. This individual beggarliness is reflected in our collective beggarliness: our free societies demand subventions and official recognition. We are the mendicant friars of science and literature.

It would be inaccurate to say that our social misery comes exclusively from the war with Chile. Certainly, defeat brings psychic diminishment, accentuates all the vices of the defeated, and is greatly dispiriting, but it does not radically or suddenly transform our social essence. A permanent conquest or secular occupation is like an plague-bearing inoculation, but a war of a few years is merely a bloodletting. It's natural for us to be anemic, but why should we suffer from gangrene? The natural thing, once the war was over, would have been for us to react and recover.

Our sickness spreads to the point of international servility: our literary and scientific societies end up being little more than corresponding branches of Spanish royal academies. Writers, lawyers, and doctors turn their eyes toward Spain in the shameful posture of begging some academic title. Lackeys of the intellectual world, our writers, lawyers, and doctors swagger around with their medallions and badges from Spanish corporations the way former plantation slaves used to strut around in the livery of their former master.

In short, Peru today is a sick organism: wherever you poke your finger, pus erupts.

III

A difficult job awaits the writer who hopes to counter the influence of the corrupt politician: his task must consist of propaganda and attack. This may not be the time for trying collective action, but for solitary, individual effort; perhaps we don't need the book so much as the pamphlet, the newspaper, the broadside. But whether we act individually or collectively, the most fiery propaganda is of little value unless it goes hand in hand with a determined assault on politics and politicians.

What has our politics always been? The art of governing men the way you run a machine or a herd of animals. And our politicians? A union of sick ambitions where by some perverse process of selection those floating to the top seem always to be the doctor without patients, the banker in the process of liquidating his assets, the journalist with no subscribers, the ruined rancher, the bankrupt shopkeeper, the engineer with no contracts, the military officer with no service record, and of course the lawyer with no clients.

In the wheeling and dealing of politics everything gets mired and corrupted in foul water. The most precious arguments about form and language—when do they fail to deteriorate into mere squabbles over vested interest and rancor between rival cliques? What do we profit from all our Byzantine digressions? From our Barbary factionalism? What freedoms have we ever won, beyond those granted in the first constitutions? We shook off the tutelage of the viceroys only to vegetate under the tyranny of military strongmen, so our true form of government is caporalism. We freed the black slave only to replace him with the yellow slave, the Chinese. The national substratum (i.e., the Indian) hasn't advanced beyond his condition under Spanish rule: immersed in the same ignorance and beaten down by the same servility. If he no longer cowers beneath the corregidor's staff, he groans beneath the yoke of the civil authorities or the rancher; if he doesn't pay taxes in gold he makes his contribution in his own flesh; if he doesn't die in the mines, he dies on the field of battle. We have even achieved the miracle of killing in him what almost never dies in a man: his hope. Our national history can be summed up in a few words: a plethora of half-baked political reforms, social progress almost nil, in other words, stagnation. The degree of civilization in a society is not measured by the wealth of a few and the enlightenment of another few, but rather by the general well-being and intellectual level of the masses. Yet politics drains away the idealism of our youth. Scarcely after graduating from the universities or, worse, while they're still sprawled on their high school benches, our adolescents have already begun to restrain their impulse for freedom, adapting themselves to the pettiness of the environment and taking on all the fawning refinement and malice of a bureaucratic sycophant worn down by years of adulation and mendacity. Don't bother asking of them any noble sentiment of independence, which in other countries constitutes the patrimony of minds recently awakened to the awareness of life. Their very physiognomy tells what they are: the humility of their countenance, the curvature of their posture, the submissive inflection of their voices—all this heralds the advent of a man doomed to mummify inside the skin of a senator, a minister, a judge, or a mere bureaucrat. Politics is indistinguishable from the judicature or the administration or careerism or parasitism. From public office one goes into politics, and from politics back into public office, so the three branches of government can be regarded as workshops where the national artifact is manufactured: the employee. Just as there were castes in India and craft guilds in the Middle Ages, so in Peru there are families of budget eaters or bureaucrats by secular inheritance. For such families, every profession, every career, every industry is a station on the way to the treasury. Men who might have left a luminous mark in art or science or industry squandered their good qualities and became intellectual invalids in the prime of life. Whenever we pass by the doors of congress, the palace, or any public office, we should recite the English poet's "Elegy in a Country Churchyard."

If politics is the evil, if politicians are the enemy, does this mean the writer should live closed off within himself, indifferent to the path his country is taking, as if he had fallen to earth from a distant star? Just because a man is excluded from politics, does this keep him from being affected and dragged along by events? When a reactionary party seizes power and passes laws restricting freedom of the press, does this not harm the writer in a direct manner? If we live near a swamp, we don't hold our breath to avoid the pestilent vapors; we try to devise a system to drain off the backed-up water. Even more to the point, although a man is unaffected by some harmful event, won't others be harmed by it? Are we to act out of an icy, cowardly selfishness and allow a dam to break and carry our neighbor away just because it doesn't threaten us? If there's anything a man should regret who has made his living by writing, it is failing to devote the best years of his life to collaborating in the task of social regeneration. And if there's anything he should take pride in and congratulate himself for, it is expressing a useful idea, extirpating a misconception, or introducing a ray of light into a mind clouded by obsessions with social class or religious sect. "When I began to write," says Zola, "I had an extraordinary scorn for politics . . . That feeling, which was the simplistic judgment of a frustrated poet, I now regard as the most imbecilic and childish notion . . . I've since come to see politics for what it really is, the burning field of battle where we fight for the life of a nation, where we sow the history of our country for future harvests of truth and justice. I've come to realize that the most elevated minds can evolve there, achieving the greatest of all goals: the welfare of others."

If anyone has the duty and the right to become involved in political issues, it's the writer, not for the purpose of becoming muddled and obliterated in them, but to furnish them with light and broader perspective; not to defend some legalistic convention or lie, but to unveil broad horizons of justice; not to investigate interpretations of the law or the survival of puerile, traditional customs, but to elevate political issues to the level of social issues. Serene amid the unleashing of evil passions and debased instincts, indifferent to personal changes that do not embody reforms advantageous to the masses, the writer defends the oppressed against the oppressor; in times of a country's greatest debasement and abuse of power, the writer is an advocate of humanity and justice. The professional politician is a soldier who in the smoke and confusion of combat can't see beyond the narrow circle that surrounds him; the writer is a sentinel who can survey from on high the movements of armies and foretell the final outcome of the battle.

There's nothing quite so limited in perspective as a man constantly enmeshed in politics. If he's loyal to his party, he operates in an orbit the size of a microbe's, can conceive of nothing beyond his group, and devotes himself to a labor of personal interest and egotism. If he isn't loyal, his life is nothing but rancor and revenge; if he's unfaithful to his party members he moves from group to group, playing the ignominious role of deserter and public pillager. Even the great statesman, that model of generosity and nobility, the prototype of the so-called civic virtues, manifests in politics something irreducible and automatic that makes us dislike him: he's always the man of high accomplishment, the man of judicious action, ever motivated by reasons of state. A secular priest, he sacrifices everything on the altar of God-state, just as the Catholic clergyman offers his sacrifice on the altar of God-Church. Though he may boast of being a freethinker and an atheist, he is the most egregious fanatic in the worst of all religions. His great fetish is the state, his pope is the chief executive, his ecumenical council the congress, his Holy Fathers the judiciary, and his Bible the constitution and the law.

That's why, when someone belittles the worth of a writer by saying "he isn't politic," we should understand this as a form of praise. Such a person is like a scalpel to decaying flesh, or disinfectant to bacteria.

In short, the writer should involve himself in politics in order to discredit it, dissolve it, and destroy it.

IV

Yes, politicians are the real enemy, and to deal with them we need to employ not only a general attack en masse, but individual expurgation so as to catch them one by one and subject them to moral vivisection. Yes, politics is the evil, and every act of propaganda should utilize all the energies wasted today in political research and conflict to bring about social reform.

Although those who adore myths and conventional slogans may be shocked, we need to do away with questions about the bases of the state and the principles of government and repeat the words of a true thinker: any government with the greatest number of individual rights and the least administrative action. When we compare the guarantees enjoyed by the *subject* of the English Crown with the harassment endured by the *citizen* of Peru, we come to understand that the forms of government have little or nothing to do with the freedom of the individual. Where would you rather live: in an autocracy ruled by Marcus Aurelius or in a republic governed by a Cáceres or a Piérola?

We have to show the people the horror of their debasement and wretchedness. There's no way to perform a good autopsy without taking the body apart, and no way to get to know a society in depth without stripping the flesh from the skeleton. Why be frightened or shocked? Whatever we have to say, don't citizens and foreigners alike already know it from experience? You don't cure leprosy by covering it with a white glove.

It is of little use to be always trampling the nation underfoot in its own mire or day and night rankling its wounds, if we aren't working simultaneously to raise the spirits of the masses scattered along the coast, if we don't shake the lethargy from the sleepwalkers forever dozing off along the slopes of the Andes, if we don't administer continuous electric shocks to an organism on the verge of paralysis. We need to poke and goad the masses, not for the malevolent pleasure of offending and exasperating them but out of the generous desire to move them toward goodness and fuel their courage to act. We don't need to fear that few will listen or hear; when a sincere, honest voice rings out, even the most ignorant will stop and listen. What we mistake as the inadequacy of the masses for understanding ideas ought to be called the impotence of the writer to make himself understood. If the technology and specific proofs of science are a dead letter for the uninformed or the uninitiated, its main conclusions exhibit such clarity and simplicity that minds with even a rudimentary education can understand them. Is it necessary to study astronomy in depth to understand that the earth moves around the sun? Or to study natural history extensively to understand that there are no unexplainable differences between man and the higher animals? Do we have to study sociology in depth to know that the human personality is sacred and that everyone has a right to a fair share of air, light, and life? Were all those who followed Martin Luther's teachings great theologians? Were Cromwell's soldiers and the volunteers of the French Revolution great sociologists?

Writers who won't allow themselves to be understood don't know how to express themselves: the art of eloquence is in large part dependent on knowing how to place oneself at the intellectual level of the audience. "Anyone who despises the masses despises Reason itself, considering it incapable of being communicated and understood; to the contrary, the only true philosophy is that which considers itself as something created for everyone and which maintains that we were all born equipped for the most exalted truth and that we all deserve our share of it, just as we deserve our share of sunlight."

Renan[1]

(1893)

I

Just as Victor Hugo turned poetry into a devastating democratic weapon, along came Renan to convert erudition into the magical art of instilling disbelief. Since Luther and Voltaire, few men have ignited more virulent polemics or unleashed more violent indignation.

When he translated the book of Job, Renan offered himself as new excommunicant among the thousand authors listed on the Index. When he lost his chair in the College of France for denying the dogmas of Catholicism, he became famous among freethinkers and scholars. But when he wrote the *Life of Jesus*, he became the object of universal abhorrence, the Turk's head that even the least violent man felt it proper to strike with his fist.

In the time of the Crusades, sinners and pious alike felt obliged to break a lance in the Holy Land; so from 1863 till 1870, the good as well as the evil disciples of the Nazarene took it as a point of honor to take up the pen against Renan. A thousand climbed into the ring, from Pope Pius IX, who called him "the French blasphemer," to Bishop Dupanloup, who threatened him with the "rigors of the secular arm."

[1] Written in Paris in 1893, the year before the publication of *Pájinas libres*, in which it appears for the first time, this piece anticipates two other articles that he wrote on the author of the *Life of Jesus*, which appeared posthumously—L.A.S., 1976.

There was more. Protestant and papist alike, who never before managed to agree on anything, tacitly conspired to denigrate the book and ridicule the author. One cannot conceive today the outrage felt by some Protestants when the son of Athanase Coquerel addressed Renan as *dear friend*.

There was even more: the freethinkers attacked him for contradictory reasons, finding the work full of circumspection, accomodation, and reticence, when they would have preferred Renan's pen to turn into a slashing, jabbing weapon, another Longinus lance.

You could put together a voluminous if not very civil library with everything written to insult Renan and refute the *Life of Jesus*. When the Franco-Prussian war broke out, they eased up on the heretic, and a whole body of literature, written by men whose good intentions compensated for their lack of genius, went into decline.

Renan, whose spirit of bellicosity was a bit underdeveloped, remained immersed in his papers, continuing his study of Syrian, Hebrew, Arabic, or Greek while the hurricane roared around him and the thunderclaps burst overhead. He hardly seemed to notice the imperial decree that ousted him from the chair in the College of France, even when blasted by repeated and malevolent attacks from Dupanloup. To engage in controversy with close-minded and ill-willed adversaries, to get down in the gutter to engage in a debate where more mud than ink was slung, hardly suited the character of the man who conjoined the mildness of Kant with the simplicity of Spinoza.

He never participated in debates. "In debates," he wrote, "you must know how to find the weak side of your adversaries and feed on them, never touching uncertain matters, never conceding anything, in short, renouncing the very essence of the scientific spirit."[2] "Slandered like none other, he never retaliated, placing no value on the efficacy of slander, persuaded that for serious minds the righteousness of the honest man was always self-evident."[3] "To feel hatred toward fools, great God! To respond to every inept attack, to waste your life in sterile combat, to put yourself at the mercy of those who insult you, granting them the right to imagine they can harm us, what madness!, when the

[2] *Etudes d'historie religieuse,* Preface.
[3] The Hebrew chair at the College of France.

world is so vast, when the universe holds so many secrets to discover, so much magnificence to contemplate" [*Feuilles detachées*].

Renan's enemies were wolves howling in vain; he, a tireless, silent termite who kept gnawing away at the wood of the Cross of Calvary.

II

Today we are amazed at the scandal aroused by the *Life of Jesus* in the hypocritical France of the age of Bonaparte. A nation with writers like Bayle, Fréret, Diderot, Voltaire, and d'Alembert, where the rationalist, secular winds of the revolution were blowing, where Dupuis and Volney reduced the entire gospel to a solar myth, where Parny sang the War Between the Gods, where Laplace, Stendhal, and Proudhon boasted of their atheism—a nation like this scandalized because a scholar denied the divinity of Jesus?

If Renan proceeds courteously, in a low key, and with circumlocutions, it should not be inferred that he is trying to write a work that will reconcile fanatic and atheist. Nor should we concur with Jules Levallois that the *Life of Jesus* provoked a unanimous uproar in the most diametrically opposed bands because "nothing separates men so drastically as a failed attempt to reconcile them" [*Deisme et Christianisme*]. True, Renan used great caution as he went about converting God to man; but all moral subterfuges, every softening of language, are mere literary recourses to win the reader's goodwill. Jesus has been depicted with such admirable and sympathetic features, has been so embellished by the adventitious adornments of the legend, and represents such a sublime example of gentleness, that if you attack him angrily and with hatred you arouse the unyielding antipathy of your readers and lose any chance of success in your attack, engaging in a harmful and counterproductive project.

If in many of his books Renan walks hand in hand with the timid and the conservative; in his *Life of Jesus* he marches with the advance guard of those assaulting old theogonies. He has calculated very carefully the magnitude of his demolition charge, knowing that it's enough to strip the divine veneer from Christ to bring down the immense edifice of Christianity. He undertakes with full consciousness a profoundly radical project, and to charge him with being a "respectful dissident" or to predict that "some day the Church will invoke him as an apologist" is an act of Machiavellian disingenuousness. . . .

No. The Church will eternally anathematize him as its worst enemy, and with good reason, for having committed the unpardonable crime of making us read him, for causing the Catholic faith the same harm as a dagger hidden in a bouquet of flowers or poison in a golden chalice. Most lives of Jesus are illegible and irritating, while Renan's is attractive, light-spirited, even winged. It has a Hellenic quality, and many of its pages transcend the Vergilian idyll. If it cannot be called a divine book, in the orthodox sense of the word, it should be called something much more valuable, a perfectly human book. When you finish reading it, you see that the son of Mary gains immensely from losing his divinity, for he is transformed from mythical and legendary shadow into a real historical person. No man would complain about having such a monument dedicated to him, and if Jesus returned to the world, he might well prefer seeing his purely human actions hyperbolized in Renan's book to seeing his thaumaturgical wonders glorified in the Gospels.

To strip the real event of its legendary incrustations by means of an inspired critique; to determine inductively and cautiously how such events could have occurred, when an impartial and conclusive narration is lacking; to analyze the indecisive or contradictory portraits in the Gospels; to fix with precise features the historical figure of Jesus, such is the project attempted by Renan. Christ, casting off the illusion of grand fetish and miracle worker, acquires an image much closer to the truth and appears humanly possible, although at times sketched with superhuman, almost divine, perfections. Without going so far as to make him a god, Renan confers exaggerated virtues on him so that he is touched with divinity. "Jesus will never be surpassed." Anti-Catholic but not irreligious, the *Life of Jesus* exhales a perfume of vague mysticism.

If perhaps Peyrat's book leaves a more lasting and effective impression in the mind of the reader, Renan's work, with all its heresies distilled into mystical-idealist clauses, offers the curious inducement of profane music played on a church organ by a supreme artist.

Supreme artist: not even his greatest enemies dared to deny it; they condemned his soul, not his style or his language.

The *Life of Jesus* has indisputable merit, an excellence that renders it imposing and eternal: its form. Renan confesses that he spent a year just revising it because the matter required complete sobriety, complete simplicity; and with his assiduous labor he achieved the feat that makes the artist most proud, the concealment of its artfulness. One quality of style stands out above the rest and seems to sum up all the rest, its clarity. You don't have to read a phrase twice to understand its meaning, you don't have to waste the time interpreting it that you could better spend meditating on it. As Joubert said of Plato, "the language is colored with the splendor of the thought."

In the *Life of Jesus* we see clearly the gift some French writers have for composing an almost original work out of foreign materials. The grave erudition of the German exegetes is converted in Renan into a pleasant dissertation. Or to put it another way, the juice of Germanic authors, subjected to the manipulation of the French stylist, takes on the clarity and crystalline quality of a diamond.

III

Renan has to be examined from different perspectives, since he isn't a sphere but an irregular polyhedron. He portrays himself as follows: "I was predestined to be what I am: a romantic who protests against romanticism, a utopian who preaches the politics of scorched earth, an idealist who works in vain to appear bourgeois, a web of contradictions reminiscent of the chimera of the Scholastics, endowed with a dual nature. One of my halves is busy demolishing the other half, like the fabulous animal of Ctesias that ate its feet without noticing it [*Souvenirs d'enfance et de jeunesse*].

A tonsured monk who hangs up his habit often becomes an implacable enemy of Catholicism and the most stubborn refuter of its dogmas. Only in an ex-papist monk like Luther is such violent rage against the popes conceivable. Renan comes off as impious without bitterness, a heretic with the seraphic unctuousness of an ecclesiastic. He speaks of Catholicism with respect, almost with veneration; he oozes an ineffable tenderness, recalling his early years in the faith; he admits that he owes to his religious education all the goodness of his nature; and he laments having saddened his earliest teachers, the venerable priests of Tréguier, with his heretical ideas. He credits them for instilling in his books a quality rare in our century: serenity. Although he appears sentimental and melancholy, he's far removed from those authors who write in a constant state of nervous exaltation. He peers down on events and persons as if he were from another planet, often like Voltaire's Micromegas.

Renan did not move from mysticism to voluptuousness. He cut short his ecclesiastical career and abandoned the seminary, when reading and meditating on certain German authors proved to him the fallibility of his former teachers. "Around 1843," he says, "I was in the Seminary of San Sulpicio when I begin to discover Germany through Goethe and Herder. I thought I had entered a temple, and everything I had formerly regarded as glory worthy of divinity began to have the same effect on me as paper flowers grown yellow and faded with age [*La réforme intellectuelle et morale*]. He admits that he had been chaste all his life, that he only loved four women—his mother, his sister Enriqueta, his wife, and his daughter—that on the threshold of old age he came to understand the words from Ecclesiastes: "Go, eat your bread with enjoyment . . . Enjoy life with the wife whom you love." However, "from childhood I beheld beauty as a gift of such supremacy, that talent, genius, virtue itself, were nothing in comparison." In his old age he writes phrases that remind us of Heine preaching the redemption of the flesh or Zola defending the dignity and nobility of procreation: "What," he says, "am I to believe that the highest work of creativity, the continuation of life, is connected to a gross or ridiculous act?" It may be that all of his senile eroticism is merely a literary recourse, a touch of naturalism. Only thus can we explain his writing the following: "The libertine is right and practices the true philosophy of life."

Renan comes off as an eccentric in his time and in his nation because of his disinterest or "detachment from temporal goods," by his own report. His works earned him very little. While novelists and dramatist accumulated fabulous sums and lived regally, he grew old in modest circumstances and, had it not been for the government of the republic, would have died in poverty. When the empire, after evicting him from the Hebrew chair, tried to recompense him, he rejected in haughtily. While he wasn't a spendthrift like Lamartine or prodigal like Dumas, he lacked Voltaire's and Victor Hugo's practical sense of life. His happiness would have consisted in having someone provide him with room and board, dressing him and keeping him warm, leaving him completely free to think and write. Not much different from the good abbot who asks for a good library but doesn't turn up his nose at a good refectory.

Contrary to the general pessimism, Renan was happy to have been born and expressed his pleasure in living. He appeared always to be satisfied, though all his satisfaction was little more than a discreet mask to cover his inner conflicts. It may be that neither his happiness nor his sadness were very profound because the true basis of his character was a smiling, amiable, and well-bred selfishness. He himself says frankly that during his clerical education he was horrified by personal friendships, that he never offered to help his friends or anyone else. It's unlikely that he lost any sleep over the sufferings of humanity. He had a good seat from which to watch the drama, and he enjoyed himself without worrying much about whether his neighbors were enjoying themselves as well. A man detached from deep passions and consequently from deep sorrows, he looked at the universe from the good side and professed an optimism so exaggerated that at times it smacked of irony. Who knows whether all his optimistic philosophy can't be explained in this way: "We owe virtue to the Eternal; but to get even, we have the right to add a touch of irony, giving it back to the one who deserves it, joke for joke, doing unto others as they did unto us."

A man of restraint and reticence, advances and retreats, he would scratch and then stanch the blood and offer a bandage, without considering that the scar would be indelible. The womanly scratches Renan inflicted on Catholicism were more harmful than the furious ax blows dealt by others. On the one hand he removed the gilding from the paper idol, and on the other he tried to gird it up with iron bars.

IV

Paul Bourget affirmed that Renan's work, considered in its entirey, is scientific. Wouldn't erudite be a better way of putting it? A series of logical connections without contradiction, a compact and unassailable assembly, in short, a great pyramid of observations leading to the affirmation of a law—that's not what we look for in Renan's writings. He acknowledges this himself when in his old age he expresses his regret at having devoted himself to investigations whose results "will never be accepted and that will always be seen as interesting considerations about a reality than vanished never to return" [*Souvenirs*].

He even believes he strayed from his true intellectual vocation, and with astonishing ingenuity he writes in his last years: "The extreme zeal that physiology and the natural sciences aroused in me leads me to believe that, had I devoted myself to them without interruption, I would have reached many of the same conclusions Darwin did, conclusions that I glimpsed" [*Souvenirs*]. But having glimpsed from a very young age many of the conclusions of Darwin does not keep him from resolving metaphysically problems that are proper to the natural sciences (e.g., the origin of language), nor from characterizing as a "false hypothesis the idea of a primitive form of humanity living in a savage and almost bestial state" [*De l'origine du langage*]. "Science," he writes, "shows that on a certain day, by virtue of natural laws that until then had presided over the evolution of things, without exception or exterior intervention, the thinking being made its appearance endowed with all its qualities and perfect with regard to its essential elements, and, consequently, to attempt to explain the appearance of mankind on earth by laws that have ruled the phenomena of our planet ever since nature ceased to create, would be to open the door to such extravagant imaginings that no serious mind would waste a single moment entertaining them" [*Études d'histoire religieuse*].

Renan brushed up against the continent of science the way an Américo Vespucci did; but he didn't penetrate it the way an Hernán Cortés or a Pizarro did. Evoking Schopenhauer, he calls love "the distant voice of a world that wants to exist"; evoking Darwin, he affirms that "love instilled beauty into the animal"; evoking Jacobi, he says that "his ancestors bequeathed him their musty economies of life, which think for them"; evoking Flammarion, he writes, "Let us imagine that everything that ever existed still exists somewhere as an image capable of being reanimated. We preserve the clichés of all things. The stars at the end of the universe still receive the images of events that happened many centuries ago. The matrices of everything that existed are still scattered through the various zones of infinite space."

When we read his *Future of Science,* when we remember that he once conceded superhuman power to future chemists, when we hear him maintain that "the world reveals to us a complete absence of deliberate design as well as the spontaneous impulse of the embryo toward life and consciousness," we begin to think of him as a modern sage. But when we witness his constant sorties into the realm of mysticism, when we hear him prophesy the immortality of the religious sentiment and affirm that "only the grossest materialism can call into question this eternal necessity of our nature," then we see he's a thousand years away from Taine, who declared that vice and virtue are as natural as vitriol and sugar, or Madame Achermann, who proclaimed that "ignorance is the common bond between religions," that "faith will disappear as science develops," that "a more civilized humanity won't need belief, only knowledge."

Let's not compare him with Darwin or Spencer, nor expect of him the audacity of Feuerbach, who razed the entire religious edifice of humanity, or Haeckel, who reconstructed the evolution of life on the planet. Without ever leaving France or penetrating the domain of the natural sciences, he can be compared with Letourneau, André Lefèvre, or Guyau. Compared to the *Irreligiosity of the Future* or the *Outline of a Morality without Obligation or Sanction,* many of Renan's books seem antiquated or reactionary. Even Vacherot[4] came to more daring conclusions concerning the psychological future of religion. His great audacity consisted in denying Christ's divinity and maintaining, although not consistently, the Hegelian concept of the universe, that is, regarding it as an entity in the gestation of God. He didn't stop to reflect on the fecund solidity of positivism. And although he rendered enthusiastic homage to the philosophical quality of Littré, he unfairly attacked Auguste Comte, accusing him of having written in poor French (an accusation between grammarians, not philosophers).

Orthodox thinkers call him a skeptic. Renan doesn't deserve that label because if he cast doubt on what was dubious, he affirmed the reality of the world of the senses, believed blindly in mathematical demonstration, and accepted the laws that were verified through observation and experimentation. In questions of morality or religion, he abstains or equivocates; regarding dogma, he affirms categorically the humility of Jesus Christ and the absence of divine revelation. He is, as Jules Simon says, "incredulous rather than skeptical."[5] Nevertheless, it is with some justification that Father Gratry calls him a sophist. Renan

---

[4] In his book *Religion,* Vacherot subsequently turned toward Catholicism and more recently affirmed the following: "God gives men politics and keeps religion for himself."—The author.

[5] *La Revue de Paris,* February 15, 1894.

argues for and against with surprising ease, not out of bad faith, but perhaps to illustrate the fragility of dialectics: he constructs a house of cards, blows it down, then puts it back together and knocks it down again. You might say he wants to satirize logic, his topic, and the reader. We're reminded of Mephistopheles making old Marta fall in love.

When Renan acknowledges Victor Cousin as "one of the inspirers of his thinking" [*Feuilles dettachés*] we realize that through his zeal to discover some truth completely, he is willing to reconcile contradictions. If some of his defects spring from eclecticism, others can be explained as the exaggerations of his critical spirit. The fear of falling victim to illusion and the obsession of believing himself to be "a refined spirit unencumbered by passion" led him at times to be reticent in his affirmations or to qualify his denials, in other words, to neither affirm nor deny and even to fall into contradictions, since he would express an idea and almost immediately, using a *however,* defend the contrary. Hence his scant popularity: the masses only comprehend and follow men who express themselves frankly and even brutally, with words like Mirabeau, with actions like Napoleon.

V

Ernest Renan, born in Tréguier on January 27, 1823, died in Paris on October 2, 1892. He, who customarily called into question the existence of God and the immortality of the soul, feared nothing so much as cerebral decline, and worried about nothing so much as his posthumous fame. "How it would grieve me," he says, "to go through a period of diminishment in which the man who was formerly strong and virtuous would end up reduced to the shadow and ruin of his former self, to the great delight of fools who would set about destroying the reputation he had so laboriously constructed! Such an old age is the worst gift the gods can concede to a man. If this fate befalls me, I refute in advance any nonsense a softened brain leads me to express or maintain. The Renan who is sound of mind and heart, as I am now—not the Renan half destroyed by death and no longer himself, as I'll become if I fall apart gradually—is the one I want people to hear and believe."

He would have preferred to die violently on the battlefield or to be assassinated in the senate chamber, and to some degree his desire was granted, as he died gently, without pain, maintaining his mental lucidity to the final moment. With him there were no religious masquerades or death legends in the style of Julian the Apostate or last minute repentance in the style of Littré and Claude Bernard. When he realized he was dying, he warned his family not to call in a priest even if in his final moments of pain and hallucination they were to hear him call out for spiritual succor. Married to a Protestant woman (sister of the painter Ary Scheffer), attended by their two sons, surrounded by loyal friends who knew his wishes, no clerical assault could even be attempted.

Having died a secular and impenitent death, Renan had sumptuous national exequies, was carried through Paris in a kind of posthumous triumph and laid to rest in the cemetery of Montmartre, beneath the same tombstone as Scheffer, not far from that of Théophile Gautier and Henri Murger.

What were his final, definitive convictions? A difficult question to answer, when we recall that Renan himself exclaimed one day: "*In utrumque paratus*. To be prepared for anything, perhaps that is the truest wisdom. To give ourselves up, depending on the moment, to trust, to skepticism, to optimism, to irony, is the way to be sure that, at least momentarily, we have possessed the truth" [*Souvenirs*].

To give some idea of his beliefs in the realm of politics and sociology, some quotations from his book, published under the pompous title of *Intellectual and Moral Reform*, will suffice:

> Egotism, the font of socialism; envy, the font of democracy; these will always produce a weak society, incapable of resisting powerful neighbors. A society is strong only if it acknowledges the fact of natural superiorities, which can be essentially reduced to one, that of birth, since intellectual and moral superiority is nothing but the superiority of the vital seed, developed under particularly favorable conditions.

> I am not rich, but I could scarcely live in a society without the rich. I am not Catholic, but I'm very glad there are Catholics, sisters of charity, village priests, and Carmelite nuns, and if it were in my power to suppress all of that, I would not do so.

> In reality, the Church and the schools are equally necessary: a nation cannot survive without either: when Church and schools are in conflict, everything goes badly.

... To educate the people, to revive their somewhat stunted faculties, to inspire them (with the aid of a good patriotic clergy) to cultivate a superior society, respect for science and virtue, the spirit of sacrifice and abnegation. ...

Considering only the rights of individuals, it is unjust that one person should be sacrificed for another; but it is not unjust for all to be subject to the higher work being conducted by humanity. It is the function of religion to explain these mysteries and to offer all those sacrificed on earth a superabundance of consolations in the ideal world.

This last dictum is the convenient system of *a religion for the people*, a system that is fraught with bloody irony on the lips of a man who did not live with much confidence of finding in the other life the rewards offered so generously to the unfortunate.

In effect, although he claimed "that he preferred hell to nature, ... that he expected and desired immortality," he did not live with any sure hope of achieving it. How could he, if he didn't even have a clear and definitive idea about God? His God fluctuates between a coming-into-being, the divine in nature, the celestial Father of Jesus, the God-the-Father, and a dirty old man delighting in the wickedness of his grandchildren. He attacked Béranger for his God of the Good Folk, and he proves to be even more irreverent than Béranger; he censured Voltaire for his impiety, and he turns out to be even more impious than Voltaire. Voltaire accuses Jupiter of having played a cruel joke by creating us; Renan contends that "the supreme seducer concealed the greatest ironies beneath our most sacred illusions." Voltaire, when he was dying, tells the priest who is trying to convince him of the merits of Jesus Christ: "Don't speak to me about that man." Renan takes off his hat when he enters a church and his friend says to him: "I thought you had a grudge against the good Lord." Renan answers: "We say hello, but we don't talk to each other."

Is there such an abyss between Voltaire and Renan? Who knows but that the *Life of Jesus* could be called another *Maid of Orléans,* not in the verse of Voltaire, but in the prose of Renan, the difference being that where Voltaire appears crude, shameless, and sarcastic, Renan seems polished, discreet, and simply ironic.

Renan is a clearer, more refined Voltaire.

VI[6]

On reading through Renan's works today, we are struck by two things: the flexibility of his talent and the immense productivity. The same man who deciphers an ancient, faded Semitic inscription also writes the *Philosophical Dramas* or the *Memoirs of Childhood and Youth*. Like Voltaire, he wields the pen with his dying hand and rests only after he sinks down into the tomb. Sickly, on the verge of death, he teaches two classes at the College of France and works tirelessly to finish his *History of the People of Israel*. More fortunate than his friend Taine, he doesn't leave any of his major works unfinished.

His adversaries, mainly the Catholics, accuse him of being frivolous and unserious, forgetting that the *Mission of Phoenicia*, the *History of the Origins of Christianity*, the *History of the People of Israel*, the *General History of the Semitic Languages*, and the *Corpus Semicarum Inscriptionum* attest to countless hours of study and profound meditation. True, Renan paid tribute to his epoch writing volumes filled with simple amenities or elaborations; but such books, often written to satisfy the voracious importunities of his editors, did not convey the quintessence or marrow of his talent: they were like the amusements or hobbies of the artist, who after constructing a basilica sat down to illuminate a miniature or engrave a goblet. Perhaps he discovers the serious depths of his character when he writes that of all his works he prefers the *Corpus semiticarum inscriptionum*,[7] which is the most arid and least accessible of his works.

Perhaps his final circumstances contributed much to the preference, since, like Taine, he proclaimed the aristocracy of the intellectual and would have liked to see the scientists transformed into a species of privileged being or earthly divinities. Not only did he look down on the common people, but in a moment of literary pessimism he attacked his contemporaries en masse and predicted somewhat morbidly that nothing or almost nothing written in the present century would prove to have lasting value. Without displaying a similar pessimism, we might ask, Which of his works will survive the coming shipwreck? Who can

---

[6] This article was included in the previous five-chapter editions.—L.A.S.

[7] James Darmesteter, *Revue Bleue*, October 21, 1893.

make an accurate prediction about what the future will choose? Quevedo, one of the wisest men of his time, lives through his ballads and miniature poems, through the superfluous products of his genius. Not even the authors themselves can predict the fate of their works: Petrarch thought he would be famous for his Latin verse. Newton esteemed his book on the Apocalypse as highly as his works on mathematics. Something similar is happening now with Renan. We forget the collaborator of Victor Leclerc, the traveler, the archeologist, the linguist and philologist, the historian of Israel and translator of Job, the Song of Songs, and Ecclesiastes, and only remember the stylist of the *Life of Jesus*. He hoped to live through his scholarship, and he lives through what he valued least or pretended not to value: literature.

Renan portrays himself as a scholar who regrets having devoted himself to scholarship and as a literary figure who prides himself on scorning literature. He says he is unafflicted by literary vanity, that at a certain point in his life he dedicated himself to literature just to please Sainte-Beuve, who was an important influence on him. However, after coming to know Sainte-Beuve intimately and after having escaped his influence, he wrote sentences, pages, and entire books of mere literature. When he affirms that "the desert is monotheistic," that "parallel lines meet in the Infinite," that "if Nature were evil she would be ugly," that "God is good, but he's not all-powerful yet, though he will be someday," isn't he writing books that are purely literary and even Lamartinian, with a Graziella in the form of Naomi?

In short, Renan achieved through German exegesis the same thing Madame de Staël and Egger achieved with Germanic literature and philology. Science can annul a portion of his work, as is now happening with the *Origins of Language*, but art will forever preserve thousands and thousands of his pages that give off a breath of eternal youth and the ineffable aroma of life. In French anthologies he will occupy a place beside Lamartine because there isn't that great a distance between *Jocelyn* and the *Life of Jesus*. If Lamartine was a poet who strayed into politics or a bee who built his honeycomb in the Phrygian cap, Renan was a poet walled in by erudition or an Ariel with library dust on his wings.

Notes on Language[1]

(1890)

I

Lamartine lamented that people and writers don't speak the same language: "It's the writer's task to transform himself and descend to a level where he can put the truth in the hands of the masses: to descend in this way is not to cheapen one's talent, but to humanize it."

Scientists have their own technical jargon, and no one demands that in books of pure science they make themselves understood by even the most ignorant individual. The relative obscurity of scientific works cannot be avoided, and to expect that an unlearned person should understand them just by opening the pages is as silly as to try to translate a language without having learned it. How can ordinary language express

---

[1] This article, dated 1890, corresponds with the campaign that, against every established truth, including language, M.G.P. was engaged in after 1886 and especially after 1888. By then he had already been excluded from the personnel involved in reorganizing the Peruvian section of the Royal Academy of the Language. Moreover, a powerful movement was under way at that moment to make the speech of Americans somewhat less dependent on the speech of the Europeans. Andrés Bello, as well as Domingo Faustino Sarmiento, took part in the polemic held in Santiago de Chile in 1842. M.G.P.'s proposals do not discover but reiterate the ways to best characterize the written expression of Spanish-speaking Americans. Rubén Darío also tried to establish the use of the contraction *del, della,* and *desto* in *Prosas Profanas* (1896), published two years after *Pájinas libres* (1894).—L.A.S., 1976.

chemical nomenclature or the theories and systems of our modern scientists? Not by writing "come to be" in place of "becoming," "otherness" for "altruism," or "throwback" for "atavism." We know that there is no labor so difficult or thankless as scientific popularization, but without the popularizer, scientific breakthroughs would be the patrimony of a privileged few. Vergil boasted that he made the jungles fit for consuls; modern popularizers do even more when they strip the truth of some of its aristocratic garb and bring it into the house of ordinary people in plain language.

The same is not true for literature. The readers of novels, plays, poetry, and so on, belong to the moderately well educated class, and they demand a straightforward, natural, comprehensible language so they won't have to be constantly looking up words in the dictionary. To attain perfect knowledge of a language takes years of assiduous concentration, and not all men are able to spend their lives studying grammars and consulting lexicons. The person who subscribes to a newspaper and buys a novel or a play wants them to speak to him clearly and comprehensibly. Reading ought to supply the pleasure of understanding, not the torture of guessing.

Masterworks are distinguished by their accessibility and do not constitute the patrimony of the initiated few but the legacy of all men of common sense. Homer and Cervantes deserve to be called democratic geniuses: a child can understand them. Talents who pride themselves on being aristocratic and inaccessible to the masses conceal their hollowness with the murkiness of their form. They have all the depth of a well that never strikes water, the elevation of a mountain whose peak is hidden by clouds.

French authors dominate and command respect because they pride themselves on their clarity, claiming that "clarity is French," that "obscurity is neither human nor divine." And let's not imagine that clarity consists of telling and explaining everything, when in fact it consists of leaving something unsaid and letting the public read between the lines. Nothing is quite so tedious as authors who explain even their explanations, as if the reader had neither eyes nor brain. The skilled artist, leaving out shadows and lines, can give life and expression to the physiognomy of a subject with only a few strokes. The good writer says neither too much nor too little and, by eliminating the gratuitous, offers his readers the pleasure of collaborating with him in the task of making himself understood [Michel Bréal, *Mélanges de Mythologie et de linguistique*].

The books that humanity reads and rereads without ever tiring of them, don't have the subtlety of embroidery but the beauty of a regular polyhedron or the grand disorder of a mountain range. Good writers, like good architects, make use of grand lines and disdain superfluous and puerile ornamentation. In good style, as in beautiful buildings, we find spacious use of light and vast connections, not intricate labyrinths or narrow mazes.

The coquetries and mannerisms of language seduce frivolous minds that are easily dazzled by academic triumphs and the applause of small cliques, but they "do not impress serious thinkers who hurl themselves bravely into the moral struggles of their century." To exert real influence on the minds of one's contemporaries, the writer must fuse the immaculate transparence of language with the fundamental substance of thought. Without clarity and naturalness, all perfection is diminished, lost. If Herodotus had written like Gracián, if Pindar had sung like Góngora, would they have been listened to and applauded in the Olympic Games?

Here are the great movers of minds in the sixteenth and eighteenth centuries: We have Luther, as devastating to popes as he was restorative to the German language, and we have especially Voltaire with his prose, as natural as breathing, as clear as distilled alcohol.

II

To fret about getting men to speak today the way they spoke yesterday is like straining to make the brass of a bugle throb like the head of a drum. The unsullied purity of language, an academic caprice. When was the Castilian language ever pure? In what epoch and by whom was that ideal language spoken? Where was there ever an impeccable and exemplary writer? Which is the perfect form of our language? Can any language become crystallized and take on a definitive form without following the evolutions of society or adapting to the environment? Nothing illustrates the instability of vital organisms so much as language; with good reason the Germans regard it as a perpetual state of becoming. In languages as in religions the theory of evolution admits no debate.

A language is not a fictitious or conventional creation, but the necessary product of the intellectual and moral environment, of the physical world and our organic constitution. All we have to do is move a people from the north to the south, or vice-versa, and their pronunciation will change immediately because it depends on anatomical and physiological causes.

In languages, as in organic beings, we can identify movements of assimilation and movements of segregation; hence, the existence of neologisms or new cells, archaic forms or detritus. As the adult maintains his personal identity, even though his organism no longer preserves the cells of his childhood, so do languages renew their vocabulary without losing their syntactic form. Gonzalo de Berceo and the archpriest of Hita now require a glossary, as will Juan de Mena and Cervantes in the near future.

Scientific discoveries and industrial applications lead to the invention of numerous words that appear initially in technical works and end up sifting down into ordinary language. Is there any vocabulary that has not assimilated Darwin's theory in fewer than forty years? Do we not have a plethora of new locutions derived from the steamboat and electricity? Even today the bicycle serves as an example. Special dictionaries abound in France, England, and the United States to define terms related to cycling, and all these words or phrases do not just constitute the jargon of a small clique. Those capable of understanding and using them number in the thousands or millions today. The bicycle has an entire literature with its books, its newspapers, and its public.

Parallel to this sifting down, there's also an ascending movement. Just run through one of the populous and active commercial centers, of port cities in particular, and you'll get a sense of the immense phenomenon of verbal fusion and renovation. You can hear every language, every dialect, every variety of slang and and jargon; you can see words seething and stirring like bacteria organized in an effort to survive and dominate. True, thousands of words pass through without leaving a trace, but there are also many that prevail and impose themselves by a kind of natural selection. An expression that resonated on the lips of sailors and porters ends up being incorporated into the speech of poets and scholars. Neologisms move from conversation to the newspaper, from the newspaper into the book, from the book into the academy.

This up-and-down movement takes place whether we like it or not:

"language follows its course, indifferent to the complaints of grammarians and the lamentations of purists."[2]

French, Italian, English, and German assault and open four huge breaches in the old castle of our language. French, like a beating drum, now penetrates the very heart of the precinct. Baralt, the stern author of the *Diccionario de Galicismos*, admitted in his last years the irresistible effect of the French invasion into the Castilian language. But some writers from Spain don't see it or pretend not to, and they go on boasting of the purity in the language, like the naive mother who praises the virtue of a daughter who has broken all seven cardinal sins.

The corruption of languages, is this necessarily bad? If through reciprocal infiltrations, Spanish, English, German, French, and Italian became so corrupted that what was spoken in Madrid were understood in London, Berlin, Paris, or Rome, would this not be a good thing? From five arroyos we would have a river; instead of five metals, a new metal from Corinth. Humanity would realize an immense saving in the mental energy that is now expended in learning three or four living languages—hundreds of words and piles of grammatical rules. What would it matter that I couldn't enjoy the pleasure of reading *Don Quixote* in Castilian, if I possess the immense advantage of being able to communicate with the man from Paris, Rome, London, and Berlin? In comparison with human solidarity, all the intranigencies of language seem petty and puerile, as petty and puerile as matters of race and borders. The people of Provençe in France, the Flemish in Belgium, the Catalonians in Spain, in short, all those who use regional languages to the detriment of national languages, are engaged in a retrograde project. To the word of great scope, used by millions of people and understood by most of the intellectual world, they prefer the restricted word, used by thousands of provincials and artificially cultivated by a few literati. To write *Mireío* in Provençal and not in French, *Atlântida* in Catalan and not in Spanish, is like giving up the railroad for the stagecoach, or the stagecoach for the horse.

The language used by the greatest number of individuals, the one most accepting of changes, the one most adaptable to the social environment, has the greatest likelihood of surviving and serving as the basis for the future universal language. So far it seems that English has

---

[2] Arsene Darmesteter, *La vie des mots*.

the advantage. It's not only the literary language of Byron and Shelley or the philosophical language of Spencer and Stuart Mill, not only the official language of England, Australia, and the United States, but the commercial language of the whole world. We might well call Spanish and Italian languages of the past, English and German languages of the future. All the neo-Latin languages, which are not so much old as outmoded, need to purge themselves of the double gibberish, legal and theological, bequeathed by the Roman Empire and the Catholic Church.

Sanskrit, Greek, and Latin became dead languages without rendering the Hindu, Greek, and Roman civilizations totally mute. Their voices were muted, but their echo can still be heard. Their best books survive in translation. Perhaps, with the poetic melody of those languages, we lost the flower of antiquity. But we still have the fruit, and who is to say that our accentual rhythm is worth less than their quantitative rhythm? When certain scholars in their enthusiasm for classical literature conclude that "our decrepit languages are barbarian babble in comparison with Greek and Latin [*Histoire des grecs*], all they're doing is applying the theological notion of human degeneration to linguistics. The creature who without supernatural aid moved from the grunt to the word and transformed the impoverished and crude primitive languages to rich and structurally admirable languages, like those spoken in India and Greece, probably tried to detain and even turn back the development of his own verbal faculties: up to Sanskrit, progress; afterward, decline, because according to the law followed by many, Sanskrit is superior to Greek, Greek to Latin, Latin to all the Romance languages. If someday books are discovered in a language older than Sanskrit, wise men steeped in theology and metaphysics will demonstrate that that language was superior to Sanskrit. We know more than our ancestors, and we don't speak as well. The function continues, and the organ atrophies or evolves. The evolution of languages—their so-called decadence—has consisted in moving from synthesis to analysis, just as understanding moved from the global, a priori concept of the universe to the particular study of phenomena and the formulation of their laws. True, we're gradually losing the ability to think in images, metaphors are being transformed into mere comparisons, the word is becoming more analytical and precise, to the detriment of poetry. But does humanity live only through epic poems, dramas, and odes? Isn't the *Origin of Species* as valuable as the *Iliad*, isn't Newton's binomial theory as valuable as the works of Aeschylus, and aren't Kepler's laws as valuable as Pindar's odes? Say what you want, we speak as we should speak, the way our cerebral constitution and the environment dictate. Not being Hindus, Greeks, or Romans, is there any way we could express ourselves as they did? A language does not represent the total progress of our species in all epochs and in all countries, but the mental evolution of a people at a specific moment. Language offers us a kind of cliché that stores the momentary image of a thing in constant transformation. The true writer is the one who, conserving his own literary individuality, manages to stereotype in a book the language used by his contemporaries. With good reason we say the language of Shakespeare, the language of Cervantes, the language of Pascal, or the language of Goethe to signify what English, Spanish, French, and German were in a particular epoch.

When our living languages become dead ones, or change so radically that they aren't understood by the descendants of those who speak them today, will humanity have suffered an irreparable loss? The disappearance will come about slowly, not violently. Like nations, like everything in nature, languages die by giving birth. Unless some general cataclysm wipes out the centers of civilization, the real treasure, the treasure of science, will be preserved intact. The civilizing conquests are not words stored in dictionaries or phrases laid out to dry in erudite dissertations, but moral ideas transmitted from person to person and achievements preserved in the books of science. Chemistry and physics, are they any less chemistry and physics in Russian than in Chinese? Did the geometry of Euclid die when the language in which it was written died? If English dies tomorrow, will Darwin's theory vanish with it?

It's inside the fortress of language that the wretched spirit of nationality takes refuge. Each people admires in its own language the *non plus ultra* of perfection and thinks everyone else babbles in some crude gibberish. The Greeks scorned Latin, and the Romans were outraged that Ovid wrote verse in the language of hyperboreans. If the theologians of the Middle Ages vilified Muhammad for having written the Qur'an in Arabic and not in Hebrew, Greek, or Latin, the Arabs regarded their language as the only one that was grammatically constructed and called the speech of Castile *aljamía*, or the language of barbarians. Behind the Frenchman who acknowledges no *esprit* outside of his Rabelais stands the Englishman who regards as inferior any foreigner incapable of reading Shakespeare in the original and the Spaniard who through the mouth of his kings praises Castilian as the best language for communicating with God.

Since language holds the sacred archive of our errors and concerns, we think it's a profanation to touch it. If we stopped using our native language, we would perhaps change our way of thinking because political convictions and religious beliefs are often reduced to word fetishes. According to André Lefevre, "out of thousands and thousands of confusions, conveyed by analogous expressions, all the legends of the divine tragicomedy were born" [*Religion*, 19].

With the national word we inherit all the morbid conceptions accumulated in the minds of our ancestors over centuries and centuries of ignorance and savagery: language molds our intelligence, deforms it as the shoe deforms the foot of the Chinese woman. So there's no greater hygiene for the brain than to emigrate to a foreign land or immerse itself in literatures from other languages. Leaving one's country, speaking another language, is like emerging from underground and breathing pure mountain air.

We regard as senile the attachment of the ultramontanist to the old vocabulary, since retrograde ideas adhere to antiquated turns of phrase the way a rusty sword adheres to the scabbard; we think too of his sacrilegious horror of new words, since the neologism, like a kind of Trojan horse, carries the enemy inside. Thus nothing is quite so logical (or laughable) as the rage of some purists against the neologism, a rage that induces them to regard words as personal enemies. Debating in *L'Académie française* over the admittance of a word that was used everywhere in France but was not pure, Royer-Collard exclaimed angrily: "If that word enters, I leave."

In the aversion of the Church toward French and its preference for Latin, we have a revival of the hatred of the synagogue for Greek and its love of Hebrew. Just as the Greek language signified irreligiosity and philosophy to the Jew, to the Catholic the French language embodies impiety and revolution, Encyclopedia and Declaration of the Rights of Men. It's the black plague, and it has to be quarantined. As Judaism lived inseparably conjoined to the Hebrew language, Catholicism has celebrated an eternal alliance with Latin. The dogma does not fit with living languages. For something dead, invariability; for a mummy, a stone sarcophagus.

II

Spanish is marked by its energy as the language of a virile, warlike people. There are more harmonious languages, richer and more scientific languages, but no language more energetic. Its phrases lay you low, like Hercules' club, or cut you in two, like Charlemagne's sword. Today we are surprised by the raw frankness and crude naturalism of earlier writers who say what they have to say without beating around the bush. It seems like we've moved into a foreign language when, after reading Quevedo, for example (Quevedo in his good moments), we turn to those neoclassical authors who use the purest and most correct phraseology.

In the sixteenth and seventeenth centuries there was in Spain a fluorescence of writers who polished and enriched the language without altering its pure and virile character. Poets, following Garcilaso's lead, completely renovated versification by assimilating the Italian hendecasyllable: with the *silva*, the sonnet, and the royal octave, it seems as though the Spanish genius sprouted new wings. To get an idea of the giant step taken in poetry, we need only compare Ayala's couplets or Castillejo's *quintillas* to the *Noche serena*, the *Canción a las ruinas de Itálica*, and the *Batalla de Lepanto*. The prose writers were not left behind, although they tried to give colossal dimensions to the period, blindly imitating Cicero. In each writer, particularly in the historians, personal physiognomy is compelling, so that no one confuses Melo with Mariana, or Mendoza with Moncada. True, none reached the level of Pascal or Luther; the heterodox weren't eminent prose writers, and the good writers weren't orthodox. The greatest defect of the Castilian authors—what separates them from intellectual Europe, confines them to Spain, and gives them an insular character—is their narrow and wretched Catholicism. You sense in their works, as Edgar Quinet says, "the soul of a great sect, not the living soul of a human being." Except for Cervantes, no Spanish author enjoys any popularity in Europe. It pains us to think what a Góngora or a Lope de Vega or a Quevedo or a Calderón could have achieved if they had thrown off the chains of dogma and flown freely or followed the saving movement of the Reformation. In the purely literary realm, Saavedra Fajardo attempted something daring and original: to strip the language of idioms or idiotisms, to give it precise, philosophical, almost mathematical form. Had he been endowed with greater genius, he would have initiated in prose a revolution as fecund as that realized by Garcilaso in verse; but seeking to imitate or improve on Machiavelli with his *Príncipe cristiano*, he was left in the great Florentine's dust.

In the mid-eighteenth century there emerged a species of prose writers, all coiffed and affected, who exaggerated the Latinism of the writers of two centuries earlier. Out of a language that was all muscle and nerves they created a substance that was all excrescence and fungus. Through their obsession to construct Ciceronian phrases and hold the meaning in suspension from the first to the last line of a folio page, they substituted for the logical sequence of ideas the capricious and arbitrary connection of the particles. They sacrificed substance to rotundity and constructed round but hollow geometrical spheres.

True, our language reflects the exuberance and pomp of the Spanish character. The Castilian language takes more pleasure in expansion than in constriction and seems organized not to crawl along, but to march with the solemnity and magnificence of a queen with her rich and velvety train. It's also true that between the natural and picturesque language of the Spanish people and the wan and artificial language of its affected writers, an abyss yawns.

The sentence loses much of its force when we start piling on articles, conjunctions, prepositions, and relative pronouns. All those the's, an's, whose's, which's, and that's make our sentences look like nets of tangled, flimsy threads. Nothing so detracts from their vigor as the overuse of the relative pronoun *que* and the preposition *de*. The abominable possessive pronouns *cuya*, *cuyos*, and *cuyas* are the source of countless ambiguities and are almost always carelessly used, even in the Spanish Academy. A thought expressed in English with a verb, a noun, an adjective, and an adverb requires, in the Spanish of many Spaniards, a whole string of pronouns, articles, and prepositions. If, according to the Spencerian theory, language is reduced to a machine for transmitting ideas, what are we to say of the mechanic who wastes energy in unnecessary friction and useless connections.

If our language cedes in concision to English, it competes in richness with German, though it does not equal its freedom in constructing new compounds from simple words, assimilating exotic words, or even inventing new ones. This last habit degenerates into a kind of Germanic calamity, for a philosopher who invents or tries to invent a new system creates a new vocabulary, which is like applying freedom of conscience to language. The astonishing flexibility of the German language is evident in its poetry. The German poets translate with masterful fidelity long compositions, using the same number of verses as the original, the same number of syllables, and the same placement of consonants. Moreover, they do not accept the idea of a conventional poetic language and, like the English, they sing with admirable simplicity about such ordinary and domestic objects that it would be extremely difficult or impossible to translate them. Whereas in Spanish the poet lets himself be carried along by the form, in German the poet dominates both rhyme and rhythm. Spanish American and Spanish poetry offer something hard, irreducible, like a substance resistant to the manipulation of the artist: hendecasyllables in particular seem like symmetrically placed iron bars. In an extremely limited number of authors, Campoamor in particular, we encounter Germanic flexibility, the sovereign power of infusing life and movement into the poetic phrase.

It isn't only in poetry that we have a conventional language, but in spoken and written prose as well. Men who speak plainly in conversation, like any of us, express themselves extravagantly and obscurely when they wield a pen. Like a prestidigitator's bottle, they pour out wine and then vinegar. It's as if they were doing a rough draft and suddenly decided to translate everything intelligible and smooth into something unintelligible and uneven. The process must not be all that difficult when people who are profoundly illiterate, so illiterate that they don't even know the rules of grammar, manage to infuse into their prose an air of stale nobility. With mile-long clauses peppered with violent inversions; using a veritable cloudburst of idioms, idiotisms, and refrains hauled in by the carload from the dictionary; saying *combing gray hairs* for *turning gray, fixing your mind on* instead of *observing, cute chic* for *lovely girl, thought I* or *said he* for *I thought* or *he said*, and right away they've pulled it off, stumbled across the end of the sentence. The use of refrains, though it's nothing new (Sancho Panza provided us with the model), has the advantage of making people laugh with jokes invented by others. This is not mental activity but manual labor: making lists of phrases or words and then inserting them into what you write. Works composed in this way seduce us for a while, but they end up boring us, revealing their bookish flavor and demonstrating that the worst enemy of literature is the dictionary.

True, the word needs specific nuance: a harangue in Club Revolution is different from gossip in a nun's parlor. Language fits the man, fits the company. In the hypocritical court of Charles the Bewitched the obsequiousness of fawning courtiers was like the affected piety of old ladies in church, whereas in the free land of Greece, people roar in a tone reminiscent of the artistic evolutions of the Pythian games and the irresistible assault of the Macedonian phalanxes.

Montaigne liked "plain, simple speech, whether written or oral, a succulent, vigorous speech, short and concise, not so much delicate and groomed as vehement and brusque." Today he would like modern speech. Is there anything more ridiculous than using archaic forms such as *magüer, aina mais, cabe el arroyo,* and *doncel acuitado,* to the hum of a telegraph wire, the creak of a steamboat propeller, as a locomotive whistles by us, and a hot-air balloon sails overhead?

In America and in our century, we need a condensed, juicy, nourishing language, like beef extract; a language as fecund as irrigation in a field; a language that unleashes its sentences with the strength and din of waves on the shore; a democratic language that doesn't get bogged down with proper nouns or phrases as foul as a soldier's oath; a language in which you can hear the hammer beating against the anvil, the screech of the locomotive on the rails, the dazzle of light in electricity, and even the smell of carbolic acid, or smoke from a chimney, and the creaking of the pulley on its axis.

Death and Life

(1890)

I

Poor or rich, ignorant or wise, born in huts or palaces,[1] in the end we
have the shroud for cloak, the earth for our bed, darkness for sun,
worms and putrefaction our only companions. The tomb, a fitting end
to the play!

Is there great pain in dying or does a comatose state precede the
final crisis? Sometimes death lets us die, at other times it kills us. Some
show signs of passing on slowly and smoothly, like a perfume that seeps
out of the flask through an imperceptible crack; others succumb desperately, as if life were being torn from them piece by piece with white-
hot pincers. In old age we surrender, but in our youth we fight back.
Who knows what death might be like: first, a great pain or a heavy
drowsiness; afterwards an invincible dream; then, a polar chill; and finally, something evaporating in the brain and something turning the
rest of the body to marble.

It's nothing more than poetic illusion or theological ploy to exag-
gerate the beauty and majesty of the cadaver. Can you imagine Romeo

---

[1] An echo of Horace's *Pallida mors aequo pulsat pede pauperum tabernas, / Regumque
turres*, which Fray Luis de León translated: "Que la muerte amarilla va igualmente—a la
choza del pobre desvalido—y al alcázar real del rey potente" and which Cervantes quotes
in the prologue to *Quixote*, I.—Translator.

finding Juliet more beautiful dead than alive? A corpse produces distance, repugnance; a statue without the purity of marble, with all the horrors and miseries of the flesh. Only on the battlefield are the dead endowed with greatness, eyes aflame with imposing virility, hands grasping a sword, lips that look as if they had just issued a final command.

The corpse in a state of decay, which Bossuet says has no name in any language, sums up for most people the most horrific and frightening aspect of death. It's as if the posthumous preservation of form implied the continuation of pain. Men imagine themselves not just dead but dying by slow degrees, over a long period of time. When the tomb is exchanged for the crematorium, when the diseased flesh is transformed into blue flame and the skeleton imprisoned in its coffin is replaced by the handful of ash in the funeral urn, fanaticism will have lost one of its most effective weapons.

Does something exist beyond the tomb? Will we preserve our personality or be absorbed into the All, like a drop of water into the ocean? Will we be reborn on earth or be transported to the stars to continue a planetary and stellar series of new and varied existences? We have no idea: a hundred granite walls separate life from death, and for untold centuries men have been trying to perforate the wall with the point of a pin. To say "this thing is possible, but that isn't" is the height of presumption or madness. Philosophy and religion pontificate and anathametize, but pontificating and anathametizing prove nothing. Where are the facts?

What hope can sustain us when we sink down into the abyss that made Turenne tremble and sent a chill up Pascal's spine? None, so we won't be disappointed or happily surprised if there is something. Nature, which is capable of creating flowers to be eaten by worms and planets to be blown to bits, can also create human beings to be annihilated by death. To whom can we turn? To no one. Once all traditional beliefs fall apart, two grand questions remain, for which no scientific proof, nor any logical refutation, has ever been formulated: the immortality of the soul and the existence of a "distinct and personal God, a God absent from the universe," as Hegel put it. To this point, what can we say about God and the soul? Two hypothetical, imagined entities devised to explain the origin of things and the functions of the mind.

If we escape the shipwreck of the grave, we have no reason to think we'll land on shores any more hospitable than earth. It may be the height of folly to boast with stoic bravado that "death is a possession that no one on earth can take from us," since we don't know whether the doorway to the sepulcher opens onto a ballroom or a bandit's grotto. Dying is bad, said Sappho, because otherwise the gods would have died. Achilles may have been right when among the ghosts of Erebus he answered Ulysses with these melancholy words: "Don't try to console me about death; I'd rather till the earth in the service of the most destitute farmer than be lord of all the ghosts of those who no longer exist.[2]

Our fear of death—is this merely one of nature's schemes to chain us to life, or is it an omen of coming misfortune? On approaching the supreme moment, all the cells of the organism seem to feel the horror of dying and begin to tremble like soldiers about to enter the field of battle.

On earth, there is never any clarification of rights, only contests of strength; in the history of humanity there is no apotheosis of the just, only the elimination of the weak. But we postpone the denouement of the earthly drama so as to give it a moral ending. We do a *berquinada:* applying to nature the system of compensations, extending to all creation our purely human sense of justice, we imagine that if nature piles evils on us today, it must be storing up treasures for us tomorrow. We open a checking account with nature, with its debits and credits. An entire doctrine of penalties and compensations is derived from the application of bookkeeping to morality.

Nature is neither unjust nor just, only creative. It shows no sign of acknowledging human sensibility, neither hatred nor love. An infinite vessel of conception, a divinity in constant labor, a mother who is all breast but without heart, it creates and creates only to destroy and create again and destroy again. In a single gust it knocks down the work of thousands and thousands of years. It doesn't hoard centuries or lives because it relies on two inexhaustible entities: time and fecundity. It regards the birth of a microbe with the same indifference as the disappearance of a star, and it would fill an abyss with human beings just to make a bridge for an ant.

---

[2]*Odyssey,* Canto II.

Is there any reason to think that nature, which is indifferent to men living on earth, will become just or merciful just because we descend into the tomb and take on another form? That's like thinking a king will cease to be deaf to cries of misfortune just because his subjects move to different houses or wear different rags. Wherever we end up going, we're not leaving the universe, and we aren't going to escape its eternal, inviolable laws.

It frightens and terrifies us to imagine where life's whirlwind will take us, how it will transform us. Being born is like stepping into a macabre dance never to emerge or falling into a dizzying whirlwind and spinning around eternally without knowing how or why.

Could anything be more desolate than our condition, more depressing than our slavery? We get born without anyone consulting us, we die when we don't want to, we end up where we wouldn't choose to go. For years and years we wander through a desert, and on the very day we set up our tent, uncover a spring, plant a palm tree, and settle down to rest, death shows up. We want to live? Then die. We want to die? Then live. What difference is there between a stone drawn down to the center of the globe and a man dragged by an invincible force toward an unknown resting place?

Why can't we be masters even of ourselves? When our head presses down on our shoulders with the weight of a mountain, when our heart writhes inside our chest like a tiger trapped but not tamed, when the last atom of our being draws back in hatred and nausea at existence, when we bite our tongues to hold back the explosion of a stupid blasphemy, why is it we lack the power to annihilate ourselves with an act of the will?

Can it be that all men desire immortality? For many, nothingness appears as a delightful immersion in a bottomless sea, a voluptuous swoon in an infinite atmosphere, an untroubled sleep on an endless night. Mirabeau, dying, rejoiced at the thought of self-annihilation. Do we perhaps always resolve the idea of immortality in this way? At times, fed up with feeling and tired of thinking, we become disconsolate with the perspective of eternal activity and start to envy the sterile idleness of nothingness; at other times we experience an insatiable thirst for knowledge, an immense curiosity, and we long to exist as an impalpable, ascending essence, to journey from world to world, seeing everything, scrutinizing everything, knowing everything; at other times we want to lie back in a kind of nirvana, recovering consciousness now and then for just an instant, so as to enjoy the good fortune of having died.

But why be afraid? Whatever comes, let it come. Fear, like the volcanic vapors near Naples, can asphyxiate creatures who keep their heads at ground level, not those who raise their heads a few feet off the ground. When death comes, let's go out to meet it, and die on our feet like the Roman emperor. Let's look straight at the mystery, even if we see furious, menacing specters; let's hold out our hands toward the unknown, even against the points of a thousand daggers. As Guyau says, "Let our last pain be our last curiosity."

There are different ways of dying: some depart from life like frightened reptiles slithering between the cracks of a cliff; others go off to the darkness like an eagle soaring over a thundercloud. Speaking without hypocrisy, it's unworthy for a man to die demanding the last place setting at eternity's banquet, like a beggar asking for a bread crumb at the door of the feudal lord who never stopped flogging him mercilessly. It's better to take responsibility for your actions and leap toward the unknown, just as the pirate hurls himself against the immensity of the sea without passport or flag.

II

We all picture the All as an endless repetition of the spectacle our eyes can see or our imagination can fantasize. But how important is the tiny radius of our observations? What objective value do our cerebral notions have? We experience the unity of physical forces and the material unity of the universe. Who knows if we aren't like the deluded spectator who mistakes the simple figures on the curtain for stage and actors!

We hold out our pygmy arms to grasp and hold what's removed from us by a temporal eternity, an immensity of space. We pride ourselves on having discovered the truth, when even in our sweetest illusions observation and experience undermine all our systems and all our religions, as the sea undermines the mounds of sand piled up by a child on the beach. Each generation boasts of having discovered the secret of life, and each one repeats the same question; but Nature answers each person with different words and eternally guards her mystery.

What difference is there between mineral crystallization, the cell of plants, and the membrane of animals? What differentiates sap from blood? Man: does he represent the final stage of earthly creatures or will he one day be stripped of his present supremacy? When we're born, do we spring from nothingness or do we simply achieve metempsychosis? Why have we come to earth? We would think it all a dream if pain didn't verify the reality of things.

Doubt, like a polar night, envelops everything. What is obvious, what is undeniable, is that in the drama of existence all of us as individuals represent the double role of executioners and victims. Living implies killing others; growing, the assimilation of multiple corpses. We are a walking cemetery where myriads of beings are buried to give us life with their death. Man, with his insatiable stomach, turns the universe into a hundred-course banquet, but we shouldn't imagine that everything in creation is resigned and vulnerable. Minerals and plants conceal their venom, the animal has its claws and teeth. The microbe gnaws and destroys man's body: the humblest creature brings down the proudest. The omnivore is eaten in turn.

Why this hunger to live? If life were something good, the absolute guarantee of losing it would be enough to turn it into something bad. If a man dies each second, how many tears are shed in a single day? How many since humankind began? The dead are replaced by those born; but do we derive any joy from coming into the world? That lump of flesh we call a newborn, that fragile being who drowses with its eyes open, as if it hadn't made up its mind to shake off the stupor of nothingness, is capable of crying, but not of laughing. Birth, is it not the sorrow of all sorrows? On the bed of the woman giving birth a duel is staged between the stupid, selfish creature straining to be born and the intelligent, selfless woman struggling to give life to another.

Why have a beautiful sun to light sad scenes? When we see children smile, when we think that tomorrow they'll die in pain or live in bitterness harsher than death, an ineffable sense of commiseration claims even the hardest hearts. If a certain tyrant wished the Roman people had just one head, so he could chop it off with a single blow; if an English humorist wished the faces of all human beings could be reduced to a single face, so he could have the pleasure of spitting in it, who wouldn't wish humanity had just one face, so we could dry all its tears at once?

There are moments of generous solidarity in which we not only love all of humanity, but even the beasts and birds, the plants and lakes, the clouds and stones; we even wish we had huge arms so we could embrace all the creatures dwelling on all the globes of the firmament. At such times we admire the Eleusines who had laws against killing animals, and we think of the exquisite sensitivity of the ancient Aryans who in their prayers to Indra begged him to send down blessing and happiness to all creatures, animate as well as inanimate. True charity doesn't end with man. Like a gigantic wing, it spreads out to shelter the whole universe.

Why deny human perversity? There are men who kill with just their shadows, like the *manzanillo* tree from Cuba or the *duho-upas* from Java. Humanity, like the ocean, has to be looked at from afar; like the tiger it deserves a bite, not a caress. Virtue engenders envy, good deeds provoke ingratitude, good brings ill with it. Our friends are like cursed fields where we plant wheat and harvest weeds; the women we love with all the warmth of our hearts are as impure as the mud on the roads, as ungrateful as vipers warmed against the bosom. Whence all this perversity? How long can a poor wretch be good and long-suffering? Lacerated flesh inevitably rebels against heaven and earth.

If man suffers crucifixion, are animals, plants, and rocks exempt from suffering? What truth is concealed in our casuistical distinctions between inanimate and animate matter, between inorganic and organic entities? Who knows what happens inside the molecules of a stone? Perhaps a single drop of water holds more tragedies and sorrows than the entire history of humankind. The great pachyderm and the harvest mite, the cedars of Lebanon and the lichen in Iceland, the boulder on the mountain top and the sand in the sea, all of these are "our companions in life," our brothers in misfortune. Ancient philosophers thought the stars were gigantic animals. The celestial harmonies Pythagoras heard, wasn't it just the moaning from all the creatures dwelling in the masses of the firmament? Wherever our imagination transports us, wherever we imagine the most rudimentary or the most complex manifestation of being, there we find bitterness and death. Existence is sorrow, and the labor most worthy of a God would be to reduce the universe to nothingness.

In this infinite martyrology, there is no irony more bloody than the imperturbable serenity of the laws of nature, no despair more profound than the intangible, impersonal quality of the forces oppressing us. Unfeeling millstones grind us down, hands we can feel and grasp strangle us, monsters with a hundred invisible mouths tear us to pieces. But the universe, is it an actor, an accomplice, an executioner, a victim, or merely the instrument and setting for evil? Who knows! Nonetheless, it could be said, and often, that amid this universal and eternal horror, *someone* is strolling along, having a time, the way Nero strolled among the agonized cries of men who were being slowly devoured by fire, turned to human torches.

What madness is it to continue in the war of all against one and one against all? If death offers no more refuge than mute submission, because all resistance is vain and foolish, in life we can act and struggle. Action stuns, intoxicates, and cures the evil of living; struggle multiplies our forces, makes us proud, and gives us dominion over the earth. Let's not just vegetate as we dig our own graves, or petrify with inaction until birds begin to nest on our heads.

A man is worth little or nothing. But do we know the fate of humanity? Do we know if the cycle of our evolution is closed? Do we know whether our species will be the springboard for a superior species? Do we not imagine that *tomorrow's being* will surpass today's man as Plato surpassed the gorilla, as Friné surpassed the Hottentot Venus? Seeing where we come from and where we are now, comparing what we were with what we are, we can calculate how far we'll go and what we'll be tomorrow. We lived in caves, in forests; now we live in palaces; we tracked through the dark hollows of bestiality, and now we feel the vigorous shudder of inner wings pushing us towards realms of serenity and light. The vicious, cannibalistic animal now produces self-sacrificing types who defend the weak, declare themselves paladins for justice, and inject themselves with diseases in order to find ways to combat them. The savage, once happy just to sleep, eat, and procreate, writes the *Iliad*, erects the Parthenon, and measures the movement of the stars.

No superhuman light shone for us in our night, no friendly voice cheered us in our failures, no invisible arm fought for us in the centuries-long war against the elements and wild animals. What we were, what we are now, we owe to ourselves. What we are capable of becoming, that too we owe to ourselves. To go forward, we don't need to look up, but ahead. We've wasted enough time peopling the firmament with the phantoms of our imagination and giving form to hallucinations forged by fear and hope; it's time to tear the blinders from our eyes and see the universe in all its beauty but also in all its implacable reality.

We didn't ask for existence; but by living, we accept life. Let's accept it, then, without monopolizing it or wanting to eternalize it for our exclusive benefit; we laugh and make love on our parents' tombs; our children will laugh and make love on ours.

II

Times of Struggle

The Parties and the National Union

(1898)

Gentlemen:

Complying with the mandate of the National Union, I come to offer a word of encouragement to the few men who still remain faithful to our cause after so many temptations and struggles. I will speak about political groups and their leaders, about the last civil war and its consequences, about the National Union and its obligations under the current circumstances.

You'll hear from my lips no reticence, no blustering or temporizing, no cowardly backstabbing: I say what I have to say clearly and directly; I attack evil public figures head on, without recourse to masks or hidden daggers. I speak neither to flatter those in power nor to serve as mouthpiece for those who dream of seizing power, but to say what I think needs to be said, no matter whose interests it harms, no matter whom it irritates.

I

What has been the general nature of our parties during recent years?—syndicates for sick ambitions, private clubs, mercantile associations. And our leaders?—agents of powerful financial groups, astute peasants who turned politics into a lucrative job, impulsive soldiers who saw in the presidency of the republic the final step in their military career.

There were, of course, men who were committed to forming homogeneous, sound parties. In the end, they found themselves isolated, without supporters or disciples, and they had to maintain permanent silence or limit themselves to conducting a lonely apostleship. Where do we look to find the members of the last Liberal Party? It's like this: in Peruvian brains there are these tiny phosphorescences, mere glimmers of emancipation. We all deny today the convictions we embraced yesterday; in our decrepitude, we trample the ideas that were the pride and honor of our youth. And if only it were the old alone who displayed such mendacity!

We do not classify individuals as republicans or monarchists, radicals or conservatives, anarchists or authoritarians, but as supporters of specific aspirants to the presidency. When we herd together, we form parties that degenerate into private clubs or, to put it more accurately, we establish private clubs that pose as parties. It's true that ideas are embodied in men; but it's also true that for many years, none of our public figures have represented even the simulacrum of an idea. Let's look at what's happening now. What groups presume to call themselves parties? Are people actually banding together behind these figurehead leaders?

Let's not even mention the civilism of 1872, that nucleus of trustees gathered together and sworn to react against Dreyfus. The choral leaders of the Civil Party were nothing but businessmen disguised as politicians, from bankers who converted the nation's gold into worthless bills through fraudulent issues to sugarcane magnates or Chinese lords who transformed the blood of hapless coolies into sugar water. The healthy part of civilism, the young who had followed Pardo, inspired by a zeal for liberal reforms, became corrupt on contact with the bad elements or, segregating themselves before it was too late, lived entirely apart from politics.

Pardo committed serious economic errors trying to renovate the system of loans and advances on guano, a system that he himself had fought against. But he suffered the effects of causes created by his predecessors; he struggled against resistances that were superior to his forces and found himself enclosed in a tightening ring of iron. We commit a serious injustice when we attribute to him all the blame for the national bankruptcy, initiated by Castilla, continued by Echenique, and sealed once and for all by Minister Piérola with the Dreyfus contract.

A responsibility far harder to evade than the bankruptcy hangs over civilism: taking a name that implied a challenge to a particular social class and then declaring war on the military, it forgot that if the lower strata of the earth rest in granite, the new societies are built on iron. This oversight contributed effectively to our collapse in the last foreign war. Chile had the immense advantage of fighting on sea against old and poorly outfitted ships, on land against squads of raw recruits led by undisciplined officers or, even worse, merchants, doctors, or landowners. Castilla, a soldier without education or knowledge, but intelligent and wary, understood very well that Peru ought to have been a sea power. *When the Chileans build a warship,* he said, *we should build two.* Pardo preferred dubious and problematical alliances to the real power of cannons, and he was in the habit of repeating with a frivolity unworthy of his suspicious nature: *My two warships are Bolivia and the Argentine Republic.* Even so, he too can be forgiven for not having built up our seapower: he had to waste the money he should have invested in warships to fend off Piérola.

With Pardo dead, who was its head and its life, the Civil Party decomposed like any cadaver. Its members, dispersed, lacking the necessary cohesion to reconstitute themselves with any stability, resigned themselves to taking on secondary roles in new groups. In succession, and even simultaneously, they have become Pardists, Calderonists, Iglesists, Cacerists, Bermudists, civicists, coalitionists, and democrats. And they do not march together in a compact mass; they have their individual tactics. When a revolution breaks out or some leader emerges with a real chance to reach the top, the impatient ones join up on the spot, while the unprincipled and cautious ones maintain the status quo, awaiting the results of the struggle so they can swell the victor's ranks. Even within the bosom of a single family we see one or two brothers enrolling in the Democratic or the Constitutional Party, while others hang back as charter members of civilism. The so-called Civil Party is for many today the art of dining at all tables and sticking their hands in all sacks.

The Civilists constitute an inevitable disaster: there's no way to govern with them because they carry the virus, and no way to govern without them because they dominate through gold and shrewdness.

Let's also exclude the Civic Union, or to put it more appropriately, the parliamentary chamber, which had hopes of emerging as the panacea when in truth it was just another pathological case. It was born with several heads and, like all monstrosities, it had a short and wretched life, though it did survive long enough to serve as a decorous bridge between civilism and Pierolism, since many who lacked the courage to make the drastic leap from civilists to democrats slipped smoothly from civilists[1] to civicists, from civicists to coalitionists, and from coalitionists to democrats.

Could the Civic Union have done any better, given its origin? We all know the history of the Peruvian congresses, starting with the one that knelt humbly before Bolívar to confer the dictatorship on him and ending with the one that has just now sanctioned the Protocol and handed over the grand lottery prize to the lush virginity of a Tartuffe. In our legislative bodies, in that deformed conglomerate of wan, feckless, and even unconscious men, the carnival of vested interest has always been at play, and seldom if ever any struggle for an idea or for the national interest. The chambers were made up of tightly controlled, disciplined majorities. When an honest, independent minority tried to speak out, it was always marginalized by authoritarian procedure or silenced amid the outcry and insults of an impudent and mercenary majority. Of all the iniquitous congresses, first prize goes to the Congress of the Grace Contract, the most audaciously venal congress, the congress that produced the Civic Union by schism.

When the Parliamentary Chamber dissolved, some of its members moved over to the Democratic Party en masse (it thought about rejecting them but ended up accepting them) while many contritely returned to the Constitutional Party because they were vitally bound to Cáceres through back room deals and bedroom secrets. If anything united the wheelers and dealers of the Civic Union, it was crime, which was also what disunited them. Before merging to form a pseudoparty, they had already perpetrated the butchery of Santa Catalina, that useless, cowardly crime that will forever dishonor Morales Bermúdez, as Thebes dishonors Cáceres.

That leaves us Cacerism and Pierolism, which should not be consid-

---

[1] Civilism, or the Civil Party, is equivalent to plutocracy or oligarchy. It took the name civilism because at its birth in 1872, it tried to win power for civilians, taking it from the military. One of its principal founders, don Manuel Pardo y Lavalle, succeeded in doing so, only to be assassinated on the steps of the senate once he became senate president (1878). Civilism announced its own death spontaneously with the fall of Leguía (1930), but in truth it lived on under various names.—L.A.S., 1976.

ered homogeneous parties but heterogeneous groupings, led by two equally abominable and sinister men: Cáceres, who formerly represented the interests of Grace, and Piérola, who for all we know still favors the Dreyfus deals. On witnessing the tooth-and-nail war between Pierolists and Cacerists, anyone would think that their leaders personified two diametrically opposed politics, one championing conservative ideas to the point of absolutism, the other carrying the banner of advanced ideas to the point of anarchy. Not at all: we challenge the keenest analyst to find a line of demarcation between Pierolists and Cacerists, and to tell us what reforms Cáceres wouldn't accept and what reforms Piérola would reject. Excluding the matter of finances, or rather, excluding Grace and Dreyfus, Cáceres would have signed any Piérola platform, just as Piérola[2] would have signed any Cáceres manifesto. Both represent a living contradiction: Cáceres is an illegal and despotic constitutionalist, Piérola a clerical and autocratic democrat.

The two antagonists hold many analogous positions, except that the dictator of 1879 cloaks himself in hypocrisy, using his left hand for strangling, his right for making the sign of the cross, while the Lord of Breña denounces the instincts of prehistoric man while conducting his blatant and unabashed escapades in the primal forest. In both of them, we see the same pride, the same spirit of arbitrariness, the same thirst for power and even the same obsession with grandeur; if the one regards himself as dictator *in partibus*, the other thinks of the presidency as the legal limit of his career. In the life of Cáceres, there's one bright moment—when he fought against Chile and was transformed into Grau on land. In Piérola's existence the shadowy figure of conspirator and deal maker always stands out. Surrounded by a few honorable, well-meaning men, Cáceres could have been a good leader; Piérola, surrounded by a ministry of Catos, would still produce the same fruits. One represents ignorance or a chest half-empty, the other bad breeding

---

[2] Piérola, Nicolás de, born in Camaná in 1839, died in Lima in 1913. He was minister of the treasury in the government of José Balta, whose administration negotiated a number of public works contracts with the North American Henry Meiggs and the French firm Dreyfus between 1868 and 1871. Supreme leader of the nation (1879–1880) and constitutional president, following a bloody popular revolution (1895–1899), he led several insurrections. Prada was his ideological and political adversary as far back as 1871.—L.A.S., 1976.

or a basket of wornout trumpery. In Cáceres, the defects are compensated by a certain military chivalry and a kind of virile arrogance: his adversaries find themselves before a man they abhore and respect; in Piérola, all his actions, no matter how natural they might seem, betray some sleight-of-hand illusion: his enemies have to contend with a second-rate comedian or clown who makes them laugh. We want to take a shot at Cáceres, to hiss at Piérola.

We've already had a look at them as dictators or presidents: with Piérola we had economic chaos, political pandemonium, military confusion, and a dictatorship anointed with military chaplain's oil and perfumed with musk of mother superior; with Cáceres, pillage of the home, flagellation in prisons and military compounds, firing squads in vacant lots, and the worst of all possible tyrannies, tyranny masked in legality. In short: what is Piérola? A comic-opera García Moreno. What is Cáceres? A Melgarejo aborted in mid-birth.

Pierolism and Cacerism make one thing evident: Peru's intellectual and moral wretchedness.

II

Yes, a wretchedness that will be incurable and eternal if the healthy and plundered majority doesn't make a heroic effort to root out the sick and plundering minority.

It's a mistake to regard the latest civil war as a healthy sign. All those wretched Indians who shed their blood on the streets of Lima weren't citizens moved by an idea of justice and social betterment, but barely conscious creatures, herded down from the heights and forced into battle on the point of a bayonet and hurled against each other the way you set one wild animal on another or ram one locomotive into another. In the revolutions of Castilla against Echenique and Prado against Pezet there were formidable and spontaneous uprisings of entire provinces, well-disciplined armies and humane though bloody battles. But in the civil war of 1894, the people remained completely indifferent and all we saw were guerrilla gangs led by bandits, quota administrators, pillagers of haciendas, hoodlums beating recruits, raping women, shooting prisoners—in short, barbarians as savage in defending the laughable legality of the government as in proclaiming the monstrous birth of the coalition. All the courage manifested in the taking of Lima, for what?

Nothing easier than to turn an ignorant draftee into a wild beast. If a thoughtful and generous courage denotes a person's moral superiority, this kind of blind and brutal rage, this thirst for blood, this killing for the sake of killing and destroying for the sake of destruction, these mark a return to primitive savagery. When two civilized men resort to dueling, the winner offers his hand to the loser; when a pair of cannibals fight over the same prey, the winner eats the loser as well as the prey.

Revolutions everywhere develop as the painful and fecund gestation of a people: they shed blood but they create light, they suppress men but they evolve ideas. Not in Peru. Did anyone derive the least benefit from it? Did anyone display any largeness of heart or superior intelligence? Did any of those splashing around and sinking down in that pool of blood salvage the pearl of a generous idea or any noble sentiment? Mediocrity and baseness everywhere, in everyone. Observe them immediately after the victory, even before the pools of blood have dried or the stench of rotting corpses dissipated: the first feat carried out by these vanquishing heroes is to swarm over the fortunes of the bloodied, impoverished nation the way vultures swarm over the flesh of a cow broken and dying at the bottom of a cliff. They stage bullfights, theatrical performances, and gluttonous banquets simultaneously. Members of the civil, civic, and democratic parties all congratulate each other as they eat and drink in cynical and repugnant promiscuity. Their brains all become extensions of their digestive tracts. Like hogs escaped from different styes, they mingle amicably in the same wallow, at the same trough. And not a word of protest! Not a single soul sick to his stomach! And they all eat and drink and don't notice the stench of death or the taste of blood in the wine! And Piérola himself presides over the funereal love-in and proffers the congratulatory toasts! Twenty-five years of spouting off against civilism, sowing implacable hatreds, leading bloody revolutions, and loading Montoya's rifle—all of it meaningless, only to end up with mutual pardons and fraternal hugs.

Could the revolution have produced better results? Where poverty is so intense that hunger ends up as a national habit, what can men do but fight over the cadaver and devour each other? A revolutionary who wins, grabs his destiny and eats, lays siege to the treasury and steals. And if the fallen is hungry and cries out, he has to be shut up, sometimes forever. What we are witnessing is the battle for crumbs, *I* and *Thou* without mercy, in the dark recesses of the forest. Our revolutions have been (and will be for a long time) illegal enterprises like smuggling, like fornication; and in the din of battle you can hear, not only the clashing of arms slashing and killing but the sound of hands grubbing about in the bottom of a sack.

With the triumph of the revolution and the presidency for its leader, Peru's fortunes, then, do not improve. What came in with Piérola is no better or worse than what went out with Cáceres. You have to wear blinders or be drunk on the festive vapors to see any difference between the rampant soldiery that imposed the leader of the Constitutional Party on us yesterday and the slavering guerrilla hordes who now subject us to the leader of the Democratic Party. The same tragicomedy goes on, with new extras but with the same leading actors. The democrats are so well aware of their inferiority that they had to call on the collaboration of civilism to mount a provisional government. In twenty-five years of preparation and training they couldn't manage to define their ideas or educate half a dozen men capable of running the ministries!

Let's watch as Piérola is installed in the seat of power, the seat of administration. The *immaculate one* grants his personal attention, his favors, and most trusted offices to men who throughout the ages and under every government have distinguished themselves for their rapacity and shamelessness; the *restorer* of individual liberties incarcerates deputies, closes down newspapers, and avails himself of any subterfuge, any lawyer's dodge to confiscate presses and seal the lips of men who speak independently and boldly; the *regenerator* turns the capital into a leper's colony of nuns and monks, turns half of Peru over to the religious communities, exiles from Cuzco the English clerics who are setting up a school, and thinks that the black stain on his conscience can be erased with the plaster applied to the towers of a church; the great *federalist* responds with threats and cannons to the initial movement in Iquitos, threatens to suppress the departmental councils and dreams up any measure he can imagine to carry out the most oppressive centralization; the great *democrat* does not receive the strikers with the sweetness and affability of a colleague but sends them away with the harsh scowl of a feudal lord, with all the insolence of power, ready to dispatch as many cops as it takes to shoot down the hungry crowd crying out for bread; in short, the *protector of the indigenous race* sets up once again on the road from Pichis the old law of the Mita or forced labor, and reenacts with the forsaken Indians of Ilave and Huanta the horrors and butchery of Weyler in Cuba and the sultan in Armenia.

In short, the latest civil war was evil, as much for the way it was carried out as for the leader it imposed on us. It's like an earthquake swallowing up cities and breaking the earth into sections, releasing floods of black water and clouds of sulphurous gases.

Still, nowhere is there a greater need for a profound and radical revolution. Here, where evil or sickly institutions rule, where the guilty form not only transitory alliances but secular dynasties, we need to begin the task of taking an axe to the forest. We're in no condition to settle for the overthrow of an administration, or new elections in the chambers of deputies, or the removal of a few judges, or even a total replacement of passive, lower-level bureaucrats. Let's ask the simple, well-meaning people, the farmers or industrial workers, the citizens who have no ties to the government and who do not prosper at the expense of the Public Treasury: they will all answer that their hearts are sick and their stomachs nauseated, that they feel asphyxiated in the hospital-like atmosphere, that they long for a breath of fresh, clean air, that they want new things and new men. What can keep us from seeing clearly now? All the institutions have been analyzed and laid bare, and today they reveal their organic infirmities. All the players have undergone anatomical dissection and microscopic examination: we know them all.

And the corruption is spreading to the craftsmen in the cities. The working class functions everywhere as the mother forest where we find the good wood for building and the good land for sowing. When the most civilized part of a nation prostitutes itself and grows weak, a fertile tide rises up from the people to regenerate and strengthen everything. The craftsmen of Lima, situated between the simple day-laborer (whom they scorn) and the upper class (whom they admire), make up a pseudo-aristocracy with all the ignorance of the lower depths and all the depravity of those above them. When they meet they establish guilds or private clubs; and since they have no convictions, since they haven't the remotest idea of their social mission or their rights, since it seems to them that the sum total of human wisdom is condensed in the shrewdness of Bertoldo combined with the roguish folly of Sancho, you see the craftsmen of Lima playing the part of courtiers or lackeys to all the legal and illegal powers, feeling quite happy today to be receiving holy water and rosary from Piérola just as yesterday they received whiskey and sandwiches from Pardo.

Happily, Peru is more than a rotten and rotting crust. Far away from the politicians and those obsessed with power, from the wicked and sick, a healthy, vigorous multitude slumbers, a kind of virgin field awaiting the good labor and the good seed. We can laugh at the sad sociologists who want to overwhelm us with their *decadencies* and their *inferior races,* easy conclusions for resolving unsolvable questions and justifying the iniquities of the Europeans in Asia and Africa. Decadence! If today we are in a fallen state, when was our shining hour, when did we ever ascend to any peak? Can those who never climbed high fall low? Our fellow citizens in Moyobamba and Quispicanchis, do they dine like Lucullus, or dress like Sardanapalus, or make love like the Marquis de Sade, do they collect pre-Raphaelite paintings and know by heart the poetry of Baudelaire and Paul Verlaine? Here we have as a national base a mass of ignorant Indians, so primitive that to this day their only culture consists of revolutions, alcohol, and fanaticism. To imagine them to be in a state of decadence, you have to confuse childhood with senility, mistaking the boy who hasn't yet mastered the use of his own limbs for an elderly paralytic. *Inferior races?* When you recall that in Peru almost all men of any intellectual worth have been Indians or men of mixed race, when you see that the few descendants of Castilian nobility produce sickly or sexually perverted offspring, when it would be hard to distinguish between the facial features of a gorilla and a venerable marquis from Lima, it's time to stop talking about racial inferiority. What we should do is admit that since the first blush of the Conquest, *whites* transformed the Indian into a *sociological race,* or better, a *lower caste* from which they continue to extract oxen for their haciendas, moles for their mines, and cannon fodder for their barracks.

If it were true that the bad elements outnumber the good, we would have disappeared as a nation long ago because no organism can endure when the disorganizing force exceeds the force for conservation. Here the truly guilty was the enlightened man, who offered copious examples of immorality when he should have been educating the people with his good example. Moral decrepitude is concentrated at the top, in the dominant classes. We're like those lands that rise up from the ocean with all the detritus of submarine life visible on the peaks. Peru is a mountain crowned by a cemetery.

III

Amid all this wretchedness and ignominy, the National Union[3] wants to form a single body of all men determined to convert good intentions into effective, vigorous, purifying action. It wants to unify and prepare them to substitute the orderly work of a collectivity for the disorganized, unplanned, and often counterproductive efforts of the individual. The Union does not aspire to win converts through ambiguous pacts or hybrid solidarities; it breaks with political traditions and seeks to organize a force to react against bad ideas and bad habits. There is only one way for us to attract sympathy and find an echo in the soul of the masses: by being intransigent and uncompromising. Why did our parties fail?—for lack of clear dividing lines, because of mutual crossing over of men from one band to another. In the political order, as in the zoological, the conjoining of species produces only hybrids and sterile beings. In Spain, one can conceive of the temporary fusion of the republican parties to depose the monarchy and detain Carlism; in France, one can also conceive of restraining the influence of clerics and Orleanists. But here alliances are inconceivable because they pursue the sole objective of seating or unseating a president. What was the result of the coalition of 1894?—to remove one man, to put another in his place and continue with the same regime. What's happening today?—the civilists are courting the democrats to shore up Candamo, while the democrats are playing hard to get because they hope to impose who knows what shadowy and indecisive personalities.

Since there is always an abundance of middle-of-the-road types and amorphous, indefinible groups, we're faced with a dilemma: we either dissolve or become a true party of combat. It's important to repeat this frankly and sincerely, to avoid misunderstandings and to draw a clear

[3] The National Union is the radical party "in the French conception," founded by Prada in May 1891. He publicly broke with it in 1902, after spending several years in Europe (1891–1898). It was a federalist, nationalist, indigenist, secular party, tending toward anarchism, which Prada definitively embraced subsequently.—L.A.S., 1976.

dividing line from this day forward. Between the National Union and all the mercantilist or personalist groups, there is absolutely no room for alliances or negotiations. If we approach any other band, it will be not to march with it but against it, not to extend our hand but to open fire.

This being said, neophytes are likely to carry their optimism to the point of folly, imagining that on entering here they're about to set out through a bed of roses. But we're off to war against powerful enemies who regard the country as their legitimate patrimony, and they will defend their spoils with all their wealth and astuteness, with force and with crime. They possess in the army a fist that can tyrannize with iron, in the press a tongue that can kill with calumny. They can count on well-paid praetorians, well-bribed spokesmen.

It's not enough to unfold our flag and shout to get supporters to join our cause. We're addressing a people who have been duped a hundred times over, who will mistrust us if our actions don't prove the sincerity of our intentions. We can achieve much with pen and word, with pamphlet and speeches, with personal letter and private conversation; but we will achieve much more with our example. The way we live will exert a slow, mute, but irresistible propaganda. For that we need brains that can think, not automatons who will speak and gesticulate; living people, not walking cadavers; converts in good faith, not deserters corrupted by the legacy of the past and by bad example; in a word, the youth of the young, not men still practicing the faith they were baptized into a quarter of a century ago and whose hearts are over a century old.

We are fully aware of how hard it is to organize. When the country was peaceful, the National Union grew slowly, without having to struggle against serious obstacles, except for setbacks all associations encounter initially. But when the leaders rose up to formulate programs, win converts, and organize clubs, then some of our adherents began to quiver like iron filings in the presence of a magnet. This agitation reached its peak in March 1894 with the outbreak of the revolution. In the very bosom of the Union, even within the tiny central committee, we saw acts of duplicity, desertions, apostasy. We were barely born, but the evil legacy was already gnawing away at us.

This sometimes makes it seem as though efforts to bring men together for a cause higher than individual convenience are vain and counterproductive. Who knows if the bell has already tolled for true parties in Peru! Who knows if we aren't still mired in the epoch when everyone preached only to himself! Perhaps it's time to hurl ourselves onto the field of battle, without trusting in the loyal collaboration of others, equally afraid of the enemy attacking us head on and the friend stabbing us in the back. And in this unequal struggle, today's colleague becomes tomorrow's enemy, while our adversary never becomes our friend. Those who march straight ahead in Peru end up alone, mocked, crucified. Perhaps all we can do is keep working like a well-trained crew courageously bailing out water to the point of exhaustion, knowing the water is rising and the boat is going to sink. But come what may, the voice of a few men true to their convictions will ring out tomorrow like a virile protest in this twilight of souls, this slag heap of characters.

Happily, the National Union is run by a solid, homogeneous majority that resists internal dissension and fights off attacks from without. If some seem to have grown weak or even delinquent, if some have presumed to seize power that no one granted them, the central committee in Lima has not made any compromising alliances or shameful deals: it has thrown out conspirators and liars. With these ambiguous and pernicious elements isolated, the danger of a split overcome, the majority of the National Union continues to hold up an unsullied banner, doing so not only bravely in Lima, where the citizen enjoys the respite of a truce, but audaciously in many towns of the republic, where people are ruled as if by Roman proconsuls, where there's no law but the obtuse will of some prefect, subprefect, governor, or party strongman. We can even boast that the most solid strength of the Union resides in the provinces, just the opposite of all our political bands, which only respond to orders from the capital. If some day the committee in Lima were to violate the program or engage in murky conspiracies, the most remote committee in the republic could become the true center of the National Union. Here we don't have, nor do we want, any men who blindly obey the orders of the group or the master.

In our development, slow but sure, nothing is owed to individual initiatives. Everything comes from collective action, and there's no charismatic, indispensable man we have to waste time praising. The Civilist Party was all Pardo, the Constitutional Party was Cáceres, the Democratic Party is Piérola: the National Union isn't any man. On occasion perhaps, succumbing to the mania for rules and the general obsession for pouring everything into parliamentary molds, we have organized presidential tables with complicated and even humiliating procedures. But it should be noted that we try to keep our adherents fully informed, so that at any given moment the most obscure and humble member can become the spokesman for our ideas and the inspiration for the group. In a word, we don't want to risk death by decapitation like the Civilist Party.

Pure headlessness, which at first glance seems to be the strength and merit of the Union, retards its development and can bring about its ruin. There's nothing so disastrous as a man without convictions at the head of a nervous and malleable crowd; nor is there anything quite so sterile as an idea living on nothing but air, failing to take tangible form or to incarnate itself in a particular personality. A cause without an apostle is a mere abstraction; and humankind only adores and follows individuals: even in the most ideal of religions, if the material symbol is suppressed, the dogma falters.

We expect that the necessary man will emerge at the opportune moment: one of those sincere, enthusiastic adherents, perhaps the most silent and least likely, will tomorrow implement the fecund ideology of the National Union. When that superior figure takes clear form among us, let's open the way, let's smooth his road, sacrificing our pride and personal ambitions. If there's merit in proclaiming an idea, there's even greater merit in standing aside for the man capable of achieving it.

While we await that day, there's much for us to do. Even today we are noted for our practicality and common sense, but despite this we are accused of being deluded, dreamers, utopians, by men of ill will or by professional politicians. Because actions count in politics, it's fair to ask, What was ever accomplished by those *eminently practical men* who were not stirred by illusions, who never formed utopias, who never dreamed? They drew up constitutions and laws without educating citizens to understand them and live according to them, they forged metal without checking to see if the mold was big enough to receive it, they decreed digestion without provision for bread. The forsaken masses of Indians would be justified in railing against them: what good is free instruction if we have no schools? what good is a free press if we don't know how to read? what good is the right to vote if we can't exercise it in an informed way? what good is free enterprise if we have no capital, no credit, not even a scrap of land to plow? Those *eminently practical men* were politicians in the style of the good doctor who kills off all his patients, the good lawyer who loses all his cases, or the good captain who sinks all his ships. Look what they're up to right now. When in the south we're threatened by even graver problems than in 1879, they raise questions they aren't equipped to answer, hoping to salvage with diplomacy and protocol territory we ought to be taking back with rifle and sword. These *eminently practical men* are trying to build a dike with a flurry of memoranda to stave off an invasion of bayonets.

Some are asking that each word or manifesto from the National Union include not only a complete and defined program but also a formula for resolving problems that have never been resolved by any country on earth. If humankind had managed to resolve all its religious, political, and social problems, the planet would be an eden, life a festival. A party cannot and should not be condemned to follow a strict and unvarying program like the credo of a religion; it's enough to set up a few guideposts and mark the course, without fixing way in advance the number of steps. The National Union could condense its program into two lines: to develop a sense of broader freedom for the individual, preferring social reforms over political transformations. It's easy to guess, then, where we would stand if we had to choose between a federal regime or freedom of cults. Although it seems paradoxical to say it, we are a political party, moved by the desire to distance men from mere politics, a sickness endemic to modern societies. Politics means treason, hypocrisy, bad faith, rot with a white glove; and when we accuse a man of principle of being a bad politician, we aren't insulting him, we're awarding him a diploma attesting to his honesty and humanity. No, from *great* and *good* politicians, the world never derived anything great or good. "Politician" is a name we reserve for Enrique IV selling out in Paris and Saint-Denis, Napoleon executing the duke of Enghien, Talleyrand squirming for advantage under every regime, Bismarck faking the telegraph from Ems, Guillermo II applauding the strangulation of Greece, Cánovas of Castille laying waste to Cuba, decimating the Phillipines, and setting up a secular inquisition in the fortress of Montjuich.

Questions of governmental reform, questions of words, of people. There's not much difference between a monarchy and a republic, when equal misery reigns in St. Petersburg and New York, when individual rights are more accessible in Belgium than in France; when the queen of all Great Britain lacks the authority to put a poor worker in jail, but a Morales Bermúdez and a Cáceres can put us in jail, exile us, or have us beaten or shot in a deserted pampa or a secret cell. This is why the world is divided today not between republicans and monarchists, or liberals and conservatives, but between two large segments: the haves and the have-nots, the exploiters and the exploited.

We who are called *deluded* prefer a small colony of free and happy farmers to an immense republic of servants and proletarians; we *utopians* recognize that there's nothing absolute or definitive in the institutions of a country, and we regard every reform as a point of departure for initiating new reforms; we *dreamers* know that it's necessary to emerge from evangelical charity to move toward human justice, that all people have the right to develop themselves as whole persons, and that there's absolutely no reason why the privileged few should monopolize for their own benefit what belongs to all humanity. We say once again to those eminently practical men: Down with politics, bring on your social reforms! We also say to them, so as to be done with them once and for all: If one day the National Union becomes a powerful and decisive force, then you'll see whether we're spaced-out idealists or men capable of conducting a fair and thorough social liquidation.

IV

Today the country's attention is concentrated on the 1899 elections, on the new revolutionary movement, and on the Protocol of Arica and Tacna.

We would deserve to be called *deluded, utopians,* and *dreamers,* if we thought we were a powerful factor in contemporary political life and tried to exert any leverage in the upcoming electoral farce. If we were to fling ourselves into the fray, we would be wasting in a most sterile and even harmful way the energy we ought to use to grow and consolidate. What dike could we throw up to stem the flood of illegality and corruption? Acting alone, we would find ourselves overwhelmed and defeated; allying ourselves with others, we would end up absorbed and invalidated. Since we do not yet have the prestige necessary to move the masses and draw them into effective and regenerative action, let's overcome our impatience and save our strength for later. Abstaining today does not signify abdicating our rights but postponing them.

Perhaps in the area of delegations or seats in the senate we could compete with some probability of success in some parts of the republic (the committees will decide this when they test their influence), but with respect to the presidency and vice presidency, it's useless to try. Why should we put up candidates only to see them uselessly slandered and abused on that field of ignominy and abomination? Whether we participate or not, the coming elections will be what they always were, a fraud legalized by Congress.

So let's achieve something more useful than climbing down into that cockpit of electoral backbiting, that bacterial stew, and let the civicists, democrats, civilists, and constitutionalists go on marching through the blood and ruins, like the grotesque masque of some sinister carnival. In the clamor of strident, selfish cries, let's be a voice that calls out day and night for the rebuilding of our army and navy, not to attack but to defend ourselves, not to conquer but to keep from being conquered, not to seize foreign territory but to recover what was taken from us with iniquity and oppression.

When the National Union announced, not long ago, that the passage of the protocol would start a civil war, the entire incense-bearing, boot-licking press maliciously misconstrued the announcement as a call to arms and accused us of inciting revolution. Naturally, the yellow journalists among them got some cheap laughs at the contrast between the weakness of our arms and the ardor of our bellicose impulses. This is the kind of logic one uses to attribute a desire for epidemic to the doctor who announces it or a desire for hurricane to the sailor who predicts it.

Have we forgotten the revolutions of Cáceres against Iglesias or of Piérola against Cáceres? If the wealth wasted in them were poured into the nation's treasury, if the men uselessly sacrificed in them were marching today with rifles on their shoulders, Chile's attitude toward us would be quite different. No, those revolutions produced nothing of value, and nothing of value will come from the one threatening us from the north. Did Cáceres annul, could he ever annul the Treaty of Ancón? Has Piérola set up a government any more legal or less arbitrary than that of Cáceres? If the resplendent revolutionaries win tomorrow, does anyone think they'll be capable of scrapping the protocol and confronting the Chileans face-to-face? If the revolution succeeded, the day after the victory Chile would send a secret agent, and everything would be settled between Chileans and revolutionaries. Just ask Ataura.

The people, instead of wearing themselves out worrying about whether Colonel Pérez is winning or Doctor García is losing, ought to be trying to find out whether, when the fighting is over, they'll be paying lower taxes, shaking off the shackles of the great landowners, and emerging from their condition as day laborers and indentured servants to become free men and small landowners. To go through a revolution just to bring about a change of players without a change of regime, is there any value in that? With civil wars like the ones we've had so far, the ignorant don't ascend a single centimeter toward the light, the wretched don't shed one ounce of the world weariness dragging them down. The ignorant and the wretched take to revolution like slaves changing masters, like sheep rising up to win themselves new shearers, new butchers. That's why, when the new revolution is announced, we cry out: Down with the new army of ambitious, the new gang of criminals! We in the National Union are entitled to such an outcry because we've no blood on our hands we have to hide; but not those of the Democratic Party, not even Piérola, who for twenty-five years has been presiding over a seat of sedition and mutiny: he has no right to repudiate and mock these new revolutionaries who are graduates of his school, his disciples.

Today, international problems are putting on a new face with the alliance, *entente cordiale*, or tacit agreement with Bolivia and Argentina. If we come together to form a triple alliance, we have a good chance of defeating Chile, annuling the Treaty of Ancón, and reclaiming the lost territories; if we don't join, we run the risk that our neutrality will be seen as a manifestation of hostility and that the Argentine–Bolivian pact will have consequences damaging not only to Chile but to us as well. An alliance between Peruvians and Chileans against Bolivians and Argentines is unthinkable. There is no government crazy enough to propose it nor any people debased enough to accept it; so the most Chile can expect from us, should war break out, is strict neutrality. In such a case, what would we stand to gain?—at most, very little honor. If Chile won, we would be where we are today, with no prospect that the country that so ruthlessly conquered us in 1879 would owe us even the slightest gratitude or grant us the slightest compensation for our valiant neutrality; if Bolivia and Argentina won, they'd impose peace terms on Chile and, without worrying too much about fairness, draw up a treaty reconciling their respective interests, making us pay very dearly for the crime of not having joined their alliance. There's no moral obligation requiring Bolivians and Argentines to shed their blood and waste their money to redeem us; and even if such an obligation existed, they're not the sort of romantic, generous countries who would rush out to sacrifice their own interests on the altar of some moral obligation.

What can we say about Bolivia? Today there is one compelling consideration justifying the alliance between us and them—the fear that if they hadn't been with us, they would have joined Chile in attacking and savaging us. The 1879 alliance between Peruvians and Bolivians is reminiscent of the brotherhood between Sancho and don Quijote, since in the *sad fortunes* of war, they saved the body and we took the blows. No one knows for sure if Bolivia was bathing in rose water while Peru was drowning in a sea of blood. What we saw is that after San Francisco, Daza's veterans vanished while the invisible and ubiquitous General Campero captured Calama twenty times over, without ever leaving Cochabamba or La Paz. After the famous retreat from Camarones, certain public figures in Bolivia began to imagine that their indolence in the war and their distancing themselves from Peru might serve as good leverage for Chile to concede Tacna and Arica to them. Some even thought that *we* would feel obliged to make these concessions, if not as remuneration for services contributed in the war (a war we entered to defend them), then maybe out of good old American solidarity or evangelical charity. Under the latter assumption, the Cavours and Metternichs of Chuquisaca did us the great honor of endowing us with the virtues of Saint Vincent de Paul and Saint Martin. But since Chile wouldn't let loose of the booty, and since Peru wouldn't let it go under any circumstances (if they happened to get it back), the Bolivians are now turning to the Argentines, hoping to make some friends who'll be a bit more complacent, more giving.

What can we say about Argentina? The people who for more than twenty years have put up with the bloody dictatorship of Rosas, the people who allied themselves with Brazil and Uruguay in order to crucify the Paraguayans, the people who when asked in 1866 to join the alliance of Peru and Chile against Spain replied (insolently and scornfully) that their interests did not draw them toward the Pacific, such a people do not deserve much trust for their civic spirit, their magnanimity, or their Americanism. And the administration of a Juárez Celman, is there any glory in that? Who knows if as an effect of optical illusion we look on Argentina from afar as an immense slaughterhouse of cattle

and a chaotic carnival of Italians who don't know Spanish and Spaniards who speak Catalan or Basque. What is certain is that everything
about that republic reminds us of export commodities, loud colors,
poorly finished furniture made of rich wood. It wouldn't surprise us,
then, if when we least expected it the Argentines agreed to a shameful
peace or, if they did have to go to war, they learned a more disastrous
lesson than the one we suffered in 1879. Meanwhile, for some ten years
now, the good gauchos have been like don Simplicio Bobadilla in *Goat-
foot:* they reach for their sword, but they can't get it out because the
blade has a spell on it and is who knows how many kilometers long.

Even so, sympathy toward the Argentines is so widespread and spontaneous in the nation today that if they ever did attack Chile, no one
can predict the effect the sound of the first cannon shot would produce.
Perhaps it would give us another opportunity to point out that the rifles
were only aimed in the direction of Iquique and Tarapacá. No one
would envy the fate of any politicians bold enough to oppose the national groundswell or dream of trying to stem the tide. The revolution
that would inevitably come about to overthrow them would be the only
good and holy revolution, the only truly popular revolution. We Peruvians can tolerate being deceived and mocked, gagged and bound,
impoverished and bled in domestic matters; but we would never tolerate
anyone merging our interests with those of Chile to the point of dragging us into a humiliating alliance in a war against Bolivia and Argentina. We mustn't attack the Bolivians, out of loyalty; we mustn't attack
the Argentines, out of convenience. If there's such a thing as Chilean
treachery, if Bolivian or Argentine treachery are imaginable, let there
be no Peruvian treachery, or imbecility.

Whether war breaks out, or is conjured up, whether we enter into
alliances or remain neutral, we should pursue one objective—to become
strong. Chile will be demanding and haughty to the extent that we are
weak and humble. With Chile, no protocol is as strong as powerful
warships, no reasons are as compelling as a large, well-trained army.
As long as it sees itself checked to the east and fearful of our joining
the Argentine–Bolivian alliance, it will continue to soothe us with lull-
abies and promises of friendship. But once it finds itself unencumbered
and safe, it will revert unapologetically to its implacable system of ab-
sorption and plunder. Think about it! Even today, threatened by a

foreign war, perhaps on the eve of a frightful civil uprising, its credit ruined, with enormous fiscal debts, almost at the edge of the abyss, when it ought to be trying to win us over with its loyalty and good faith, Tarata (Cochabamba) mocks us with an insidious protocol, in which far from conceding us some hope of regaining Tacna and Arica, it embroils us in an endless series of questions to keep us off balance, to lull us to sleep, to manipulate us.

To conclude, gentlemen. If Chile has discovered its national industry to be war with Peru, if it won't give up the hope of coming sooner or later to ask us for another pound of flesh, let's arm ourselves from head to toe, let's live in a state of formidable armed peace or latent war. The past speaks to us with great clarity. What good does it do us to be rational human beings, if yesterday's harm doesn't open our eyes to avoid tomorrow's. To breathe the optimism reigning in the official precincts, to see the confidence lulling all the social classes to sleep, anyone would think there aren't any foreign threats, that Chile is impotent and disarmed, that we won the last war. However, it wouldn't be a bad idea to remember from time to time that Piérola didn't rout the Chileans in San Juan, that Cáceres didn't make them bite the dust in Huamachuco. If we didn't learn any useful lessons from our misfortunes, if we didn't try to fend off the new storms gathering over our heads, we'd deserve for the Chileans, Argentines, and Bolivians to fall upon us and turn us into a South American Poland.

It's not a question of rushing into a stupid and reckless war, weak and poor as we are today, nor of throwing together in a few days an entire fleet and a whole army; what's needed is a project conducted with meticulous detail, underground, something like the work of a mole and an ant. We have to accumulate money, one sol, one cent at a time; build up war supplies, one cannon, one rifle, one cartridge at a time. Nations live very long lives, and they don't tire of waiting for the hour of justice. And justice isn't attained on earth through reason or pleading: it comes on the point of a bloody sword. True, war is the ignominy and bane of humanity; but that bane and that ignominy ought to fall upon the unjust aggressor, not on those defending their rights and their lives. From colonies of infusorians to human societies, we see struggle without respite and abominable victories by the strong, with one single difference: all of nature suffers the harsh law, but man rejects it and rises up. Yes, man is the only creature who issues a call for justice in the universal and eternal sacrifice of the weak. Let's heed the call and rise up against injustice and win reparation; let's grow strong. A lion so foolish as to pull out his claws and teeth will die on the fangs of wolves; a nation that won't bear iron in its hands will end up dragging irons on its feet.

The Intellectual and the Worker

(1905)

Gentlemen:

Don't smile if we begin by translating some verses by a poet.

> In late afternoon on a hot day, nature drowses in the rays of the sun, like a woman languishing under the caresses of her lover.

> The field hand, bathed in sweat and panting, goads his oxen; but all of a sudden he stops to greet a young man walking along humming a tune:

> "You're the lucky one! You spend your life singing while I, from the time the sun rises until it sets, wear myself out plowing these furrows and sowing wheat."

> "You're quite wrong, worker!" answers the young poet. "We both work just as hard, and you could even say we were brothers; because, if you spend your time sowing the earth, I spend mine sowing hearts. Your work is as productive as mine: the grains of wheat nourish the body, the songs of the poet delight and nourish the soul."

This poem teaches us that planting wheat in fields is as important as planting ideas in people's minds, that there's no difference in hierarchy between the thinker who works with his intelligence and the worker who works with his hands, that a man at his desk and a man in his shop, instead of marching separately and regarding each other as enemies, should walk side by side.

But is there such a thing as purely cerebral work or exclusively manual labor? Think about it: the blacksmith forging a lock, the stonemason leveling a wall, the printer setting type, the carpenter fitting boards together, the miner pounding his pick into a vein; even a man kneading clay thinks and meditates. There's only one kind of work that's blind and purely material—the work of a machine; wherever a man's arm works, we can see a mind at work. It's just the opposite with so-called intellectual activities: the nervous fatigue of the mind thinking or imagining is accompanied by the muscular weariness of the organism at work. They're worn out and exhausted: the painter by his brushes, the sculptor by his chisel, the musician by his instrument, the writer by his pen; even the orator grows tired and exhausted from the use of the word. What could be less material than oration and ecstasy? Then consider: the mystic succumbs to the effort of kneeling and holding his arms crossed.

Human endeavors take life from what they steal from us in terms of muscular effort and nervous energy. There are railway lines where each cross tie represents the life of a man. As we travel over them, let's imagine that our coach is moving along rails nailed onto a series of cadavers; but when we stroll through museums and libraries, let's also imagine that we're walking through a kind of cemetery where paintings, statues, and books enclose not only the thoughts but the lives of the makers.

You (we're speaking just to bakery workers now), you stay up all night kneading the dough, watching over the fermentation, and monitoring the heat of the ovens. At the same time, many who don't make bread also keep watch, minds focused, wielding pens and struggling to stay awake: I'm speaking about newspapermen. When the daily paper comes off the press damp and tempting early in the morning just as the sweet-smelling, provocative loaves of bread are coming out of the ovens, we should ask ourselves: who got the most out of the night, the journalist or the baker?

True, the newspaper contains the encyclopedia of the masses, knowledge prescribed in homeopathic doses, science clothed in the simple garb of ordinary language for ordinary people, the book for those who have no library, reading matter for those who barely want or know how to read. And bread?—the symbol of nourishment or life—it isn't happiness, but there's no happiness without it. When there isn't any in your house, it produces night and discord; when it comes, it brings light and tranquility: the child receives it with cries of joy, the old man with a smile of satisfaction. The vegetarian who abominates infected and criminal meat, blesses it as a healthy, regenerative nourishment. The millionaire who banished crystal-clear water from his table can't find a substitute for it, can't do without it. With great sovereignty, it rules in the dwelling of a Rothschild and in the hovel of a beggar. In the faraway times of fable, queens cooked bread and gave it to hungry pilgrims as provisions for their journey; today it's kneaded by the poor, and in Russia they offer it as a sign of hospitality to czars visiting a village. Nicholas II and all his progeny of tyrants show how to respond with whip, sword, and bullet when bread is offered.

If the journalist were to boast that he performs a more important task, we would respond, Without the stomach the brain doesn't function; there are eyes that don't read, but no stomachs that don't eat.

II

When we proclaim the union or alliance of intelligence with work, we aren't proposing that due to some illusory hierarchy the intellectual should set himself up as tutor or guide to the worker. The whole caste system is a product of the idea that the brain performs a more noble labor than the muscle: from the great empires of the Orient, we have examples of men who arrogate to themselves the right to think, reserving for the masses the obligation to believe and work.

Intellectuals serve as lights; but they shouldn't pose as guides for the blind, especially in tremendous social crises where the arm carries out what the mind has conceived. True, the gust of subversion stirring the masses today comes from thinkers or isolated individuals. It was always so. Justice is born of wisdom, for those who are ignorant don't know their own rights nor the rights of others, and they think that force constitutes the entire law of the universe. Moved by that belief, humanity habitually evinces the resignation of the dumb animal: it suffers in silence. But suddenly, the echo of a great word rings out, and all those who were resigned flock to the redeeming word, as insects are drawn to the beam of sunlight that penetrates the darkness of the forest.

The greatest problem thinkers have to deal with is the notion that they alone know the truth and that the world should move in the direction they urge and as far as they ordain. Revolutions come from above and function from below. Illumined by the light from the surface, the oppressed at the bottom see justice and rush to attain it, without worrying about the means or fearing the results. While moderates and theorists conceive of geometrical evolutions or embroil themselves in details and trivial matters of form, the multitude simplifies matters, brings them down from the nebulous heights, and confines them to practical terrain. Follow the example of Alexander: don't untie the knot, cut it with a sword.

What does the revolutionary want?—to influence the multitudes, shake them, awaken them, and hurl them into action. But it happens that the people, once shaken from their slumber, aren't content to obey the initial impetus, but begin to exert their latent forces, march and keep marching far beyond the objective conceived and desired by those who stirred them to act. Those who thought they were moving an inert mass find they're dealing with an organism bursting with vigor and initiative; they must deal with other minds that want to spread their light, other wills that want to impose their law. This is the source of a phenomenon common in history: the men who seemed so bold and progressive when starting up the revolution, are charged with being timid and reactionary in the clamor of the struggle or in the hours of victory. Thus Luther shrinks back in dismay when he sees that his doctrine is causing an uprising among the German peasants; thus the French revolutionaries guillotine each other because some are moving forward while others prefer to mark time or even turn back. Almost all revolutionaries and reformers are like children: they tremble at the apparition of the ogre that they themselves conjured up with their shrieks. It's been said that humanity, once it gets under way, starts beheading its leaders. It doesn't start out that way, with sacrifice, but it usually ends up with executions, because friend turns into an enemy, inspirational leader into an obstacle.

Every revolution, once it arrives, tends to become a government based on force, every triumphant revolutionary degenerates into a conservative. When was there ever an idea that didn't get degraded in the application? What reformer didn't lose his prestige when he came into power? Men (politicians in particular) don't keep their promises, nor does reality ever match the hopes of the disenfranchized. A revolution's fall from honor begins on the very day of its triumph; those who dishonor it are its own leaders.

Once the revolution gets under way, true revolutionaries ought to follow through with it in all its evolutions. But to change with circumstances, to cast out wornout convictions and assimilate new ones, this has always been repugnant to the human spirit, to man's presumption of believing himself to be the emissary of the future and the revealer of ultimate truth. We grow old without registering it, fall back without noticing, thinking we're always young, always heralds of the new, never allowing ourselves to admit that what comes after us has access to a broader horizon by dint of having climbed one step further up the mountain. Almost all of us live milling around a coffin we mistake for a cradle, or we die like worms, never fashioning a cocoon or transforming ourselves into butterflies. We're like those sailors who in the middle of the Atlantic said to Columbus: let's not go any further, there's nothing there. But America was there.

But we started out speaking of intellectuals and workers, and somehow we're discussing revolutions. Anything odd about this? We're operating in the shadow of a flag that's trembling amid the fires of the barricades, we're surrounded by men who sooner or later are going to cry out for social restitution, and it's May 1, the day that has earned the name of Easter for revolutionaries. The celebration of this Easter, not only here but throughout the civilized world, reveals to us that humanity has ceased fretting about secondary matters and is demanding radical change. No one expects any longer that the happiness of the wretched will be decreed by parliament or that some government is going to rain down manna to satisfy the hunger of all our stomachs. The legislature fashions loopholes and establishes taxes that weigh heaviest on those who have least; the governmental machine doesn't function on behalf of nations, but for the benefit of the dominant classes.

Once we recognize the inability of politics to provide for the greater good of the individual, all controversies and arguments about forms of government and governors are relegated to a secondary level, or better, they disappear. What remains is the *social question,* the grand question that the proletariat will resolve by the only effective means—revolution. Not one of those local revolutions that brings down presidents or czars and turns a republic into a monarchy or an autocracy into a representative government, but world revolution, that will erase frontiers, do away with nationalities, and summon humanity to its rightful possession and benefit of the earth.

III

If before concluding we had to sum up in two words the quintessence of our thinking, if we had to compose a shining banner to guide us on a straight path through the vicissitudes of existence, we would say: *Be fair.* Be fair with humanity, fair with the country we live in, fair to the family that raised us, and fair with ourselves, helping all our brethren to take and enjoy their share of happiness but not forgetting to pursue and enjoy our own.

Justice consists in giving all men and women what they are legitimately entitled to; let us give, then, to ourselves our fair share of the goods of the earth. Being born imposes on us the obligation to live, and this obligation gives us the right to take not only what's necessary but also what's comfortable and pleasurable. Man's life can be compared to a voyage across the sea. If earth is a ship and we are passengers, let's do whatever is possible to travel first class, enjoying fresh air, a good cabin and good food, instead of resigning ourselves to staying down in the hold, breathing stagnant air, sleeping on wood rotted by moisture and living on the leftovers from those more fortunate. Is there an abundance of provisions? Then everyone should eat according to his need. Are supplies scarce? Then everyone should be rationed, from the captain to the lowest cabin boy.

Resignation and sacrifice, practiced unnecessarily, would make us unfair to ourselves. True, because of the sacrifice and abnegation of heroic souls, humanity is gradually entering the road to justice. Not kings and conquerors, but those humble individuals who put the happiness of their brothers before their own, who poured the living waters of love into the barren sands of selfishness, deserve to live in history. If man could ever be transformed into superman, it would be through sacrifice. But sacrifice has to be voluntary. It's not acceptable for those in power to say to the powerless: sacrifice yourselves and win heaven, while we take control of the earth.

What we're entitled to, we have to take, because it's most unlikely that those with the monopoly will ever give us what's ours in good faith and in a spontaneous outpouring of generosity. August 4 is always more show than reality: the nobility give up one privilege, and right away they demand two new ones; the priests give back the tithe today, and tomorrow they demand the tithe and also the firstfruits. As a symbol of ownership the ancient Romans chose the most significant object— the lance. We should interpret this symbol as follows: ownership of a thing isn't based on justice, but on force; the owner doesn't reason, he strikes; the heart of the owner has the same attributes as iron: hardness and coldness. According to those who know Hebrew, Cain means *the first owner.* It shouldn't surprise us if a nineteenth-century socialist, seeing in Cain the first usurper of property as well as the first fratricide, should avail himself of this coincidence to reach a frightening conclusion: *ownership equals murder.*

If some people strike and don't reason, what should others do? Since we don't deny nations the right to rise up to overthrow bad governments, we ought to accord humanity that same right to rid themselves of those who exploit them mercilessly. And that concession today is a universal credo. Theoretically, revolution comes about because no one can deny the iniquities of the current regime, nor the need for reforms to improve the lot of the proletariat. (Isn't it true that there's even such a thing as Catholic socialism?) In practice, it can't occur without fighting and bloodshed because the very ones who acknowledge the legitimacy of social reparation refuse to give up the most infinitessimal part of their privileges; they talk justice, but in their hearts they hold on to their ill-gotten gain.

Many fail to see or pretend not to see the phenomenon that is under way at the base of modern societies. The death of belief tells them nothing, nor the diminishment of love of country, nor the solidarity of the proletariat, without regard to race or nationality. They hear a distant clamor, and they fail to see it's the cry of the hungry who are on the march to win bread for themselves; they feel the trembling of the ground, and fail to realize it's the revolution marching by; they breathe an atmosphere permeated by the stench of corpses, and fail to perceive that they're the ones, they and the entire bourgeois world, who stink of death.

Tomorrow, when waves of the proletariat rise up and crash against the walls of the old society, the plunderers and oppressors will feel the quaking and know the hour has come for the final, merciless battle. They'll call up their armies, but the soldiers will have joined the rebels; they'll cry out to heaven, but their gods will turn a deaf ear to them. Then they'll run off to pull in the drawbridges of their castles and palaces, thinking that help will come to them from somewhere. When they realize that help isn't coming and they see the angry faces swarming toward them from the four points of the compass, they'll turn to look at each other, full of self-pity (they who never pitied anyone) and they'll cry out in alarm: *The barbarians are coming, we'll be inundated!* But a voice, made up of the din of countless voices, will answer: *We aren't the flood of barbarism, we're the flood of justice.*

Our Judges

(1902)

I

Mariano Amézaga was not only a sincere and virile writer but a lawyer of proverbial honesty, a true character in the best sense of the word. If a malicious litigant tried to get him to take on some innocuous case, Amézaga would discourage him gently: "Friend, since there's no merit to your case, I won't represent you." If the cause seemed just, he would take the case, but most of the time it turned out that they wouldn't pay his fee. Maybe in the tumult of forensic give-and-take the litigant would say to him roguishly, "Doctor, sir, to tell the truth, I just learned from the reverend father N.N. that you have published a book attacking the dogma of our holy religion; and I, as a good Catholic, cannot continue to hire a heretic as my lawyer." The point? It would be prudent for all the legal hacks in Lima to engrave the following little addendum to their nameplate: *Attends mass regularly.*

Actually, the addendum goes without saying, given the psychology of the corporation. If there are a few young lawyers who deplore the decadence of the Latin race, proclaim themselves Anglo-Saxons, and talk about Spencer, Le Bon, Giddings, Hoeffding, and Gkumplowicz, the old ones accept nothing new, firmly adhere to the teaching of their day, and declare that sociology is a science of which they know and wish to know nothing. Instead of a brain they have a phonograph record crammed with laws and decrees; instead of a heart, a bundle of petitions and motions; instead of science, a monster engendered in the cohabitation of theology with Roman law. It isn't only sociology that doesn't exist for them; neither do natural history, chemistry, physics, mathematics, prehistory, or geography. They care even less for literature and would likely mistake Shakespeare for a Russian writer and Homer for a German judge. The only Bible they worship is the dictionary of legislation, and all they know are its codices, its forensic practice, and the rules of order of the court. They accept nothing new because they were huddled inside their medieval shells, because their briefcases are stuffed with university degrees and their brains pickled in antediluvian incrustations. Like a sheep lagging behind the flock, they follow those in front; like the beaver, they build rooms just like those all beavers build; like the oyster, they were born, they multiply, and they die in the same oyster bed where their parents were born, multiplied, and died.

Nonetheless, in Peru we have a hard time acknowledging that a man can have any intellectual worth or any store of knowledge unless he's got himself a law degree; no sooner does an individual give a speech, write a play or novel, or publish a book of history, and right away he's granted the title of doctor by unanimous acclaim. We were a bit surprised that when General Mendiburu published his dictionary, they didn't take away the general and promote him to doctor; but we were not at all surprised, and we even think it's politic and sensible, that our revolutionaries have stopped calling themselves colonels and have taken to calling themselves doctors. The masses are unaware that knowing nothing but codices is a very poor kind of knowing.

There's no one on earth as subject to professional corruption as a lawyer. What stout heart wouldn't get bent by the habit of trying to decipher justice in the random rulings of a judge? What mind is exempt from the perversion caused by years of scheming and legal shenanigans? What word, what language, wouldn't be corrupted by the use of judicial jargon? What good taste wouldn't be spoiled by daily exposure to codices, rules of law, and courtroom compromise? In the practice of law, as into a voracious, insatiable tomb, many good minds have sunk prematurely, perhaps the best in the country.

Dead to science and art, many of them live for their profession, and they degenerate calamitously. Rome isn't despised so much for its inhumane conquests as for its Roman law and all its pettifogging lawyers.

The lawyers were perhaps even more fearsome than the proconsuls and praetorians. Juvenal doesn't lavish much praise on them, Tacitus compares them to the vendors in the marketplaces, and the Consul Caius Silius proclaims on the floor of the senate that the money they earn stems from iniquities and injustice just as doctors traffic in disease. There were so many *defenders of justice* in the empire that even women did it; but one matron (we aren't sure if it was Aphrania or Calpurnia), furious at losing a judgment, turned her back on the judges, pulled up her tunic, and so on. Thanks to that expressive gesture women were forbidden to practice law, and humanity was freed of the burden of double or triple the number of pontificating humbugs. But the species multiplied anyway; thus, when the Greco-Latin world collapsed in ignominy, lacking the vigor to fend off the barbarians, the empire was swarming with sorcerers, cooks, gladiators, and rhetoricians, that is, all the prime ingredients for cooking up lawyers.

Today their ilk continue to swarm over the world, from the huge metropolitan centers where they weave the net the millionaire uses to catch and maim small businessmen, to the tiny villages where they bait the hook the wealthiest citizen uses to strip bare those who have nothing. The lawyer always serves as fawning escort to the usurer. If the despot is insufficiently abusive on his own initiative, the lawyer is there to goad him on, because in Spanish America the worst rulers, the most abusive and reactionary, have always been lawyers.

And we have said nothing about their influence in collective bodies, legislative bodies in particular. As a single vial of vinegar can embitter a whole vat of wine, so too the tongue of a lawyer is all it takes to whip up antagonism and confusion in any group where harmony and concord reign. On hearing the juridical-legal dissertations of a doctor of law, no one agrees with anyone, and the simplest questions of fact are turned into vague and irresolvable wars of words. If five hundred people are gathered together, they come up with 499 ways of solving a problem. It seems most likely to us that in the Tower of Babel, the problem wasn't a confusion of tongues but a tangle of lawyers.

II

Before proceeding to consider the administrators of justice, we have stopped off to admire these pontificating frauds because the judge comes from the lawyer, just as the excessively devout and hypocritical old woman comes from the party girl, just as the cop and the snitch come from the retired pickpocket.

Alcibiades, who was no fool, said, "When a man is summoned to appear in court, he's a fool to show up, common sense should tell him to disappear." And there was a man from Paris, who surely knew as much as Alcibiades, who used to delight in saying, "If they accused me of stealing the towers from Notre Dame, I'd head for the hills." The citizens of Peru, if they happen to be charged with a crime and discover on assessing their financial resources that they don't have enough cash to tip the scales of justice, ought to do the same thing. If the figure of Justice in classical times wore a blindfold over her eyes, a sword in one hand, and a set of scales in the other, American Justice keeps her hands free to grab whatever comes her way and her eyes open to see on which side the soles are shining.

Take away our sense of shame and supply us with a few pounds sterling, then watch and see if we don't persuade the judges to declare us owners of the World Fair and the cathedral of Notre Dame as well. Give us a massive transfusion, say, of all the money of a Carnegie or a Rockefeller, and we promise we'll violate two or three thousand articles of the Penal Code with impunity. There's no iniquity that can't be perpetrated, no penance that can't be avoided, when you have money, influence, or power; those unfortunates growing anemic in a cell or wasting away in a penitentiary simply failed to find a protector or protectress, or simply lacked tangible assets.

And proofs or rights are worth nothing. Just as you find a thug to pull off a swindle, in complicated cases all you need is a judge to quash an indictment, issue a new one, and pronounce a verdict absolving the guilty and condemning the innocent. If by some rare chance you come across a judge with integrity who resists all seduction (masculine or feminine), then you have recourse to a series of recusals, until you find one who's reachable, who's venal. If by another rare chance you don't find the judge you need in the town you live in, you just send for him and he'll come from two or three hundred miles away.

If you want to get a sense of the independence of the national courts, just call to mind how they ruled in cases of major financial litigation and how they go about electing members of the Electoral Commission: they inevitably follow the suggestions or will of the government, so they elect democrats if the Democratic Party is in power, civilists if the

Civil Party rules. If men display this kind of malleability in the public eye, what will they do behind closed doors, when no one is watching or listening? We would be hard put to say whether those who collaborate in the falsification of popular elections will feel the least scruple in absolving criminals or condemning the innocent.

Knowing how the Judicial Corps is elected, it all becomes clear. According to the Constitution: "The public prosecutors and judges of the Supreme Court will be appointed by Congress who will offer a short list of three to the executive power; the public prosecutors and judges of the Supreme Court will be appointed by the president, who will offer a short list of three to the Supreme Court; and the superior court judges and fiscal agents will presented to the respective Superior Courts in short lists of three." Differences in form only because in substance the true and only elector is the president of the republic: Courts and Parliaments should be called dependents of the executive power. There are judges and prosecutors who appoint themselves, thanks to a newly invented and highly comfortable procedure. Serving as ministers, and even in the Justice Department, they step down from their offices for a few hours and have themselves nominated or appointed by the colleague who is sitting in for them. Almost always, a high judicial post is a reward for services lent to the government. Because such services reek of suspect integrity, it would be advisable for people to observe a hygienic measure: after shaking hands with certain judges, wash with cleansers and disinfectants.

It isn't at all surprising that such men are not instruments of justice but tools of power and that they have earned the terrible accusations of Salazar and Mazarredo. "What follows (said the furious royal commissioner in a note addressed on April 12, 1864, to our minister of foreign relations) is not meant to characterize the courts in Peru but only to recall that the current undersecretary of foreign commerce from Great Britain, Mr. Layard, recently stated in the House of Commons, on discussing the recall of Captain White, that said British subject, treated cruelly like many others, had had the misfortune to fall into the hands of what only for the sake of courtesy is called the Court of Justice."

Since we're hiring English engineers to lay sewers in the villages, Belgian agronomists to teach agriculture, and French officers to train soldiers, we could hire Germans or Swedes to administer justice. We won't deny that for each court there are a couple of honest, upright judges worthy of remaining in their posts; but we won't name them, thus allowing all of them, if they happen to read this, to enjoy the pleasure of thinking they are the healthy sheep in the sick flock. There are honest judges: not all snakes nor all mushrooms conceal fatal poisons. In spite of everything, judges enjoy the kind of veneration and respect reserved for things divine. Just as a black savage turns a can of sardines or a boot into a fetish, so we deify the members of the courts, especially the Supreme Court.

No one can touch them or look directly at them; everywhere, everyone gives them the seat of honor and lavishes them with the most exquisite considerations. His Honor is entering the room?—every head bows down. His Honor is taking his seat?—everyone does the same. His Honor is speaking?—everyone grows silent and drinks in his words, even if he's uttering platitudes the size of the Himalayas and vulgarities the size of a planet. Vulgarities and platitudes are never lacking because many of our great judges, like the god Serapis of Alexandria, have a rat's nest in their heads.

III

Nothing so clearly manifests the corruption of a society as the decline of the judiciary. Where justice sinks to become a weapon of the rich and powerful, a vacuum is created for individual vengeance, an excuse is provided for the organization of a Mafia, a regression to prehistoric times is encouraged. Perhaps we would gain by returning to the cave and the forest, if we could do so without hypocrisy or compromise. The savage state where the individual takes the law into his own hands is better than a fraudulent civilization where the few oppress and devour the rest, casting a glaze of legality over the greatest iniquities. Between the rule of force and the rule of hypocrisy, we prefer force. We want to find ourselves in a jungle confronting a savage with his sling and cudgel, not in a palace of Justice confronting a shyster armed with briefs and official papers.

The tyranny of the soldier is less frustrating than a judge's; the first can be toppled with a popular uprising or the elimination of the individual; the second can't be destroyed even with social upheavals and political turmoil. We can execute, hang, set fire to the Gutiérrez brothers; but we wouldn't dare try that with all those venal, prevaricating judges. We didn't put up with those three violent, bullying soldiers for even a week; many judges, who are even more pernicious and guilty than the Gutiérrez brothers, we tolerate for half a century. Although governments and chambers of deputies disappear, the courts of justice remain unchanged, as if they were endowed with the incorruptibility of gold.

The tyrant takes responsibility for his acts of violence, willing to concentrate in his person the hatred of the masses; the judge does his harm without having to deal with the consequences, barricading himself behind the codices and attributing excesses of personal malice to deficiencies in the Law. A court of justice is an irresponsible force that chips away at our property, our honor, and our lives, as millstones grind and pulverize the grains of wheat. Their statue-like impassivity is like the gutless greed of an anonymous corporation.

And yet no class enjoys more security or greater privileges. The military can crush us underfoot or run us through with swords; but they give their lives for us when the country is threatened by a foreign invasion. The priest puts us to sleep with his monotonous chants from days long past and exploits us with his sacraments, his indulgences, and his guilds; but he visits the sick, consoles the dying, and exposes his body to the arrows of savages. The judge wins everything without risking anything: he rests while others grow weary, he sleeps while others keep watch, eats while others fast, practicing the kind of knight errantry where Sancho does the work of don Quixote. What does he care about civil wars? He lives sure in the knowledge that, whether the revolutionaries or the government troops win, he will go on enjoying his honors, his influence, his obscene salary, and public veneration. In moments of national shipwreck, he represents the plank that stays afloat, the bladder that rises to the surface. Even better, he's a bird nested high on a cliff. The storm that sinks the ships doesn't touch him, nor does he concern himself with the cries of the wretches drowning at sea.

If it's true that no one on earth is as subject to professional corruption as a lawyer, just imagine what an administrator of justice will be like after fifteen or twenty years in office. We recognize the professional cyclist instantaneously because, even when he's sprawled in a chair, he looks like he's pushing the pedal and steering the wheel; we can tell the judge from other men by his air of seeming to be leafing through a deposition or thundering down a verdict, even when he's wielding a fork or shaking our hand. And the corruption isn't just evident in physical terms: by virtue of hearing just and unjust cases defended with equal passion, the judge ends up by squeezing justice into a simple interpretation of the law, so an article of the code lets him uphold today the opposite of what he affirmed yesterday. They say that the Areopagus in Athens never handed down an unjust sentence. It would be interesting to hear from the Athenians who lost their cases.

The laws, no matter how clear and straightforward they may seem to us, entail enough obscure and complex elements to serve an honest man or a scoundrel, perhaps the scoundrel even more than the honest man. But assuming that they were models of justice and fairness, what good are good laws with bad judges? Let a Marcus Aurelius judge us under a draconian code, but please don't let a Judas administer Christ's laws to us.

Before the implementation of the division of labor, each man exercised on his own behalf the triple function of litigant, judge, and enforcer of the sentence. Today, when these functions are perfectly defined and separated, the judge applies the law, the jailer guards the guilty, the executioner carries out the sentence. In this abominable trio of executioner, jailer, and judge, the judge appears as the most odious figure, provider of gallows and mass graves, activator of jailers and executioners.

We say it again: the swamp of the judiciary cannot be drained. From His Excellency sitting on the Supreme Court to His Honor presiding over the lower courts, all judges have the same motto inscribed on their foreheads: I can't be touched. And no one touches them, and children and old men venerate them like priests of some intangible religion. Someone claimed that the Canary Islands were the remnants of Atlantis, and Teide Peak the fragment of a mountain range. If Peruvian society sank down tomorrow into a sea of blood, the judiciary would emerge unscathed: it is our Teide Peak.

Our Indians[1]

(1904)

I

The most prominent sociologists regard sociology as a science in formation and long for the advent of their Newton, their Lavoisier, or their Lydell; however, there was never a book throbbing with such

[1] This article was not included in the first edition of *Horas de lucha*. We have included it in this edition because we believe the ideas expressed in it are in harmony with the spirit of the work. We should point out, however, that the author never finished "Nuestros indios," and he certainly never provided definitive corrections to the pages he had sketched. And we have decided to publish it as he left it, respecting the spontaneous style of the author, instead of incorporating changes in which our good intentions would not always have managed to excuse our clumsiness, so as not to deprive the public of knowing the author's opinion concerning a topic of such national importance—A.G.P.

Following this article by Prada on the Indian, the approach to this topic in Peruvian sociological literature changes radically. Already in 1888 doña Clorinda Matto de Turner had dedicated to Prada her famous indigenist novel *Aves sin nido*, and prior to 1900 Prada had written what would later be titled *Baladas peruanas*, poems of vehement revindication on behalf of the Indian. The essay brought about a violent change of perspective in indigenist works and directly inspired the works of Pedro Zulen, Víctor Haya de la Torre, José Carlos Mariátegui, José Uriel García, and Luis E. Valcárcel. According to Prada's interpretation, the Indian does not represent a biological race but a social race, since he is dependent on his economic condition. However, concerning the Chinese and the Negro, Prada's opinions were more traditional, as can be seen in the statement of principles of the National Union, as well as in his essays on the Peruvian aristocracy.—L.A.S., 1976.

dogmatic or arbitrary affirmation as those works written by the heirs or epigones of Comte. We could call sociology not only the art of giving new names to old things but the science of contradictory claims. If a great sociologist enunciates a proposition, we can be sure that another sociologist, no less great, will uphold one diametrically opposed. Just as some pedagogues remind us of the preceptors of Scribe, many sociologists call to mind the doctors of Molière: Le Bon and Tarde aren't that far removed from Diafoirus and Purgón.

We can cite race as one of the points on which the authors most diverge. While some see it as the principal factor in the social dynamic and sum up history as a struggle of races, others reduce the impact of ethnic actions to such an extent that they might repeat with Durkheim: "We know of no social phenomenon that can be attributed to the undeniable dependence on race." Novicow, even though he regards Durkheim's opinion as exaggerated, does not hesitate to affirm that "race, like species, is to a certain point a subjective category of our mind, with no exterior reality." In a generous outburst of humanity he claims that "all the so-called limitations of the yellow and black races are figments of sick minds. Anyone audacious enough to say to a race: you can go this far, but no further, is blind and a fool."

What a convenient invention ethnology is in the hands of certain men! Once we accept the division of humanity into superior and inferior races, once we acknowledge the superiority of whites and consequently their right to monopolize the running of the planet, what could be more natural than to suppress the Negro in Africa, the redskin in the United States, the Tagalo in the Philippines, the Indian in Peru. Since the supreme law of life is manifested in the selection or elimination of those who are weak and cannot adapt, those who use violence to eliminate or suppress can claim they are merely accelerating the slow and indolent work of nature. They are replacing the dogged crawl of the turtle with the gallop of the horse. Not many will put it in so many words, but you can read it between the lines, as in Pearson when he refers to "the solidarity between civilized men of the European race confronting nature and human savagery." Where it reads "human savagery," we can translate "men without white skin."

In addition to decreeing the suppression of black and yellow peoples, within the white race itself they are devising classifications designating which peoples are destined to grow great and live and which are doomed to degenerate and die. Ever since Demolins published his book *A quoi tient la supériorité des Anglo-Saxons,*[2] the impulse to praise Anglo-Saxons and disparage Latins has intensified (although some Latins might call themselves Anglo-Saxons, as Atahualpa called himself Galician and Montezuma Provencal). In Europe and America we are witnessing the blossoming of many Cassandras who live prophesying the burning and disappearance of the new Troy. Some pessimists, believing themselves to be the Deucalions of the next flood, or even Nietzsche's supermen, look on the disappearance of their own race as if it were happening to prehistoric beings or happening on the moon. It hasn't been formulated yet, but there's an axiom here: crimes and vices of Englishmen and North Americans are things inherent to the human species and in no way signify the decadence of a people; on the other hand, crimes and vices of Frenchmen or Italians are anomalies and signify the degeneration of the race. Happily, Oscar Wilde and General MacDonald weren't born in Paris, and the round table of the Emperor William never met in Rome.

It seems gratuitous to say that we don't take dilettantes like Paul Bourget or wags like Maurice Barrés seriously when they thunder against cosmopolitanism and bewail the decadence of the noble French race, just because the daughter of a syphilitic count and a marquesa with lung disease lets herself be seduced by a strapping young man with no patent of nobility. With respect to Monsieur Gustave Le Bon, we ought to admire him for his vast knowledge and high moral character, even though he represents an exaggerated extension of Spencer, just as Max Nordau exaggerates Lombroso and Haeckel exaggerates Darwin. He ought to be called sociology's Bossuet, not to say Torquemada or Herod. Even if he hadn't become notorious for his observations on the black race, we would say that he is to sociology what the leech is to medicine.

Le Bon advises us that the term "race" should not be used in the anthropological sense because long ago the pure races disappeared, ex-

---

[2] Don Víctor Arreguine has answered him with the book *En qué consiste la superioridad de los Latinos sobre los Anglo-sajones* (Buenos Aires, 1900). According to Arreguine, Demolins's long work, the expansion of a chapter by Taine on English education and its virtues, far from being a work of impartial serenity, is an Anglomaniacal harangue in exaggerated pedagogical style, despite the fact that it upset many Latin sensibilities with what we might call its novelty.

cept in savage lands, and so we'll have a safe road to march along, he concludes: "In civilized lands, there are only historical races, that is, races totally created by the events of history." According to LeBonian dogmatism, the Spanish American nations now constitute one of those races, but a race so rare that it moved with dizzying speed from childhood to decrepitude, spanning in less than a century the trajectory covered by other peoples in three, four, five, and even six thousand years. The twenty-two Latin American republics,[3] he writes in his *Psychology of Socialism*, "although situated in the richest regions of the planet, are incapable of developing their immense resources . . . the ultimate destiny of this half of America is to revert to primitive barbarism, unless the United States does them the immense favor of conquering them. . . . To reduce the richest regions of the planet to the level of the black republics of Santo Domingo and Haiti—this is what the Latin race has accomplished in less than a century with half of America."

It could be said of Le Bon that he mistakes the skin rash of a child for the senile gangrene of a ninety-year-old, the adolescence of a youth for the homicidal psychosis of an old man. When did revolutions ever signify decrepitude and death? Not one of the Spanish American nations exhibits today the political and social misery that reigned in Europe under feudalism; but the feudal epoch is regarded as an evolutionary phase, while the period of Spanish American revolutions is seen as an irreparable, terminal condition. We could also set Le Bon the optimist against Le Bon the pessimist, as we do Saint Augustine the bishop against Saint Augustine the pagan. "It is possible," affirms Le Bon, "that following a series of horrendous disasters, upheavals never before seen in history, the Latin peoples, having learned from sad experience . . . might attempt in their own crude fashion to acquire the qualities they lack to succeed in life in the future . . . Apostles can work wonders because they can change people's opinions, and opinion rules the world today . . . History is so full of surprises, the world can anticipate such profound changes, that it's impossible to predict today the

[3] How does the author arrive at this figure of twenty-two republics? This is not a typographical error because in a note on page 40 he writes, "One would have to be totally ignorant of the history of Santo Domingo, Haiti, and of the twenty-two Spanish American republics and of the United States."

fate of empires." If no one can predict the fate of nations, how is he able to announce the death of the Spanish American republics? What the Latin empires are capable of accomplishing in Europe, couldn't people of the same origin try to achieve in the New World? Or are there two separate sociological laws, one for the Latins of America, and another for the Latins of Europe? Maybe so; but fortunately, Le Bon's affirmations are like nails, you use one to pull out the others.[4] It's clear, then, that if Auguste Comte sought to make sociology an eminently positive science, some of his heirs are beginning to transform it into a muddle of digressions without any scientific base.

II

In *The Struggle of the Races*, Luis Gkumplowicz writes: "Every strong ethnic characteristic seeks to make every weak element it encounters, or that penetrates its radius of power, serve its own ends."[5] First the conquistadors, then their descendants, established in the countries of America an ethnic characteristic strong enough to subjugate and exploit the indigenous peoples. Although the charges leveled by Las Casas are exaggerated, it cannot be denied that thanks to the avaricious cruelty of the exploiters, in some American countries the weak element is on the verge of being extinguished. Ants that domesticate aphids in order to milk them do not make the mistake of imitating the "white man's lack of foresight—they don't destroy the productive animal."

To Gumplowicz's formula we should add a law that has great influence on our way of doing things: when an individual rises above the level of his social class, he usually becomes its worst enemy. During the period of black slavery, there were no fiercer guards than the blacks themselves; today, there are perhaps no oppressors of the native American crueler than the natives themselves who have been Hispanicized and invested with a certain authority.

The true tyrant of the masses, the one who uses one group of Indians to fleece and oppress others, is the half-breed, a term referring equally to the mountain cholo or mestizo and to the coastal mulatto or zambo.

---

[4] Here he says that "*apostles can work wonders because they can change people's opinions,*" etc. On pages 451–452 he says just the opposite: "*Nos pensées,*" etc.

[5] Anonymous translation appearing in *España Moderna*, Madrid.

In Peru we see an ethnic superpopulation: excluding the Europeans and the very limited number of national whites or American-born Spaniards *(criollos)*, the population is divided into two groups quite unequal in number, those of mixed blood *(encastados)*, who tend to dominate, and the native Indians, who are dominated. Fewer than 200,000 individuals have taken control of the lives of 3 million.

There exists an offensive and a defensive alliance, an exchange of services among those who run the capital and those who run the provinces: if the highland chief serves as political agent to the political boss in Lima, the political boss in Lima defends the highland chief when he savagely abuses the Indian. Few social groups have committed so many atrocities or have such terrible reputations as the Spaniards and half-breed Indians in Peru. Revolutions are nothing compared to the half-breed's cold-blooded ruthlessness in squeezing juice from human flesh. The suffering and death of his brethren concern him not at all as long as that suffering and that death yield him a few soles of profit. They decimated the Indians with taxation and compulsory labor; they imported blacks to slave and suffer under the foreman's whip; they devoured the Chinese, giving them a handful of rice for ten or fifteen hours of work; they brought yellow-skinned slaves from their islands to die of nostalgia in the huts on their haciendas; today they're trying to bring in the Japanese. Blacks seem to be dwindling, the Chinese are disappearing, others of yellow skin have left no trace, and the Japanese show no signs of embracing slavery or indentured service; but the Indian remains. Three or four hundred years of cruelty haven't managed to exterminate him—the son of a bitch insists on living!

The viceroys of Peru ceaselessly condemned abuses and tried diligently to guarantee survival, humane treatment, and relief for the Indians; the kings of Spain, succumbing to the merciful instincts of their noble Catholic souls, devised humanitarian measures or supported those initiated by the viceroys. The royal seals abounded in good intentions. We don't know if the laws of Indies were heaped as high as Chimborazo Peak, but we do know the evil continued unabated (although there were from time to time exemplary punishments). It had to be that way. The exploitation of the conquered was officially decreed, and those carrying out the exploitation were urged to do so with humanity and justice; the idea was to commit atrocities humanely and perpetrate injustice fairly. To eradicate the abuses, it would have been necessary to abolish the taxes and the compulsory labor, in other words, to thoroughly transform the colonial regime. Without the labor of the American Indian, the Spanish treasure chests would have been empty. The wealth sent from the colonies to the metropolis was nothing but blood and tears converted into gold.

The republic continues the traditions of the viceroyalty. The presidents in their messages urge the redemption of the oppressed and call themselves "protectors of the indigenous race." The congresses enact laws that leave the Declaration of the Rights of Man in the shade; the ministers of government issue decrees, pass notes to the prefects, and appoint investigative delegations, all "to the noble end of guaranteeing the continued well-being of the dispossessed." But messages, laws, decrees, notes, and delegations are reduced to hypocritical jeremiads, words without echoes, timeworn expedients. The authorities from Lima who send their admonishing instructions to the departments know they won't be obeyed; the prefects who receive the admonishments from the capital also know they'll suffer no consequences if they don't obey them. What the marquis of Mancera said in his 1648 *Memoirs* still bears repeating today, substituting governors and ranchers for corregidors and chiefs: "These poor Indians have as enemies the greed of their corregidors, priests, and chiefs, all bent on growing rich on their sweat; one would have to have the zeal and authority of a viceroy for each one of them; by virtue of the distance, obedience is mocked, and there's not enough energy or perseverance for them to complain a second time."[6] The phrase "obedience is mocked" carries some weight on the lips of a viceroy; but even more weighty is the statement made by the defenders of the natives of Chucuito.[7]

There are many champions of the Indians who in their individual or collective initiatives behave just like governments in their official actions. Associations formed to liberate the doomed race have not progressed beyond being political gunrunners cloaked in a philanthropic banner. Defense of the Indian has degenerated into little more than sentimentality, just as the invocation of Tacna and Arica is a cheap display of patriotism. For the redeemers to proceed in good faith, they

---

[6] *Memorias de los Virreyes del Perú*, Marqués de Mancera y Conde de Salvatierra, published by José Toribio Polo, Lima, 1899.

[7] *La Raza Indígena del Perú en los albores del siglo XX* (page 6, second folio), Lima, 1903.

would have to undergo a moral transformation overnight, they'd have to draw back in horror at their own iniquities, make an inviolable resolution to obey the law, transform themselves from tigers to men. How likely is that?

Meanwhile, and as a general rule, the dominators approach the Indian to deceive him, oppress him, or corrupt him. And we should remember that it's not only our Peruvians of mixed blood who conduct themselves with such inhumanity or bad faith: when the Europeans become wool merchants, miners, or ranchers, they prove themselves to be excellent extractors and magnificent torturers, worthy rivals of the former corregidors and present-day ranchers. The animal with white skin, no matter where he's born, is afflicted by the obsession for gold and ultimately, gives in to his instinct for rapacity.

III

Under the republic, does the Indian suffer less than under Spanish domination? If there are no longer corregidors with their land grants from the king, there is still compulsory labor and recruitment. The suffering we inflict on them ought to bring down on our heads the condemnation of the human race. We keep the Indian in a state of ignorance and servitude, we humiliate him in the barracks, brutalize him with alcohol, send him out to die in civil wars, and on occasion we even organize manhunts and massacres like those in Amantani, Ilave, and Huanta.[8]

It hasn't been written into law, but it is observed as an axiom that the Indian doesn't have rights, only obligations. In his case, any personal complaint is regarded as insubordination, any group demand an uprising. The Spanish royalists killed the Indian when he tried to shake

---

[8] A reliable and well-informed person provides us with the following information: "*Massacre in Amantani.*—No sooner was Piérola's first dictatorship installed than the Indians of Amantani, an island on Lake Titicaca, lynched a chief who had been foolish enough to make them conduct military exercises. The response was the expedition from Puno of two warships that bombarded the island from six o'clock in the morning till six in the evening. The slaughter was horrible, with no way to calculate the number of Indians who died that day, without regard to age or sex. All that's left is skeletons, the upper bodies bleaching and protruding from cracks in the cliffs where they had sought refuge." Ilave and Huanta occurred during Piérola's second administration.

off the conquistadors' yoke, we citizens of the republic exterminate him when he protests the onerous taxes or grows weary of enduring in silence the atrocities of some satrap.

Our form of government is nothing but a monstrous lie because a state in which 2–3 million individuals live outside the protection of the law does not deserve to be called a democratic republic. If it's true that on the coast there is a glimmer of legal safeguard under a pseudorepublic, in the interior there is the most blatant and palpable violation of every human right under a true feudal regime. There are no codes in force there, nor any rule of law, because ranchers and caciques handle all cases, arrogating to themselves the role of judges and executioners. The political authorities, far from supporting the weak and the poor, almost always abet the rich and the strong. There are regions where justices of the peace and governors are appointed from among the servants of the hacienda. What governor, what subprefect or prefect would dare oppose the will of the owner of the hacienda?

A hacienda is made up of the accumulation of small farms stolen from their legitimate owners, and the *patrón* exerts the authority of a Norman baron over his peasants. Not only does he control the appointment of governors, mayors, and justices of the peace, but he arranges marriages, designates heirs, distributes any inheritance, and to make sure that the sons satisfy the debts of the fathers, he subjects them to a servitude that lasts a lifetime. He imposes horrendous punishments, such as the stocks, flagellation, suffocation by inserting a rifle into a soldier's belt and twisting it tight, and death; humorous punishments include head shaving and cold-water enemas. It would be a miracle for a person who has no respect for lives or property to show any concern for the honor of women: every Indian woman, single or married, can serve as a target for the brutal desires of the master. Abduction, rape, sexual abuse mean nothing to a man who assumes that Indian women are meant to be taken by force. In spite of everything, the Indian never addresses the master without kneeling and kissing his hand. Let's not imagine it's out of ignorance or lack of breeding that the territorial masters behave in this way: the sons of many hacienda owners are sent to Europe as children, are educated in France or England, and return to Peru with all the appearance of civilized human beings. But as soon as they shut themselves up in their haciendas, they lose their European polish and proceed with even more cruelty and violence than their fathers. Once they don their sombrero, their poncho, and their spurs, the beast reappears. In short, haciendas are kingdoms in the heart of the republic, and the owners play the role of autocrats in the middle of a democracy.

IV

To put the best face on the government's negligence and the inhumanity of the expoiters, some pessimists in the lineage of Le Bon mark the Indian's forehead with a shameful stigma: they say he resists civilization. You'd think splendid schools bristling with well-paid teachers were being built in all our villages, and that the classrooms were empty because the children, obeying their parents' instructions, were refusing to be educated. You'd also think that the natives were failing to follow the fine moral example of the ruling classes or that they were crucifying without scruple anyone who came along advocating generous and elevated ideas. The Indian took what they gave him: fanaticism and whiskey.

What then do we mean by civilization? Like the dazzling point of a great pyramid, morality shines over industry and art, over erudition and science. I'm not speaking of theological morality based on posthumous sanction, but human morality, which needs no sanction and wouldn't seek it at some remote remove from earth. The ultimate morality, for individuals as well as societies, consists in transforming the war of human being against human being into lifelong mutual harmony. Where there's no justice, no mercy, no benevolence, there's no civilization; where the struggle for survival is proclaimed as social law, barbarism reigns. What good is it to acquire the knowledge of an Aristotle if you have the heart of a tiger? Or the artistic talent of a Michelangelo if you have the soul of a pig? It's a higher calling to go through the world distilling the honey of goodwill than spreading the light of art or science. Societies where doing good is no longer an obligation but a habit, where generosity has become instinctive act—those are the truly civilized societies. The rulers of Peru—have they attained that level of moral excellence? Do they have the right to regard the Indian as a creature unfit for civilization?

The political and social organization of the ancient Inca empire amazes European reformers and revolutionaries today. True, Atahualpa didn't know the Lord's Prayer, and Calcuchima didn't meditate on the mystery of the Trinity. But the cult of the sun was perhaps less absurd than the Catholic religion, and perhaps the high priest of Pachacamac was less ferocious in victory than Father Valverde. If the subjects of Huayna-Capac accepted civilization, we see no reason why the Indian of the republic would reject it, unless the entire race had suffered some irremediable physiological decline. Morally speaking, the indigenous population of the republic is inferior to those discovered by the conquistadors; but moral depression caused by political servitude is not the same as an absolute incapacity for civilization due to organic constitution. Even if it were, who would be to blame?

The facts bely the pessimists. Whenever the Indian has access to instruction or learns through simple contact with civilized persons, he acquires the same level of morality and culture as the descendant of the Spaniard. We are constantly coming into contact with yellow-skinned people who dress, eat, and think like *the mellifluous gentlemen from Lima*. We see Indians in parliaments, municipal offices, judgeships, universities, and athenaeums, conducting themselves with no greater venality or ignorance than members of other races. It's impossible to determine responsibility in the spectrum of national politics to say whether the greater evil was caused by the mestizos, the mulattoes, or the whites. There is such promiscuity of blood and color, each individual represents so many licit or illicit mixtures, that in the presence of a multitude of Peruvians we would be loath to determine the portion of black and yellow constituting each of them. No one deserves to be characterized as pure white, even if his eyes are blue and his hair blond. We need only recall that our most broad-minded and enlightened head of state was of the indigenous race: his name was Santa Cruz. A hundred others have been equally so, and valiant to the point of heroism, like Cahuide, or faithful unto martyrdom, like Olaya.

Novicow is right to affirm that "the so-called limitations of yellow and black races are the figments of sick minds." There is no generous act that cannot be accomplished by any black or yellow-skinned person, just as there is no despicable act that cannot be perpetrated by any white person. During the Chilean invasion in 1900, the yellow-skinned people of Japan gave lessons in humanity to the whites of Russia and Germany. We don't recall if the blacks in Africa gave similar lessons from time to time to the Boers of the Transvaal or the English of the

Cape. We do know that the Anglo-Saxon Kitchener proved himself to be as savage in the Sudan as Behanzin in Dahomey. If instead of comparing a group of whites with other groups of dark-skinned people, we compared individual with individual, we would see that in the midst of white civilization there's an abundance of people who are savages [kaffirs and redskins] inside. As flowers of their race or genuine representatives, let's look at the king of England and the emperor of Germany: Edward VII and Wilhelm II—is there any way they deserve to be compared with the Indian Benito Juárez and the Negro Booker T. Washington? Men who before occupying a throne live in taverns, gambling dens, and whorehouses, men who from the summit of imperial power order the merciless slaughter of children, old men, and women, have white skins, but their souls are black.

Is the decline of the indigenous race merely a function of ignorance? True, the national ignorance seems like something out of a fable when you consider that in many villages in the interior there's not a single person capable of reading or writing, that during the War of the Pacific the natives looked at the conflict between the two nations as a civil conflict between General Chile and General Peru, that not that long ago the emissaries from Chucuito went to Tacna thinking they would find the president of the republic there.

Some pedagogues (worthy rivals of snake-oil vendors) imagine that if a man knows the source of the Amazon River and the average temperature of Berlin, he's well on his way to resolving all our social problems. If by some supernatural phenomenon the national illiterates woke up tomorrow not only knowing how to read and write but having university diplomas, the problem of the Indian still wouldn't be resolved: the proletariat of the ignorant would be followed by the proletariat of those with bachelor's degrees and doctorates. Doctors without patients, lawyers without clients, engineers without jobs, writers without a public, artists without customers, teachers without pupils—these abound in the most civilized nations, making up an innumerable army of enlightened minds and starving bellies. In a country where the haciendas on the coasts measure four or five thousand acres, where the ranches in the mountains measure thirty or even fifty leagues, the nation must necessarily be divided into masters and servants.

If education has the power to transform the impulsive brute into a reasonable and magnanimous being, instruction guides him and lights the path he should follow to avoid getting lost at life's crossroads. But to glimpse a path is not the same as following it to the end: you need a firm will and strong feet. You also need a mind that isn't afflicted with pride and rebelliousness or the submissiveness and excessive respect for authority we see in the soldier and the monk. Instruction can keep a man in an abject state of servility: the eunuchs and grammarians of Byzantium were well instructed. To occupy the place on earth you choose instead of accepting the place they assign you; to demand and take the food you need; to claim a roof over your head and your plot of land, this is the right of every rational being.

Nothing changes human psychology more rapidly or more radically than ownership: when you banish slavery from your gut, you grow ten feet tall. Just by owning something, the individual climbs several steps up the social scale because classes are nothing but groups classified by the wealth they own. Just the opposite of a hot air balloon, the more you weigh, the higher you rise. If they tell you "school," tell them "school and bread."

The Indian problem, more than pedagogical, is economic and social. How to resolve it? Not long ago a German conceived the idea of restoring the Inca empire. He learned Quechua, introduced himself to groups of Indians in Cuzco, began to win supporters, and might even have organized an uprising, if he hadn't suddenly died on his way back from a trip to Europe. Is such a restoration possible today? Even if we tried it, even if we wanted to achieve it, the result would be a pale imitation of past grandeur.

The condition of the native can be improved in two ways: either the heart of the oppressors must be moved to recognize the rights of the oppressed, or the spirit of the oppressed must acquire sufficient virility to punish the oppressors. If the Indian used all the money he wasted on alcohol and fiestas to buy rifles and cartridges, if in some corner of his hut or in a hole in some cliff he hid a weapon, he would change his lot and make them respect his property and his life. He would respond to violence with violence, punishing the boss who steals his wool, the soldier who tries to recruit him in the name of the government, the guerrilla who steals his livestock and pack animals.

We shouldn't be preaching humility and resignation to the Indian, but pride and rebellion. What has he gained by three or four hundred years of conformity and patience? The fewer authorities he tolerates, the freer he'll be from harm. There's one revealing fact: the villages farthest from the great haciendas are the ones that enjoy greatest prosperity; the villages least visited by authorities are the most peaceful, the most orderly.

In short: the Indian will be saved by his own efforts, not by the humanization of his oppressors. Every white man is, more or less, a Pizarro, a Valverde, or an Areche.

III

New Free Pages

Poetry[1]

(1902)

I

The time has passed when queens kissed sleeping poets on the mouth or kings were as flattered to have a sonnet engraved in their honor as a crown placed on their heads. Today, even those who write verse take pleasure in denigrating poetry, and a Chateaubriand (who lives through the sentiments and imagination of his books) maintains that "becoming a poet is the same as losing one's strength of mind." Still, to a Chateaubriand we can oppose a Victor Hugo. The author of *Hernani* and *The Legend of the Centuries*, the man who wrote poetry for sixty years and regards poetry as a sacred calling, says that the poet has a spiritual function and doesn't hesitate to affirm that "twenty verses by Vergil occupy a loftier place in human genius and even in the progress of civilization than all the speeches ever written or still to be written."

Antiquity offers us a very curious contrast. While Plato sees poetry as an art harmful to society, Aristotle looks at it as something more

[1] An essay published for the first time in 1902 (?) in *La Nación* of Buenos Aires. It has been reproduced frequently in newspapers and journals in Spanish America. Several broadsheet editions of it have been produced in the Republic of Argentina.

We have already indicated in the *Advertencias* the very minor emendations that this text has undergone, which we complete with two quotations by the author in the margin of the clipping.—Editor.

philosophical and more serious than history. Who was Plato anyway? A poet roaming free in the nebulous regions of metaphysics, a kind of pagan Chateaubriand. And who was Aristotle? A man of science cloistered in the realm of nature, the Bacon and Darwin of Greece.

Several years ago there was a prolonged debate in a European literary society about whether poetry was doomed to disappear with the advance of the sciences and industry. As we do not know the verdict of that learned assembly or literary conclave, we will simply suggest that if poetry ceases to live, its death will not be caused by industry or science.

The notion that "that will be destroyed by this" is now being played out in the field of literature: prose tries to eliminate verse as gas eliminated the candle, as electric light is now eliminating gas. And it's understandable. If in ancient times, poetry encapsulized all the science, religion, and philosophy of an epoch, today the living sap and marrow of human thought is summed up in prose. Although the scientists and philosophers of Greece composed rich, solid poems in which they synthesized their concept of the universe and of life,[2] the rhymesters and poetasters of our century throw together pompous, feeble stanzas in which they analyze the pathological changes in their bodies. There's a paucity of true poets, but we're swarming with good versifiers—men gifted in concealing beneath the cloak of verse the deformities that would leap out at us in the austere nakedness of prose. Who knows whether a bankrupt prose writer is lurking beneath innumerable versifiers! In certain individuals the art of rhyming has become confused with the mechanical function. They write a silva or a sonnet the way a craftsman turns a column on a lathe or plies layers of cloth together with glue to make buckram.

Since no one thinks in verse or feels true sentiments or breathes new life into wornout, clichéd images in verse, we can affirm that poetry flourishes at some distance from poets themselves. Isn't there more inspiration in Spencer, Darwin, and Haeckel than in the rhymes of their contemporaries? Does Núñez de Arce have metaphors as rich as those of a Guyau, does Zorrilla have the feeling of a Dickens, or the

[2] *Marginal note by the author:* Philosophers like Xenophanes of Colophon, Parmenides, Empedocles, etc., wrote long poems in which they developed their theories. Solon composed a poem of five thousand hexameters and wondered whether he should publish his laws in prose or verse.

coloration of a Goncourt? Even linguistic harmony has sought refuge in prose writers. No one would dare deny that Campoamor has a fecund and varied talent, though he usually poetizes in metaphysical terms and practices metaphysics in poetry. But pick up *Madame Bovary* or *Salammbô* after reading the *Doloras* or the *Pequeños poemas*, and then decide in which of these texts there's a more harmonious style, and whether the verses of the Castilian poet is equal to the prose of the French novelist.

The main defect of the poets, what most alienates them from the reader, is that they do not enter fully into the rhythm and flow of the times, that they drag and bump along while the world flies by, that they would rather regress than move forward. If we depicted humanity as an army advancing in a forced march, our modern troubadors would be the ones lagging behind. What is it that they generally glorify? Today it's the Catholic religion (or call it error confirmed behind the walls of a church), and tomorrow it will be country (call it egotism embodied in a geographical denomination). Rarely do they soar free or high enough to discern in scientific truth the only religion worthy of elite minds or to recognize in the universe the only country worthy of civilized men. Because religious or ecclesiastical poetry never goes beyond rhymed sermons or theology in full rhyme, and because patriotic or official poetry is little more than glossed politics or editorials in verse, how languid, how insufferable, how soporific the rambling of our true believers and patriots!

A king of Persia had been told he was destined to die of a yawn, and since according to the proverb people yawn when they're sleepy, hungry, or bored, the courtiers watched over him to make sure he went to bed early, ate well at mealtime, and was always surrounded by merry, amusing people. The very first thing they did was to remove from the royal library all the books on jurisprudence, ethics, and theology. Thanks to this enlightened hygienic system, the king lived for half a century and seemed likely to live to a hundred. Unfortunately, when he least expected it he found himself alone in the company of a stranger who begged him to listen to a reading of a classical tragedy, in verse, five acts, and its two unities of time and place. Who doesn't comply when begged? The king agrees and lends an ear; but before the reading of the first scene is concluded, he yawns and dies.

It's understandable these days that some men start to tremble at the mere sight of a book of verse, especially if it's in Spanish. Almost all South American and Spanish poets breathe in a medieval atmosphere, like living anachronisms. Instead of emanating nectar and ambrosia, they smell like incense and gunpowder or, worse, like the dampness of a crypt or the stale smell of a barracks.

And it's even worse: since in their minds brilliant versification makes up for the lack of images and ideas, they sound hollow, as if their souls were nothing but air and had the consistency of a balloon. Some, those who hold the record, toss off silly, hybrid compositions in which they fuse patriotism with idolatry, putting the helmet of Mars on Jesus, Pallas Athena's shield on the Virgin Mary. So even if the poets have stopped murdering us with classical tragedies, they continue to put us to sleep with religious hymns and national anthems.

The failure of Spanish poetry translated into other languages or, more precisely, the impossibility of making them accessible and popular among sophisticated Europeans, is less a function of inflated, bombastic language than of their regional, provincial spirit. In its hatred of foreigners and its love of religious traditions, the Spanish nation bears a close resemblance to the ancient people of Israel. In Castilian poetry you can hear the noisy drumming of a sect or a party, but you can't feel the beating heart of humanity.

II

When someone called the poetry of the future *The Song of Reason*, he expressed quite clearly that the poet and the believer would not go on being mixed in the same mold. Even if there is a category of reason that's deistic and pious, there's also a reason that's irreligious and atheistic. The men of antiquity didn't stop singing hymns to religion when they glorified nature because at that time the human and the divine marched along inseparably united, knowledge and superstition forming a kind of indistinct and formless whole. In Greece there was no unbreachable abyss between heaven and earth, nor did the Creator crush his creatures under the weight of the infinite. The gods were like gigantic projections of man on high.[3] Since humanity was divine and the

---

[3] An image repeated in *Jesucristo y su doctrina*, p. 33—Editor.

divinity human, when people glorified the divine in song, they also glorified the human.

It's not like that today, for an irremediable schism has come about: on one side knowledge, on the other superstition. Man's place in creation and the earth's place in the universe have been established. When we regress to religious poetry, confusing the human with the divine and truth with falsehood, we try to unify what has been made separate, attempting an inverse evolution. At times, this leads to impiety and heresy. According to Tolstoy, art seeks to communicate to men the sentiments felt by the artist, and since the highest and most noble features of an epoch are preserved in religion, true art and, consequently, true poetry should glorify religious feelings. But it should be noted that Tolstoy did not profess Roman Catholicism or Greek Orthodoxy, but a kind of disinfected Christianity, an altruistic, humanitarian deism. An irreligious religion, without dogmas or cult.

Catholicism has already bloomed, has already proffered its fruit in the intellectual and moral order; its mission now completed, it only has the right to its page in the history of religions. Even if a Catholic Homer or a Catholic Vergil were to appear tomorrow, we doubt if they could bring about the miracle of resuscitating those wornout dogmas or injecting new virility into those puerile legends. They would achieve little with the brillance of their images and the pomp of their versification: the void of meaning would clash with the beauty of form. Vermillion and ceruse can lend the cadaver the physiognomy of a living person; nothing can falsify the fire of a gaze or the beating of a heart.

Must poetry that is negative or skeptical be accused of sterility? Must inspiration be ineluctably linked, if not to the dogmas of Catholicism, then at least to a faith in the immortality of the soul and the existence of a supreme being? Ask Lucretius, Shelley, Leopardi, and Vigny whether inspiration leaves a man just because he denies or doubts life everlasting. As long as we practice fairness and goodness, whether we admit or reject the immortality of the soul, we can still write excellent poetry, whether we put our faith in the effectiveness of providence or see in nature "an oblivious cause that never hears us and never answers us."

We stand before the universe like a child on the shores of the ocean: we observe certain phenomena and discover certain laws, without embracing the whole or ascertaining the supreme law, in the same way that a child plays with the peaks of foam without comprehending the profundity or extension of the waters. Not knowing why we've come or why we're going away, we struggle to know, redoubling the activities of the soul. If we could tear away the darkness of the cradle and tomb, we would cut short the wings of conjecture and hypothesis and swing monotonously back and forth like a pendulum between two lights. Doubt and uncertainty provide our imagination with limitless space to evolve. When we doubt, we affirm our personality, we grow, we feel more like men. Doubt lays a seal of virility on our thinking; woman and child believe, man doubts. And what value or meaning does thinking have if doubt is eliminated from our mind?

A kind of melancholy, serene, stoic poetry springs from submissive but skeptical minds; from rebels and contraries, a bitter, despairing, and bellicose inspiration. The most famous passages from anthologies, the verses that shine brightest in the poetic treasury of humanity, are steeped in negation and doubt, not in mystical vapors or dogmatic deliquescences. Compare the Catholicism of a Zorrilla with the irreligiosity of a Quintana, the skepticism of an Espronceda with the faith of a Laprade. You could even say that the very same poet grows languid and anemic when he enters the religious sphere: he continues to fly, but with lead in his wings. In Leconte de Lisle of *La Passion* we hardly recognize the Leconte de Lisle of *Midi*. And what could be more natural: an antiquated belief in a modern man is like a tropical tree in a northern greenhouse.

III

If faith depresses genius, neither does patriotism uplift character.

A man enclosed in the circle of a country lives morally alone, and isolation converts the poet's song into a voice crying out in the desert. Anyone who speaks of himself, his family, or his nation deserves a limited audience; but anyone who speaks in the name of humanity has the right to be heard by all. If Valmiki, Homer, Shakespeare, Goethe, and Lamartine figure among the universal geniuses for excellence, it isn't because they glorified exclusively Hindustan, Greece, England, Germany, or France. They struck humanity's most sensitive chord, and all men responded. Despite different languages, different nationalities, and the passage of years, we live in Valmiki's Rama, in Homer's Hector, in Shakespeare's Hamlet, in Goethe's Faust, and in Lamartine's Jocelyn. Who could live in the bellicose outbursts of writers like Tyrtaeus, Arndt, Gallego, Prati, or Déroulède?

A person who loves his nation more than all other nations is likely to love his village more than his nation, his neighborhood more than his village, his home more than his neighborhood, and his bedroom more than the rest of his house. The next step is to convert his ego into the center of creation. In this excessive love of country there is something contrary to our sense of generosity and abnegation, an undercurrent of secular fanaticism that is as absurd and narrow as religious fanaticism. Killing for a shield and a flag or killing for a cross or a half-moon are the same. Yet we don't see it. Hypnotized by classical traditions and chivalric legends, we accept crimes committed in the name of Roman brutality and feudal barbarism as heroic actions, worthy of imitation.

People of true distinction, true supermen, are guided by love and justice, while the unconscious majority of peoples acknowledge no other god or king than selfishness and force of arms. A mind abject enough to limit its evolution to a swath of land is often matched with a heart hard enough to see an enemy in the man who speaks a different language, professes another religion, or comes from a different country. If a wild beast is asleep within each man, the surest way to awaken that beast and set it in a frenzy is to whisper in his ear the name of his country. The grand virtue of the masses, the grandeur of those who have no greatness of soul, is concentrated in their patriotism.

The peaceful love of a plot of ground and a shack, or a village and a house, which we might call an innocent or passive patriotism, reminds us of the adhesion of the mole to its molehill, of the mollusk to its rock, of the infusorium to its drop of water. Regressive, war-mongering patriotism, that incarnation of the troglodyte in the man of today, isn't limited to less civilized nations; it flourishes with equal intensity in the desire of the Englishman to conquer the Boer, of the Spaniard to re-conquer the Cuban, of the German to mangle the Frenchman, in the Yankee to enslave the Filipino, in the Russian to oppress the Finn, and in the Turk to exterminate the Armenian. When the emperor of Germany orders his soldiers in China to give no quarter to children, women, or old men, he is merely expressing the sentiments that germinate in the hearts of good patriots. Like Zola's La Mouquette, Wilhelm II reveals what others conceal.

If popular poetry reflects the sentiments of the masses, national or patriotic poetry usually favors the interests of a party, a faction, or a man. Anyone who exalts individual and collective egotism under the rubric of love of country, or celebrates the apotheosis of brutes and scoundrels in the name of glory, usually ends up becoming the Homer of a party, the Vergil of a faction, or the Dante of a powerful nobleman. Behold Déroulède in France, Carducci in Italy.

The national anthems and patriotic odes of South American bards are generally nothing more than exercises in rhetoric, *all shrill notes, no harmonics.* If the Spanish had triumphed in Junín and Ayacucho, we would have "Iberian lions" clawing at "Andean condors," instead of "gods of freedom" stomping the "throat of tyranny." Bello, before he started deifying the heroes of the independence, had already burned incense to Carlos IV and his favorite, Godoy; Olmedo, before writing his *Song to Junín,* had called the same Carlos IV and María Luisa the beloved monarchs, mother and father, gods of Spain. Happily, the most famous warrior poets are gradually falling into oblivion, and within a few years they'll belong to paleontology, like the vertebra of a mastodon or the jaw of a megatherian.

There's nothing quite so nauseating as Alfred Austin celebrating *Jameson's Raid,* or Kipling and Swinburne turning themselves into the Apollos of Roberts, Cecil Rhodes, and the English rabble. "Strike, strike bravely!" exclaimed the "radical" Swinburne, like some redskin, kaffir, or Wilhelm II. Do you think Milton, Shelley, or Byron would ever have written poetry like that? The poet of a civilized nation has an obligation to substitute the country of mountains, fields, and rivers with the country of ideas and sentiments—to proclaim that our true brothers are not those who share the same nationality, but all who fight for truth and justice. When the popular masses roar for their neighbor's flesh or purse, the true poet becomes beastmaster, takes whip and iron in hand to restrain the wild animal.

IV

How do we fortify and renew anemic, wornout poetry? By administering a kind of scientific inoculation.

I'm not suggesting that poets should set atmospheric changes to royal octaves or express diagnoses of fever in five-verse paired stanzas, parodying the versifiers who set down in rhyme *The Genius of Christianity* or *Democracy in America,* but they should observe nature, live it, and sing it, without going so far as to say, like Núñez de Arce, that the Indian fig grows in his branches, or like Zorrilla that lilies have communion cups, or like Felipe Pardo that mines produce bronze, or like Néstor Galindo that gazelles spread their wings. In technical works the light comes to us directly; in works of the imagination, more diffusely. What Guyau said about the novel also applies to poetry; though it isn't the same as a book of science a collection of verses should manifest the scientific spirit. The poet can be didactic, not to popularize the specific laws of a science, but to enunciate through rhythm and image the general conclusions of human knowledge. The singer worthy of his epoch ascends to what is most excellent in order to demonstrate how far men have climbed in their ascent toward truth. He constructs a bridge from the light into the darkness.

No poetry will never acknowledge ignorance as her mother. The appearance or efflorescence of masterworks coincides with the apogee of civilization. Progress should be plotted by a series of parallel lines: the lines of the philosopher, the scientist, the moralist, or the industrialist should be paralleled by the artist. No Valmiki, Firdusi, Homer, Dante, or Byron ever sprang forth spontaneously from an ignorant, barbaric people. No matter how much genius a man born into a rudimentary civilization might have, he would lack the materials to conceive and achieve an *Iliad* and a *Prometheus*: he would lack the language, which is a product of advanced civilizations. As the Nile is called the father of Egypt, the great poets are Egyptians who owe their existence to the powerful river of knowledge and the traditions.

Science, like a colossal explosion of light, reveals summits hidden by shadow and accentuates profiles veiled by mist. With its advent, the vague becomes distinct, the darkness becomes light, the hidden is made manifest. Then man is no longer perceived as a unique and privileged being, but as one among the many animal species; then the earth is no longer perceived as the center of the universe, but as a mere grain of dust in the vortex of worlds. Along with an amplified concept of nature comes the feeling of solidarity, and the animal struggle for existence is transformed into the humane affirmation of life.

Art becomes new and grand. The symbolism exhumed from mythology is transformed into the metaphor inspired by the *marvelous positive*, and the imagination, once regarded as the madwoman of the house, becomes wingéd reason. When the intimate relationships between things are revealed, rhetorical figures burst forth, expanding the poetic horizon. Versification, disdaining onomatopoeia and all the other senile puerilities, conforms the rhythm of the word to the silent rhythm of the idea. Language, far from becoming enslaved to rhyme or petrifying in archaism, flies free and modernized, rejecting the dictates of official academies and recognizing no authority but usage. We only have to study the verbal renewal brought about by the works of Comte, Darwin, and Spencer to be convinced that languages owe more to philosophers and scientists than to scholars and grammarians.

Is there a greater store of poetic treasure anywhere than in observation and experiment? More beautiful things take place in a chemist's retort and under a physicist's microscope than in the mind of innumerable poets. To see a sun turn to crystal or air to liquid tells us more than the reading of countless odes and the performance of countless plays. Herschel deciphering the nebulae, Haeckel filling the gaps in organic evolution, Pasteur observing microbes, Charcot hypnotizing hysterics, Trousseau writing down the symptoms of his own death, and Claude Bernard detecting the first heartbeats of a pullet *create* more poetry than the authors of all the *Evangelical Legends* and all the *Soldier's Songs*.

The divergence between Plato and Aristotle in their assessment of poetry is even now being renewed between philosophers and writers. While the versifiers and pseudoscholars divorce the poet from the scientist and even affirm the incompatibility of art with science, the artists and scientists think just the opposite. "Study science first," says Leonardo da Vinci, "and then adhere to the art born of it."[4] "As for me," exclaims Claude Bernard, "I do not believe in the possibility of such a contradiction. Since the truth can never be differentiated from itself, the truth of the scientist can never contradict the truth of the artist. Rather, I believe that science poured from a pure spring will become more luminous for everyone and that in all areas science and art will

---

[4] *Marginal note by the author:* "Il n'y a, d'ailleurs, aucune incompatibilité entre l'exacte et le poétique. Le nombre est dans l'Art comme dans la Science."—Victor Hugo.

clasp hands, interpreting and explaining one another reciprocally." We see, then, that if a little knowledge takes us away from poetry, great knowledge brings us back.

In summary, the poet who wants to march in the vanguard of civilization and not seem retarded or backward will need a heart generous enough to beat for humanity, a mind enlightened enough to be guided by the scientific philosopy of our century.

A Moment of Philosophy[1]

(1884–88)

I

Lessing said that "in certain centuries the label 'heretic' implies the highest recommendation of a wise man to posterity."[2] We could make a similar statement concerning the skeptic. Instead of judging him to be inconsistent and frivolous, let's regard him as a serene and thoughtful spirit who, not seeing sufficient proofs to deny or affirm, maintains a balance. His condition mirrors the state of balance in the man of faith.

Skepticism does not signify absolute negation, but rather a triple series of affirmations: affirmation of *pros,* affirmation of *cons,* and affirmation of the equality between contrary arguments. To avoid deception, what could be saner than to suspend judgment? Where irrefutable proofs are lacking, prudence lies in doubting. Doubt represents the most luminous state of the soul, the state in which all sides receive different lights without being dazzled by any single light. However, for ordinary intellectuals, the man who neither affirms nor denies is an Achilles with two vulnerable heels.

If skepticism served as a refuge for thinkers who weren't hallucinated

---

[1] An unpublished and unfinished essay, probably written between 1884 and 1888.—Editor

[2] The same quotation appears in *Catolicismo y Ciencia,* p. 56.—Editor

by the prejudices or errors of their time, is there any reason to condemn the skeptic for his doubts? No, just as there's no reason to scorn the believer for his faith. The individual doesn't doubt or affirm because he wants to, but because the environment and his cast of mind induce him to believe or not believe. Depending on the circumstances, we think one way or another just as we sweat at the equator and shiver at the poles. We become believers or are born believers in the same way we become fat or are born with blond hair. To tell a skeptic: *have faith*, is as silly as telling a bird: *be an elephant*.

Only a fanatic draws a dividing line to judge the proponents of a doctrine as good and worthy of respect, and those defending the opposite as evil and despicable. The belief in absurdity and falsehood does not imply bad faith on the part of the believer, nor do we deduce the truth of a martyr's belief from his martyrdom: apostles, martyrs, and saints abound in even the most grotesque and inverisimilar of religions.

Just as a man can attain heroic stature or sainthood believing in falsehoods and committing unjust acts, it should also be accepted that moral perfection doesn't depend on possessing the truth or forming a precise concept of justice, but on professing what we believe to be true and doing what we believe to be just. A person who kills in the conviction that the killing will result in good exceeds in morality someone who distributes alms believing that the good deed will cause harm.

The man of good faith isn't recognized for his tenacity in embracing received ideas or his systematic rejection of all innovations in the interpretation of the laws of the universe; he's recognized by the logic of his actions or by the harmony he achieves between his exterior life and his inner life. Any suspicion of bad faith vanishes when actions constitute a materialization of principles. If a Turk dies to sustain a belief from one of the chapters of the Qur'an and a Christian dies to defend the opposite belief from a verse in the Gospel, they could both be wrong. But certainly neither of them is operating in bad faith.

Since there are no indisputable proofs except in mathematics, all other sciences being an accumulation of provisional truths or a series of approximate concepts, we ought to regard our convictions as a simple garment we wear today but may change tomorrow for one that fits better or is more befitting to our station in life.[3] We don't accept an

---

[3] He expresses a similar thought in *Los Viejos*, p. 113.—Editor.

inheritance without an inventory; let's not go on professing yesterday's ideas without subjecting them to a new analysis: our mental life should be subjected to a perennial adjustment of perspectives.

If creatures and things change constantly, if the universe is nothing but perpetual motion, is it fitting that our minds should be emptied into a fixed mold and remain forever unchanged? We possess some 60 trillion cells that are constantly acting and reacting among themselves. What room is there for motionlessness if the appearance or disappearance of cells produces a change throughout the organism? If our soul isn't like a traveler who has taken lodging in the inn of the body, but rather a product of innumerable contingent, multiple, mutable forces, it has to change with the alteration of each force. It has been said that the displacement of a single drop of water in the sea has a repercussion in the disk of the most distant star. Won't the functions of our brain change, then, as each one of our 60 trillion cells is transformed?

The identity of the individual? A chimera: we don't possess a unique soul, but a series of souls; we aren't one identical man, but many successive men.[4] In the depths of our being, we've all seen many personalities come to life and die: we all represent a long chain of diverse and even contradictory individuals. One personality is born today where others died yesterday: each one of us could be precisely portrayed by a cradle surrounded by graves.[5] Let's study ourselves, let's evoke the past, and we'll conclude that we live as far removed from our personality of ten or fifteen years ago as from the passerby we glimpse in the street. We don't have and don't want to have any individuality other than the present; we don't answer today for what we did yesterday, nor will we answer tomorrow for what we do today. Today we answer for today, tomorrow we'll answer for tomorrow. So there's nothing more unfair than the punishments reserved in eternity for those who sin in life. In one the guilt of another is being punished.

[4] *Marginal note by the author:* A self is a state of the soul, and in the course of life there aren't two equal souls.

[5] *Marginal note by the author:* Let's attend our own evolution and observe the transformations of our own being. Far from being saddened by what we feel dying, let's rejoice over what we see being born, considering that what has died leaves us the sweetness of its memory and what is born offers us the pleasure of novelty.

II

When we consider the blind determinism of nature and see that when an evil man slanders us or stabs us with a dagger he's displaying the same irresponsibility as the viper injecting its poison into us or the stone crushing our skull, then we understand the insanity of harboring grudges and the unfairness of acts of revenge.[6] An aura of ineffable pity and infinite forgiveness soothes the fury of the human animal.[7] Serenely, we witness the spectacle of the universe, without wallowing in the tragic pessimism of Schopenhauer or Hartmann or falling into the foolish optimism of imagining that the divinity causes rivers to pass through the center of cities or provides us with melons cut into slices so the family can eat them more easily.[8] Disavowing every human prejudice, elevating ourselves to the serene contemplation of things, we glimpse horizons of unexpected clarity. The higher and farther we look, the more clearly we see. We see that our political and religious systems are as valuable as candelabras in a marsh; we see that humankind is like a cloud of insects suddenly swarming up in a forest, drinking in their share of sunshine, flitting their wings, and then vanishing.

It's important to insist on such concepts as nature and humankind in order to do away with dogmatism and permit a spirit of mildness and tolerance to take root in human hearts. Why should our truth alone be the true? We're like the child sticking his hand into a sack in which

[6] *Marginal note by the author:* Perhaps there are no good or bad creatures, but only organisms that function blindly; there are no crimes or virtues, only acts that are amoral or that stem from ineluctable laws.

[7] *Marginal note by the author:* Let's be compassionate and merciful, even though the life of a man is as valuable as the life of a microbe.

[8] Two independent notes appear in the margin of this paragraph:

First marginal note by the author: If fleas argued the way some philosophers do, they would deduce that men were created for them alone, since they find in us the blood to nourish themselves, warmth to keep them comfortable, and nooks and crannies for shelter.

Second marginal note by the author: We shouldn't confuse a clairvoyant, healthy skepticism with a sickly, blind pessimism; pessimism, like optimism, is marred by the serious inconvenience of being a categorical affirmation. We cannot label existence a good or an evil because we don't know whether nature is following a plan or whether said plan . . . as a necessary condition the . . . [illegible in manuscript] of good and evil.

there's a gold ball and ninety-nine copper ones. How can we be sure the child will pull out the gold ball? *What is truth?* Pilate asked Jesus. What is truth? we ask the dogmatics who adore one doctrine and condemn the rest. The mouths sealed by the hands of sectarians may well have been destined to enunciate some redeeming idea.

Our refusal to declare ourselves infallible, or to impose our convictions, implies a concomitant refusal to subject ourselves to the convictions of others or to acknowledge individual or collective authorities: what we grant others, we claim for ourselves. Neither sacred laws nor infallible sovereignties. Even if certain select beings reached the summit of wisdom, we would deny them the right to impose *their truth* on those who sincerely persist in their error: our ignorance deserves as much respect as the wisdom of Solomon, our person demands the same consideration as the person of the czar or the supreme pontiff.[9]

When we step outside the realm of mathematical demonstrations or abandon experimentation and observation, we begin to theologize. And who among us doesn't theologize from time to time? Theologians no longer speak Latin only, but also English, French, or German. At times, Büchner and Haeckel leave Saint Augustine and Saint Thomas Aquinas behind. To deny the existence of God and the immortality of the soul is equivalent to sustaining the idea of redemption or the Eucharist. When the materialist decides categorically, "without brain and phosphorous there is no thought," he proves to be less of a philosopher and more of a theologian than the poet when he murmurs: "there are more things in heaven and earth than those dreamed by your philosophy."[10]

We don't see realities but appearances. We glimpse the universe through our senses: "Nothing is either true or false; everything is what it is because of the color of the glass through which we look at it,"

---

[9] *Marginal note by the author:* In recognizing the fallibility of religious creeds and political and philosophical systems, we posit absolute independence in the search for truth.

[10] *Marginal note by the author:* And what basis shall we use to come to any conclusion? In the presence of the universe we are little more or less than spectators in a theater, where we don't hear the voice of all the actors or understand the language of those we *do* hear. Do we know what the plant or animal say? Do we know what the grain of sand says or the molecule inside a stone? The infusiorium in the drop of water or the bacterium in the globule of blood have as much right to boast of their knowledge of the universe as we men on the surface of the earth.

exclaimed Campoamor, the great poet of the *Doloras*. True. But the appearance of everything also depends on the constitution of the eye that beholds it. If we were to acquire a wondrous visual power, our psychology and our concept of the world would change radically. The purest waters and the most beautiful faces would cause us repugnance and horror. Thus, for men there may be no definitive concept of the universe, no eternal truth: today's truths can become errors, just as many of the truths of yesterday are becoming errors today. So we have to love our truth as we love a bird that's bound to fly away, a crystal that will inevitably break, or a flower doomed to wither and die.

Will we abandon ourselves to inaction and discouragement? If we possessed the seed of a tree that would only bear fruit a hundred years after being born, we should sow it with the hope of harvesting the fruit;[11] if happiness were the shadow of a bird that never comes down to earth, we ought to pursue the shadow with the hope of catching the bird. Not eating the fruit, we anticipate the pleasure of eating it tomorrow; not attaining happiness, we have the joy of seeking it. And who's to tell us that the desire is not worth more than the possession? Let's suppose that in the blind determinism of nature we enjoyed greater freedom; let's also imagine that the intervention of our will influences the action of the cosmic forces and that we can accelerate the slow, majestic movement of nature, which is heading we know not where. No one blamed the ant who rode on the horns of an ox and then boasted of having plowed the field.[12] Let's practice autosuggestion until we think we're tasting honey when we eat bitter aloe. Let's fight for our current convictions and even give up our lives for them, but not without harboring in some intimate part of our soul a smiling skepticism, never forgetting that we may be fighting for an illusion or sacrificing ourselves for something foolish. Grand faith requires a dose of simplicity or naïveté. But since nothing good is ever achieved without a miracle of credulity, let's make ourselves believe we believe in something.

---

[11] A thought repeated *in ¿Qué hacer?* p. 89.—Editor
[12] A phrase repeated in *Catolicismo y Ciencia*, p. 59.—Editor

IV

Diogenes' Cask

Our Mother[1]

(1896–98)

Situated at one end of the Continent, fused to the Pyrenees the way the appendix adheres to the trunk, Spain lives breathing in the digestive exhalations of the French stomach. Germany smells like gunpowder, England like coal, the United States like oil and printer's ink, but Spain smells of mold, incense, and fried olive oil.[2]

What was its penultimate king? A satyr born of the union of a tabula rasa and a cretinoid. Alphonso XII died young, undermined by his pathological ancestral stock and his vices, but he had time to marry twice and to leave an heir who conjoined in his veins the rancid aqueous humor of the Borbonnes and the pale red cells of the Austrians.[3]

What are Spanish politicians? An incoherent pullulation of those marching band noisemakers the Chinese call shadows. In parliament,

---

[1] Upublished and unfinished article, written during González Prada's residence in Spain (1896–1898), but with numerous changes and additions from later periods. It has three different titles in the manuscript: Poor Spain, Marrying Grandmother, and Our Mother. We speculate that the latter is preferred by the author, since it also appears in an index. The idea for the second title probably served González Prada in composing Epigram 14 of *Nótulas de viaje (primera parte)* in *Grafitos.*—A.G.P.

[2] *Marginal note by the author:* As the coccyx is an atrophied tail, Spain is a residue of a nation.

[3] *Marginal note by the author:* Alfonso XIII, mated with a woman of mixed English and Jewish blood, spent all his time shooting pigeons and propagating the race of syphilitic, tubercular cretinoids.

you see on one side the shadow of a minister who pronounces the shadow of a speech to defend the shadow of a portfolio, and on the other side the shadow of a deputy attacking the shadow of a government to acquire a shadow of power and smack his lips over the shadow of a budget.[4]

What are the Spanish literati? Litters of languorous retards who emit vapors from a prehistoric cave and whose heads are stuffed with antedeluvian incrustations. Castellar, with the naïveté of a child, thinks he's casting a golden statue[5] when he combines in the same crucible the pure metal of science and the dregs of the old theogonies; Menéndez y Pelayo converts his erudition into drugs and strips of linen to mummify the cadaver of his Catholic ideas; Campoamor imitates Siamese twins, muttering versified blasphemies with his left head and prose retractions or acts of contrition with his right; Núñez de Arce chants deep-sounding hymns to glorify the conventional lies of religion and politics, dig up moth-eaten memories, curse Voltaire, and flay Darwin. We only need to remind ourselves that the national poet of the Spaniards was and still is Zorrilla, that walking corpse, that unburied cadaver who opened his eyes every now and then to confuse the visions of his medieval mind with real beings. In Spain, the rare thinking or free men are asphyxiating and dying, like insects enclosed in the bell of a pneumatic pump.[6]

What are the Spanish people? A community of untonsured monks who have hidden their habits. From the academician to the street tough they all wear a cassock between their shirts and their skin. Because just a few provinces sweat and strain so the others can eat and lie around, the best symbol of Spain would be a serpent eating its own tail. The Spaniard takes his siesta after lunch, gets tired of resting, and then rests some more from having rested. He doesn't work in summer because of the heat, in winter because of the cold, nor in spring or autumn because they are unhealthy, in-between seasons. In his zeal for the Dog Star, every self-respecting son of the Cid goes around cloaked in a huge cape that shelters him as well as his mount. You should know that when a good Spaniard orders a cape made, he climbs on his mule so the tailor

---

[4] *Marginal note by the author:* A macabre dance in which the skeletons display enormous long fingernails like those of Chinese mandarins.

[5] *Variant:* "thinks he's discovering the philosopher's stone, when he combines . . ."

[6] *Marginal note by the author:* Academics who know only half of the grammar, i.e., the gram.

can take *double measurements*. (And he's quite right to do so because the mule is more useful than the steam engine or electricity. When you send a telegraph from any Spanish city, you send a note by train to alert them that the message is on its way, and when the train departs, you send a mule to announce that the train has left.) Spaniards of good stock treat their wives like neighbor's wives, Vizcayan donkeys like peasants, applaud Frascuelo and hiss at Pi y Margall, anxiously await the return of don Carlos, and eat codfish on Fridays. But they're still capable of blandishing a razor. "Here," says Demophilus referring to Spain, "the passions are in such a primitive state that they can't be satisfied except with death." For a glass of wine, for a mere glance, for a harsh-sounding word, they'll pull out a razor and bury it up to the handle in a fit of maniacal rage. There are no gradations to the penalty. Beneath the skin of even the most learned Spaniard, you can see the horns of a bull from the Jarama, ready to charge at the slightest insult.[7]

According to the spontaneous confession of a writer from Madrid, Spaniards, from fighting bulls so long, have turned into yearling bulls.[8]

---

[7] *Las Dominicales del Libre Pensamiento,* Madrid, December 17, 1887. *Demophilus* was the pseudonym of don Fernando Lozano.—A.G.P.

[8] The following notes appear on the last page of the manuscript:

First marginal note by the author: The Spaniard's most serious defect is aggressiveness. Like all primitive men, he reacts immediately and thinks later.

Second marginal note by the author: Things original to Spain are the young woman with her Manila shawl slung diagonally across her face, the tough from Albacete slashing with his razor, the Alhambra crumbling, the Megatherium held up with iron hooks, the Castilian sun causing fever everywhere it shines, and the wind off the Guadarrama giving everyone pneumonia. Praying and blaspheming, Spaniards seem to have been born in the incubus of Santa Teresa and the devil, when actually they are the sons of Sancho Panza and Maritornes or of Don Quixote and the Holy Virgin. When you leave France and enter Spain, either through Hendaye or Port-Bou, the first thought that crosses your mind, after speaking with two or three individuals, is that the Spaniard has a thick head. The Frenchman, even if he doesn't understand a word of the language we're speaking, understands us or, more precisely, he figures out what we mean. The Spaniard, even if we speak to him as clearly as a member of the Spanish Academy, doesn't understand us at all or only half of what we say. When you deal with him, you get the urge to drill holes in his head and pour the words in, the way you lard meat into tripe.

Third marginal note by the author: The *summum* of national aspirations in economic terms would be to go back to the convent soup line.

Fourth marginal note by the author: A country where the traveler sees fifteen readers in the Biblioteca Real and fifteen thousand spectators in the *plaza de toros*.

V

Anarchy

Anarchy

(1907)

If we ask a *serious person* what he understands by anarchy, he will tell us, like one answering a question from the catechism: Anarchy is social dislocation, a permanent state of war, the return of man to primitive savagery. He will call the anarchist a sworn enemy of the life and property of others, an evil spirit obsessed by a universal and destructive phobia, a kind of feline demon wandering lost in the heart of cities. For many people, the anarchist sums up his ideals by doing evil for the pleasure of doing it.

It isn't only serious people of little learning who have that childish way of seeing things. Enlightened men, who on other subjects carry on a lucid, balanced discourse, become pitiably nonsensical when they start talking about anarchy and anarchists. They go the way of the holy fathers in their dealings with heresies and heretics. Lombroso and Le Bon remind us of Tertulian and Saint Jerome. The author of *El hombre criminal*—didn't he go so far as to suggest that anarchists should be handed over to the mobs, that is, subjected to the law of lynch? There are plenty of secular Torquemadas, every bit as ferocious and terrible as the priests.

Anyone who judges anarchy by Bresci's revolver, Caserio's dagger, and Ravachol's bombs is no different than those run-of-the-mill free-thinkers who judge Christianity by the Inquisition's autos-da-fé and the musket shots of Sainte-Barthélemy. To measure the extent to which enemies will go in heaping insults on their enemies, we might think of the Pagans and Christians of the first centuries mutually accusing each other of being assassins, arsonists, lechers, dabblers in incest, corruptors of the young, homosexuals, enemies of the empire, blemish on the human race, and so on. Carthage historied by Rome, Athens by Sparta: these will give you an idea of anarchy judged by its adversaries. Our contemporaries give the same impression in their political and religious controversies. If for the radical socialist a monarchist represents an indictable criminal, for the monarchist a radical socialist deserves the gallows. For the Anglican, there's no one quite as depraved as the papist; for the Roman Catholic, no one is as deserving of abomination as the Anglican. To affirm in political or religious debates that a man is an imbecil or evil simply means that that man doesn't think as we do.

Anarchy and anarchist signify the opposite of what their detractors charge. The anarchist ideal could be summed up in two lines: unlimited freedom and the greatest possible good for the individual, with the abolition of the state and private property. If the anarchist is to be condemned for anything, let it be for his optimism and his trust in the inborn goodness of man. The anarchist, expanding on the Christian idea, sees in each man a brother—not an inferior, destitute brother in need of charity, but an equal brother in need of justice, protection, and defense. He rejects charity as a hypocritical falsification of justice, a bloody irony, an abject and demeaning gift from the usurper to the usurped. He acknowledges no sovereignty of any kind or under any form, not even excluding the most absurd of all: that of the people or the country. He rejects laws, religions, and nationalities, acknowledging one single power: the individual. A person subject to a king or a pontiff is as much a slave as one enfeoffed to the mob of plebiscites or to a parliamentary majority. Authority implies abuse and obedience manifests abjectness of spirit because the truly emancipated man does not aspire to dominion over his equals nor does he accept any other authority than that of a person over himself.

Yet, that doctrine of love and kindness, that exquisite sublimation of humanitarian ideas, seems to many writers to be designed as a school for evil, a glorification of hatred and crime, even as the sick product of unbalanced minds. There are even some who equate anarchist with borderline psychopath. But is there nothing but insanity, crime, and hatred in the doctrine professed by a Reclus, a Kropotkin, a Faure, and a Grave? Anarchy did not emerge from the proletariat as an explosion of rage or a simple desire for vengeance on behalf of a single class. Calmly elaborated by men born outside the popular masses, it comes from above, without, however, conceding to its initiators the right to constitute an elite with the mission of illuminating and ruling the rest of mankind. Select natures, trees with lofty crests, produced that fruit of salvation.

Anarchy shouldn't be thought of as an empirical idea or a simplistic and unscientific conception of societies. It doesn't reject Comtian positivism; it accepts it, stripping it of the God-humanity and the educational priesthood, that is, any semitheological, neo-Catholic residue. Auguste Comte improves on Descartes, amplifies Condillac, steadies the compass of Claude Bernard, and serves as an advance corrective to the Bergsons of the past or still to be born. If Darwinism poorly understood seemed to justify the domination of the strong and a despotic imperialism, understood clearly it comes to humanitarian conclusions, recognizing the powerful influence of mutual aid, the right of the weak to their existence, and the reality of the individual in counterpoint to some vague metaphysical concept of species. Science has its own anarchist affirmations, and humanity tends to orient itself in the direction of anarchy.

There are periods in which certain ideas float to the surface, become part of the atmosphere, and pervade the organisms most resistant to receiving them. Even Spencer, even that great apostle of conservative and antirevolutionary evolution, has flashes of anarchy. Now and then, even the representatives of official (university) enlightenment come up with ideas so audacious, they seem taken from a Bakunin or a Proudhon. A professor from the University of Burdeos, Duguit, has no qualms about asserting: "I think a new society is in the making, one which is going to reject equally the idea of the right of the community to control the individual and the idea of the right of an individual to impose his personality on the collectivity of other individuals" (*Las transformaciones del Estado,* translated by A. Posada).

This doesn't mean we're on the verge of establishing an anarchist society. Between setting out and arriving there are empires in ruins, lakes of blood, and mountains of victims. A new Christianity is born, without Christ but not without its persecutors and its martyrs. And if the world could not be Christianized in twenty centuries, how long will it take to be anarchized?

Anarchy is the luminous, distant point toward which we are heading through an intricate series of falling and rising curves. Even if the luminous point were moving away as we move toward it, and even if the establishment of an anarchist society were no more than a philanthropist's dream, we would still have the great satisfaction of having dreamed it. Would that men always had such beautiful dreams!

The Universal Holiday

(1905)

May 1 is for humanity what December 25 is for the Christian world: a date of joy, hope, and regeneration.

Christians celebrate the birth of a man who, without considering himself God, speaks in a way that they judge him divine: by calling himself the son of a father who probably doesn't exist, he comes to redeem us for a sin we surely didn't commit. According to history or legend, that man let himself be crucified for us, but the sacrifice doesn't do much good, considering that today most of humanity is condemned for not knowing the Christian guru or his teaching. A savior who could have saved us from hunger, giving us a simple recipe for transforming pebbles into bread and water into milk, would have done more than Jesus Christ with all the sermons and so-called miracles of the Gospels.

Today, revolutionaries greet tomorrow, the coming of an era in which the liberation of all oppressed peoples and the brotherhood of all races will be achieved. The believer and the atheist, the Muslim and the Jew, the Buddhist and the Hindu, as well people of black, yellow, and white skin, all human beings, in a word, have the right to come to rejoice, all are welcomed to take shelter beneath the folds of the red flag. Christians reserve heaven for some, hell for others; revolutionaries seek an earthly paradise where there'll be room for everyone, including their implacable enemies.

May 1 would be irrelevant, and could be confused with religious and patriotic holidays, if it did not signify the revolution of everyone to emancipate everyone. The revolution of one class to rise up and impose itself on all others would be nothing but a parody of earlier political convulsions.

It has been said and it continues to be repeated: the emancipation of the workers has to come from the workers themselves. We will add, in order to broaden the perspective of the social revolution and to humanize and universalize it: the emancipation of the working class must be simultaneous with the emancipation of all the other classes. It isn't just the worker who suffers from the iniquity of our laws, the vexations of power, and the tyranny of capital; all of us, to some extent, are mocked and exploited, we are all caught up in the immense tentacles of the state. Excluding the cloud of parasites swimming in luxury and luxuriating today without worrying about tomorrow, the masses struggle desperately to clothe their naked bodies and defeat hunger.

We are all under an obligation to offer our share of light and energy to help the worker throw off the capitalist yoke. The worker is also under an obligation to help other oppressed peoples destroy the chains of other masters and lords.

Men's instincts aren't transformed overnight by violent convulsions. With the guillotine you can cut off the heads of a few evil men; with laws and speeches or with stormy changes of leaders you can't change hearts. Each person has to heal and educate himself to be free of two equally abominable plagues: the habit of obedience and the desire to rule. If we have the souls of slaves or rulers, we move only toward slavery or tyranny.

That's why we believe that a revolution of workers alone, for the benefit of the workers alone, would lead to the same results as the insurrections of the praetorians and the political movements. Once the working class prevails and takes possession of the machinery of oppression, it will be transformed into a mandarin class of bourgeoisie as oppressive and selfish as the feudal lords and the modern dictators. There will be a regression to the caste system, with just one difference: a reversal in the order of the oppressed.

Whether we're workers or not, we all long for redemption, which could never come from the individualism taught by the economists or from multiform socialism, preached in a new way by each of its countless apostles. (It is important to remember that just as there isn't one religion but many religions, there isn't just one socialism but many socialisms.)

Can't we conceive of anything other than individualists and socialists? At some far remove from depressing socialism, which whatever its form is still a kind of slavery or an imitation of life in the monastery; and at some equally far remove from the selfish individualism that teaches: *let it be, just let things happen,* and *every man for himself, each man in his castle,* we can glimpse a distant peak on which is written a single word: *anarchy.*

The Responsibility of the Anarchist[1]

I

When we say anarchy, we say revolution.

There are two revolutions: one in the field of ideas and one on the field of action. Neither takes precedence over the other, since the word often reaches where the rifle cannot, and a book can demolish fortresses the cannon cannot. Voltaire, Diderot, and Rousseau are just as much revolutionaries as Mirabeau, Danton, and Robespierre. Luther does not take a back seat to Garibaldi, Comte to Bolívar, nor Darwin to Cromwell.

Consciously or unconsciously, the initiators of every political, social, religious, literary, or scientific revolution are paving the way for anarchy. By removing the errors or obstacles from the path, they facilitate the march of the individual toward complete emancipation, playing the role of anarchists without intending or even wanting to do so. Ampere, Stephenson, and Edison have achieved results no less liberating, with their discoveries, than Bakunin, Reclus, and Grave with their books. The Jesuits, thanks to their subliminal casuistry, have contributed to the dissolution of bourgeoise morality; and thanks to their theories on

[1] Unpublished.

tyrannicide, they justify the propaganda by the deed. Mariana has no reason to repudiate Bresci or Vaillant.

The absurd and classical dualism of theoretical versus practical man derives from the pernicious antagonism between the cerebral and the practical anarchist, when in fact all we have are two travelers heading toward the same place along converging roads. The pen is as much a tool as the hoe, the chisel, or the trowel; and if the working man uses muscle power, the writer uses mind power.

There's no use repeating that revolution in the field of ideas precedes revolution on the field of action. You can't harvest without sowing, you can't win converts without persuading them. The apostle precedes the martyr; the encyclopedist precedes the true believer; the meeting or club precedes the barricade. Trying to achieve radical reforms without having first proselytized, we run the risk of having no collaborators and lacking the power to control the inevitable and powerful reactions. Every unpremeditated advance leads to retreat. "There's only one worthwhile action," said Ibsen: "to revolutionize souls."

True, nothing would be better than a quick world revolution leading to the establishment of anarchy in a single day and without bloodshed or great devastation. But how likely is that? The instantaneous redemption of humanity could not be achieved except through two equally unachievable phenomena: the sudden emergence of a spirit of generosity in the hearts of the oppressors, compelling them to give up all their privileges, or an explosion of conscious energy in the minds of the oppressed, driving them to take back everything stolen by the oppressors.

The first is not conceivable in the hearts of beings suckled on class selfishness and accustomed to viewing others as mere machines of production. Isolated examples can be cited, individuals who freed their slaves, redistributed their wealth, and even gave up the throne in order to bury themselves in a cloister. But we know of no societies that through a sudden outburst of fairness and commiseration gave up all privilege and granted to the dispossessed the means to live in comfort and ease. After popular revolutions, winds of justice blow through the bosoms of the collectivity (blowing in particular through the legislatures, it is to be hoped), but the wind stops suddenly and those collectivities take back one at a time the privileges they gave up en bloc. Generally, they take back more than they gave up. Thus the French nobles and clergymen who so magnanimously renounced their privileges on August 4, didn't take long in coming to their senses and declaring themselves enemies of the revolution.

The second is also inconceivable. There are many, many anarchists scattered through the world: they work in solitude or in tiny groups; they don't always march in step and sometimes even fight against each other. But even if they joined together and tried to initiate a swift, worldwide revolution, they would lack the means to carry it out. Can we imagine London, Paris, Rome, Vienna, Berlin, St. Petersburg, and New York, suddenly transformed into anarchist populations? For that achievement, the most stupendous achievement in history, the necessary mass is lacking.

The masses, being a mixture of infantile and senile humanity, have the emotional maturity of a child and the lack of focus of the old. They go on believing in the phantoms of their imagination and deluding themselves with the promise of posthumous happiness. They inspire fear and mistrust by their fickleness and easy adaptability to their environment. Donning the working man's cotton shirt, they prove to be rebellious and undisciplined; when they put on their draftee's uniform, they turn submissive and officious. The soldier who shoots down the striker, where does he come from? The huge armies, are they perchance made up of capitalists and noblemen? Millions of German socialists are fighting today in the Kaiser's legions. Nonetheless, those masses run off to fight and die for an idea or a man, whether it's on the battlefield or behind the barricades. In the masses there is always some hero who throws himself into the sea to save a drowning man, or runs through fire to save a child, or even risks his life to save an animal.

Great works come from collective efforts stirred by individual force: unconscious hands gather building materials; only conscious minds can conceive beautiful and lasting monuments. Hence the need to instruct the masses so as to transform the most humble worker into a conscious colleague. This doesn't mean that the revolution will come only after the multitudes have acquired the encyclopedic knowledge of Humboldt or Spencer. The general conclusions of science, truly great truths, are so simple and clear that you don't have to be Aristotle or Bacon to understand them.

Not all Christians were Saint Paul nor all Puritans Cromwell; not all French conscripts were Hoche, nor all South American rebels Bolívar. But those pagans, those Puritans, those conscripts, and those rebels, fell in love with an idea and believed in their own goodness, although perhaps they only understood it in part. Love gave them the thirst for sacrifice and made them invincible. It isn't enough to adopt a conviction halfheartedly, wearing it on our sleeve as an object for display and decoration. We have to caress it, give it a place in our hearts, and wed it to our most intimate being until it becomes flesh of our flesh, life of our life.

If the conservative or reactionary spirit persists in the ruling classes, the germ of rebellion, the passion to move forward, stirs the worker in the crowded cities. The masses are like the fledgling migratory bird on the eve of its first migration. It doesn't know the way, but it's moved by the irresistible urge to take flight.

To destroy in a few hours the labor of humanity over centuries, all it takes are fire, flood, and explosives; but it takes an extraordinary and long-term effort to erect edifices that will last a thousand years or to establish anarchist societies. It's important to remember: Anarchy promotes universal concord and harmony of individual interests through generous and mutual concessions; it does not engage in class struggle just to bring about the rule of a single class—that would not be consonant with the revolution of all individuals against the entire range of evil of society. The proletariat itself, if it managed to monopolize the victory and take charge, would become bourgeois, just as the wealthy burgher dreams of ascending to nobility. It would substitute the same social order with a mere change of personnel: a new flock with new shepherds.

Humanity doesn't need shepherds or guides, but lighthouses, torches, or guideposts along the way. And those posts, those torches, and those lighthouses should come from the masses themselves, rejuvenated and cured of their secular illusions.

II

If bourgeois society can't be uprooted in a single day and in a single assault, it can be undermined little by little, through many successive attacks, not in a decisive battlefield victory but in a prolonged siege with victories and defeats, advances and retreats. What is needed is a series of partial revolutions. Since no country can boast the human being in full possession of the capacity to realize the most intense and expansive life, there are always plenty of reasons to launch a revolution. Where the individual doesn't suffer the tyranny of a government, he must endure the tyranny of the law. Decreed and sanctioned by the ruling classes, the law is nothing but an iniquity justified by the masters. The excessive rigor of the penalties assigned to crimes against property makes it clear who inspired the codes. Duguit writes: "It's been said, with good reason, that the Napoleonic Code is the code of property and that it must be replaced by the code of labor" (*Las transformaciones generales del Derecho privado desde el Código de Napoleón*, trans. Carlos G. Posada).

Wherever the political and civil rights of the individual are fully guaranteed by law and custom, social problems persist or, more accurately, they surface with greater intensity as an inevitable consequence of political evolution. If socialists are legion in the United States and Europe, we shouldn't imagine there are many in Dahomey. When men have the right to vote and hold office, when they enjoy civil and political equality, then they can try to erase economic inequalities.

In minimally advanced nations the revolution displays the triple character of religious, political, and social, as happens in some South American states that retain a medieval atmosphere, where despite free constitutions people live in a state of political barbarism, and civil wars are nothing but a reproduction of Spanish edicts.

"I don't understand," said a French writer, "why a republican doesn't become a socialist, which is the same thing, a man far more concerned with the humanitarian question than with merely political questions" (Henri Fouquier). Even harder to imagine is an anarchist detached from the social question. Anarchy strives for improvement of the proletarian class in the physical, intellectual, and ethical realm. It concedes great importance to the harmonious organization of property, but it doesn't view the evolution of history as a series of economic struggles. No, man is more than a stomach; he hasn't been fighting forever for the sole purpose of eating. History proves it.

University professors or spokespersons of official science would not dare say with Proudhon: "Property is theft." But a number of them would go along with Duguit: "Property is not a subjective right but a social function" (*Le Droit Social*, etc.). We cannot know how future societies will exercise that function—whether through communal confederations, professional unions, or in some other way. It's enough to know and attest that even declared enemies of anarchy deny to the individual today his traditional and sacred right to property.

And with good reason. The conquest and urbanization of the earth, the enormous accumulation of capital (understanding by capital not only material goods but also the sciences, arts, and industries) is not the work of a people, a race, or an epoch, but the labor of humanity down through the centuries. If we live in beautiful, clean cities; if we travel swiftly and economically on trains and steamboats; if we enjoy museums and libraries; if we have at our disposal weapons against pain and sickness; if, in a word, we succeed in savoring life's sweetness, we owe it all to the ceaseless and fecund labor of our ancestors. Humanity of yesterday produced and accumulated capital, and humanity today is entitled to inherit that capital: what belongs to everyone belongs to everyone. What right, then, does the individual have to monopolize anything? If one individual claims the fruit from a tree, another individual can do the same because he's as much a child of earth as the first, as much humanity's heir as the other. We would laugh at a person who said *my* steamboat, *my* electricity, *my* Parthenon, *my* Louvre, or *my* British Museum, but we hear people speaking in all seriousness about *their* forest, *their* hacienda, *their* factory, and *their* houses.

The common man with an education (the most frightening kind of common man) perceives anarchists as wanting to resolve the social problem with a single act: the violent redistribution of material goods down to the dollar, per capita equality. The dollars of Morgan, Carnegie, Rockefeller, and the other Yankee multimillionaires would be divided among poor waifs, beggars, and the proletariat of the United States; the same would happen in France with Rothschild's francs, and all over the world with the money of all the rich. It's vain to tell him that anarchy seeks the methodical organization of society, and that this kind of violent redistribution would imply a scientific barbarism. Moreover, this would entail the negation of anarchist principles, since to transfer the property of the collectivity to the temporary use of the individual would be to sanction the individualist regime and, by that very act, deny that property was nothing but a social function.

Anarchy is neither religious nor irreligious. It seeks to extirpate from human consciousness atavistic religiosity, that powerful regressive factor.

Colossal works of ingenuity and logic that are based on absurd premises, religions pervert man from childhood, inspiring in him an erroneous concept of nature and life. They represent reason's heresies. They can be regarded as the rudimentary science of ignorant peoples, as a purely fantastic interpretation of the universe. To regard the theologian as a wise man today is the same as calling a witch a doctor, an astrologist an astronomer. Man, when he kneels down inside a temple, merely worships his own ignorance.

For resolving social problems, Christianity—and especially Catholicism—is as useful as a block of granite in a field: it has to be eliminated. By seeking to resolve earthly problems in the other life, by offering rewards or compensations beyond the tomb, Christianity sows resignation in the spirits of the oppressed, lulls the spirit of rebellion with the fraud of celestial music, and helps perpetuate the reign of injustice in the world. By sanctifying pain, deprivation, and misfortune, it places itself in direct opposition with the universal instinct to live a happy life. The right to happiness is not acknowledged in bibles or codes, but it's engraved in human hearts. Religion that denies such a right pursues a depressing, dissolute, and antisocial goal because there are no true social bonds in nations where there are two classes of human being—those born to enjoy the earth and those born to enjoy heaven—, where serious conflicts are resolved with the hope of posthumous remuneration, and where the individual, instead of rising up against iniquity, resigns himself to appealing to the decision of a divine and problematical judge.

It wouldn't be a problem if the members of each religion would confine themselves to believing in their dogmas, practicing their liturgy, and spreading their doctrines. But some sects (in particular, Catholics) move outside the realm of the ideal, infuse religion into politics, and fight to become an exclusive controlling element. The Roman Catholic priest incarnates the principle of authority and has always allied himself with the rich man and the soldier with the intention of governing or replacing them. Not satisfied with dominion, he dreams of empire. So it is that in certain countries the anarchist has the obligation to combat religion and be aggressively anticlerical. Or, let's say, defensively anticlerical, because the aggression more often than not begins with the clergy. While the philosopher and the revolutionary doze, the priest keeps vigil. Convinced that he's engaged in a divine work and believing he has a monopoly on the truth, he would suppress industry, art, and science just to impose the tyranny of dogmatic superstitions on the world. He accepts no light other than the *black light* of fanaticism.

Politics is a religion that is solidly organized, positing its great providential fetish in the state, its dogmas in the constitution, its liturgy in regulations, its priesthood in its bureaucrats, its devout in the citizen mob. It has its blind, zealous fanatics who sometimes turn into martyrs or inquisitors. There are men who kill or get themselves killed for the hollow verbalism of popular sovereignty, the right to vote, democratic republic, parliamentary system, and so on.

If there are people who reduce everything to religion, there are also certain individuals who lump everything into politics: social relations are politics, marriage is politics, childhood education is politics, as are one's way of speaking, writing, and even eating, drinking, and breathing. They never emerge from it, they live and die in it as aerobia in air or infusoria in liquid. They constitute a subspecies of the human: they aren't men like the rest of us, they are politicians.

The true anarchist is just the opposite, and proud to be so. He knows that due to the effects of politics the most exalted moral character is diminished and the most elite intelligence dulled, leading one to concede highest importance to trivial questions of form and to postpone human interest to party priority. How many men have nullified and even corrupted themselves breathing the foul air of a parliament, that sanctum sanctorum of politicians! We'll let the radicals answer that, or the radical-socialists, or Marxist-socialists, or social-internationalists, or socialist-revolutionaries, and so on. We don't know whether some Hamon has published *The Psychology of the Professional Parliamentarian;* but can anyone be unfamiliar with the idiosyncrasies of the senator and the deputy? They incarnate the refined, sublimated, quintessential politician. No one should presume to call himself statesman until he has received the lesson on the way things are in the life of parliament.

According to Spencer, "yesterday's great political superstition—the divine right of kings—has been replaced by today's great superstition: the divine right of parliaments." Instead of a single head anointed with sacerdotal oil, nations now have several hundred heads consecrated by the vote of the masses. However, legislative assemblies, from the

German Reichstag to the British Parliament, from the French Parliament to the congress of the latest and tiniest Spanish American republic, are beginning to lose their divine aura and to become objects of aversion and mistrust, if not shame and derision. Day by day the number of deluded souls who look to a parliament for public happiness grows smaller. There are countries currently experiencing voter boycotts. The citizens let the government fix the elections, not caring who gets elected, knowing that the most honest man will most likely turn overnight into the most corrupt representative.

There's too much government and too many laws. The individual is not absolute master of his own person but slave to his political or social condition, and right from the cradle he has been assigned the pigeonhole in which he's destined to operate, without hope of ever getting out. He has to work on his plot of land, in the mine, or in the workshop, so others can reap the profits: he has to die aboard a warship, on the battlefield, or end up an invalid so others can enjoy their wealth free of worry.

According to Victor Considérant, "the phalansterians conceded little importance to governmental forms and considered political and administrative matters to be eternal sources of discord." Augustin Thierry, to the outrage of worshipers of myths and platitudes, wrote, "Any government, with a maximum of guarantees and a minimum of administrative actions." Every system of political organization deserves to be called a house of words. The question of governmental forms is just a question of words: in the last analysis, there are no good or bad forms of government, just good or bad governors. Would anyone prefer the constitutional presidency of a Nero to the autocracy of a Marcus Aurelius?

Given the general inclination of men to abuse power, every government is bad and every authority is a tyranny, just as every law is traduced by the sanction of ingrained abuse. By resisting governmental forms, authorities, and laws, by standing against all political power, the anarchist smooths the road for revolution.

The State

(1904)

Enslavement to a political cause is equivalent to subservience to a religious cause: slaves of a dinner jacket or sport coat are no different from servants of a cassock or a habit. To acknowledge the omnipotence of a parliament is, perhaps, even more absurd than to confer infallibility on an assembly of bishops. Even in the highest ecclesiastical councils men versed in Latin and canon law engage in false logic and erroneous claims, while gentlemen who can scarcely tell you how many fingers they have on each hand pontificate and quibble over complex legal matters in congresses everywhere.

You can be as much of a Domingo de Guzmán or a Torquemada in the civil order as on ecclesiastical councils. Lay inquisitors, politicians trade God and Church for God and state and reject the mysteries of Catholicism only to profess the dogmas of the law. The spirit moving priests isn't that different from the spirit driving public figures. Tonsured or not, they all carry on and will continue to carry on in the same manner. Politicians can't blast their foes with excommunication or burn them at the stake, but they can outlaw them, jail and deport them, or execute them by firing squad: they go as far as the social milieu allows and wouldn't hesitate to excommunicate and burn if they had the power to excommunicate and burn.

In former times it was thought there could be no morality without religion; today one can't conceive of order without laws, the individual unfettered by authority, wild beasts without their tamers. Just as love of God and fear of hell have become meaningless factors that have no influence on the conduct of inherently honest people, neither do respect for authority or fear of the law engender righteousness in well-formed hearts: without constables or jails, honest men will continue to behave honestly, just as evil men will proceed with their evil ways despite jails and constables.

People who in this day and time cannot conceive of social movement without the motor of the state are like the benighted folk who in the mid-nineteenth century could not understand how a train could come and go without being pulled by animals. Or like the peasant who could understand everything about the automobile except how it could move without horses.

The individual has been reduced to the point of becoming a body without a soul, unconditionally subservient to the power of the state. For the state, he sweats and wears himself away in the mine, on the land, and in the factory; for the state he fights and dies on battlefields. In the Middle Ages we were cloth for sewing a cassock; today we're the same piece of cloth for sewing a dinner jacket. And we endure it all like cowardly sheep! Thanks to countless centuries of slavery and servitude, we seem to have developed a fear of being free, of being our own masters. Even when we are free, we grope like blind men without their guides, tremble like children in the darkness.

So the victims themselves join their voices to those of the executioners to shout down the courageous reformers preaching total emancipation of the individual. But we don't believe that mental aberration will afflict the masses forever. The seeds sown by the great anarchists of Russia and France are germinating in America and Europe. The most frightened members of the bourgeoisie are beginning to see in Anarchy something that did not end with the bombs of Vaillant and Ravachol.

Those who come tomorrow will judge the present enemies of the state as we judge the former adversaries of the Church: they will see in anarchists and rebels what we see today in the impious and the heretics of earlier times.

Authority

(1904)

According to the ancients, almighty Zeus, when he took away man's freedom, took half his virtue. Quite true. We lose the greatest and best of our being when we endure the humiliation of slavery; but what do we gain the moment we ascend the ladder of authority? Let's pick the most inoffensive creature we can find, give him the tiniest particle of authority, and we'll see how, instantaneously, as if touched by a magic wand, he'll turn into an insolent and aggressive despot.

Very few men maintain the virtues of their private life once in office. The touchstone for evaluating a soul should be sought not in misfortune but in power: let's elevate the just man to the throne, and there we'll discover flaws we never noticed at ground level.

Nothing is so corrupting or perverting as the exercise of authority, no matter how temporary and short-lived it is. Is there anything quite so odious as a child monitoring his playmates, a servant playing the role of master, a day worker acting as foreman, a prisoner acting as prison guard? If we could appoint the lowest worm constable, even substitute constable, right away we'd turn him into a viper.

An old Yankee asked an immigrant newly disembarked in New York:

"Are you a republican?"

"No, I'm not a republican.

"Are you a democrat?"

"No, I'm not a democrat."

"Then what?"

"I belong to the opposition; I'm always against the government."

This little dialogue sums up the sentiments of a free soul, rejecting the principle of authority and declaring war against it wherever he finds it. If only we all thought like that!

In the opinion of fanatics wisdom resides in the fear of the Lord; in the concept of free men the wisdom of a people resides in its scorn for authority. The terms *contempt of court* and *lèse-majesté* have no meaning for emancipated people; they only have meaning for the swarm of palace sycophants and courtiers.

How it would turn our stomachs if we knew how many crimes and despicable acts were symbolized by a president's sash, a bishop's mitre, a judge's medallion, or a general's epaulettes. How many genuflections and bows! How many promises and false rumors! How many perjuries and bribes! How many mothers and sisters and wives and daughters prostituted! The higher the rank, the greater the ignominy because you have to crawl through gutters to rise so high.

The masses shouldn't be taken in by pompous titles or let themselves be bedazzled by uniforms or rococo costumes. They need to repeat to themselves night and day that command implies no superiority over obedience, that the laborer's work clothes need not be intimidated by the president's tails. If there's any difference between the chief of state and the simple citizen, it's to the credit of the second: the citizen pays; the chief of state gets the pay; one is the master; the other is the servant. The nation's lesser and greater dignitaries are never more than lackeys, servile to a greater or lesser degree; every uniform is livery, every salary a tip.

So let's hate authorities just for being authorities: by the very act of seeking and exercising command, they betray the perversity of their instincts. Anyone who imagines himself endowed with the soul of a king, has the heart of a slave; anyone who thinks he was born to command, was born to serve. The truly good and free man has no desire to command or to obey: just as he resists the humiliation of acknowledging masters or lords, he rejects the iniquity of owning slaves and servants.

The Beginning

(1905)

This year for the first time we've celebrated May Day, not only in Lima but in several other cities or towns of the republic. We've marched through the streets and squares waving a flag that symbolizes social revolution; things that none of us have ever heard or read before have been spoken in public meetings and printed on flyers and in newspapers. It's as though the authorities and forces of law and order were in agreement to let such things be said and done. Will it be the same this coming year?

Surely, many of those who took part in the demonstrations held on May 1 were not fully aware of what it all meant, since alongside the red flags they were holding aloft the banners of their religious guilds, and shortly after applauding speeches of the purest internationalism, they went out to sing the music and lyrics of the national anthem.

The mere fact that they came together of their own free will to attend ceremonies that had nothing to do with politics or religion proves that the entire country is not made up of the groveling dogs at whom most electoral platforms seem to be addressed, that a wholesome segment of the population aspires to head toward something new and fecund. This is also demonstrated by their applause for certain ideas that would have provoked a veritable storm of outrage a few years ago.

Something undeniable is happening in our country today: the appearance and propagation of anarchist doctrines. Every day newspapers are being started up that follow more or less logically the lead of the Kropotkins and the Reclus. In Lima recently we've seen the emergence of *Simiente Roja, Redención*, and *El Hambriento*, which added to *Los Parias* make four publications of the same character in the capital alone. And we shouldn't be all that boastful, considering that in Trujillo *La Antorcha, El Zapatero*, and *El Rebelde* have recently started up. In Chiclayo, *Justicia* is adopting a more defined tone, probably through the influence of Lombardozzi. *El Ariete* in Arequipa isn't that different from *Simiente Roja* or *Redención*, since Francisco is more a rebel in the Juan Grave style than a run-of-the-mill Peruvian politician. The list could go on if we wanted to include every publication with even the slightest socialist or anarchist bent.

The hosts will continue to grow, heads will continue filling with light, and what is today the conviction of only a few will someday be the doctrine of many. The unconscious impulse to travel toward unknown or imagined lands will be gradually transformed to a conscious march toward regions clearly delineated and known.

If there's any region open to the reception of anarchist ideas, it's undoubtedly South America and Peru in particular; here there are no deeply rooted traditions that in the old societies vehemently oppose the germination of everything new; here the mania for pronouncements that stirred our parents and grandparents has been turned into a spirit of rebellion against all power and all authority; here, where the people have lost faith in public figures and in political institutions, there's not even the restraining force of religion because all beliefs are vanishing with astonishing speed.

Many Peruvians are anarchists without knowing it; they practice the doctrine but they're afraid of the name.

The Sword

(1904)

A general, an empty cask; an army on the march, the plague.

SWIFT, *Gulliver's Travels*

Nowhere is the influence of authority so palpable as in the soldier. The habit doesn't make the monk; but the suit he wears has great influence on the formation of the tiger. Merely by pouring a man into a military uniform, you infuse him with abjection before his superiors and despotism toward his subordinates. How insolent the arrogance of a colonel in his contact with the humble recruit! How repugnant the servility of that same colonel in the presence of the fatuous general! An army's chain of command should be depicted as a mountain where men climb, each kissing the ass of the one ahead, each kissed in the same spot by the one behind.

Yet many sociologists recommend obligatory military service as the fastest, surest way to civilize nations. Hence, instead of the teacher with a primer, the lieutenant with his swagger stick; instead of the classroom where the intelligence is set free, the parade ground or courtyard where the brain is atrophied to the point where it becomes a mere motor for automatic responses. To comprehend the civilizing action of the barracks, just compare the conscript at the moment of being recruited with that same man after a few years of service: the one who started out honest, compassionate, and hardworking ends up a scoundrel, a brute, and a loafer. Our villages are aswarm with a type of idleness and delinquency that is the sum total of all vices and uselessness: the former soldier. A metamorphosis in reverse, a butterfly transformed into a caterpillar, that's what you get when you turn a peasant into a soldier.

Many years ago the monk was the target of satirical poets and fanatical heretics, but isn't the soldier just as worthy of gibes and calumny as the monk? A batallion isn't that different from a monastery; an abbot and a colonel differ in that the first stammers his prayers and the second vomits blasphemies. If the one beats his head against a wall trying to translate the Latin from his breviary, the other barely understands the tactical jargon he spouts. For moral abasement, there are uniforms and habits everywhere you look, degrading barracks and monastery equally, since it's the same thing to obey the clanging of a bell or the rattle of a drum, to subject yourself to military commands or the *rules of a monastic order*. If monks and soldiers are equals in passive obedience, they are quite different in other matters. The monk eats and drinks like a glutton, gambles, and seduces women. The soldier not only debauches himself in these ways but also robs, burns, rapes, and kills. The monk shows up with buckets of wine, his cassock stained with greasy stew; the soldier is splattered with mud and blood. The tonsured one is an avatar of Priapus, the sword bearer resuscitates Cain. We laugh at Priapus, but Cain horrifies us. The tonsured pigs will never arouse the horror produced by the beasts with gold ribbons.

True, the inquisitor and the guerrilla are offshoots of the monk, as illustrated by Santo Domingo de Guzmán and the Carlist monks; the Jesuit sprouts from the soldier, as Saint Ignatius de Loyola proves. If error is enunciated by the habit, it is sustained by the uniform. Without brute force or military support, neither the great religious persecutions nor the autos-da-fé would ever have been possible. Alongside the inquisitors and executioners, at the foot of the burning stake, stood the soldier, always. Even today, swords serve as points of the cross.

Only moral perversion can make us call six shirtless peasants looting on the outskirts of a city *criminals* and six thousand uniformed bandits invading a neighboring territory to seize property and destroy lives *heroes*. What's bad in the individual we call good in the group, reducing good and evil to a simple question of numbers. The enormity of a crime or a vice transforms it in our eyes into an action worthy of praise, a virtue: the theft of millions we call business; slashing the throat of entire nations we call a glorious deed. For a murderer, the gallows; for a warrior, apotheosis. But the unknown day-laborer who kills his neighbor, whether to avenge an insult or to steal his purse or his wife, doesn't deserve as much ignominy or punishment as the noble soldier who kills twenty or forty thousand men to win glory or earn a battlefield promotion.

Looking closely at things and without conventional biases, what were Alexander, Caesar, Napoleon—all of them official heroes we offer as examples to the young in our manuals of civic instruction. Slaughterers of human cattle. But we denounce animal sacrifice and glorify manslaughter.

Happily, the legendary prestige of the uniform is fading. The Dreyfus affair has served to pluck a few feathers from the jackdaw, no longer so resplendent following the capitulation of Metz and the firing squads of the Commune. Free spirits are springing up everywhere, who see no difference between a Deibler and a Moltke, or between a Cartouche and a Kitchener. Those famous generals who look so dashing for having traded the feathers savages wear in their loincloths for three-cornered hats are beginning to make us laugh. Pretty soon our gouty, soft-bellied sergeants will have no one left to admire them but women, children, and boobs.

When mankind manages to isolate and control his atavistic ferocity, war will be remembered as a period of barbaric pre-history, and the famous warriors (so admired today) will be featured in the rogues gallery of *red souls*, alongside assassins, executioners, and mass murderers. Napoleon's cranium will be exhibited next to the skull of a gorilla; Kropotkin's spine will lie beside the arrows of a wild Indian.

The barracks have never been and never will be a school for civilization: it's a remnant of primordial jungle incrusted in the bosom of modern cities.

Military science in its entirety has never been anything but the art of brutalizing and turning men to savages: consequently, any attempt to civilize with the sword is like using soot to remove stains or sulphuric acid to soothe burns.

Socialism and Anarchy

(1906)

Though we may praise the good intentions of all those who spoke or wrote at the beginning of May, we cannot but lament the confusion some have displayed about men and things, giving certain individuals a place they do not merit and regarding as equal or similar ideas that exclude or contradict each other. And let us not imagine that this happens only in Peru, where we live in a kind of intellectual infancy. In Europe, just as among us, many are sincerely seeking a fixed orientation, but the soundness of their intentions doesn't prevent them from groping aimlessly in the dark. They feel the presence of the light, and they mistake twilight for dawn; they hear the sound of wings, and they mistake vultures for eagles.

We do not expect a host of anarchists to emerge overnight, nor even that the wretched peasants from the haciendas will profess ideas as clear as those of Peter Kropotkin or Sebastien Faure. We do expect that those bringing enlightenment to our masses will help the ignorant comprehend the vast distance separating the public man from the true reformer, political change from social transformation, socialism from anarchy.

True, in a single day a revolution can take place and a secular empire be overthrown. But it takes years to educate men capable of bringing about such revolutions. When the demolition word and the anarchist book reach social strata where today the only light shed is that emitted by ignorant priests, self-serving politicians, and hack journalists, then the masses will acquire clear and definite ideas, will distinguish between one and another kind of man, and will go forward with sufficient energy to bring down in a few hours the edifice raised during four centuries of iniquity.

Anarchists or not, workers pursuing a noble end must of necessity avail themselves of a saving means: distrust all politicians. Distrust them all, especially those clowns who cloak themselves in the rags of liberalism and shake the rattles of electoral reform, universal suffrage, civil rights, and federalism. To avoid the spread of tuberculosis through saliva, authorities in charge of hygiene hang this sign in public places: Spitting Prohibited. Likewise, since it's a matter of preventing moral contamination, workers ought to put up huge posters at all their public gatherings: Political Spouting Prohibited.

Anarchists should remember that socialism, in any of its multiple forms, is oppressive and rule-bound, quite unlike anarchy, which is utterly free and rejects all rules or any subjection of the individual to the laws of the majority. Socialists and anarchists can march together or participate in a common action to bring about an immediate goal, as is happening today to win the eight-hour day, but never a lasting alliance or a fusion of principles. Whenever a vital question is examined, difference emerges and the struggle begins.

We can see this today. While the anarchists declare themselves enemies of the country and consequently of militarism, the socialists proceed jesuitically, trying to reconcile the irreconcilable, calling themselves internationalists and nationalists. Bebel said at the height of the Reichstag, confusing himself with the savages bound by their insignia as servants of the emperor, "We socialists will fight to preserve Germany and give our last effort to defend our country and our lands." We could find similar statements by men like Millerand, Clemenceau, and even Jaurès.

As for the so-called tolerance of the socialists, we need only recall that Liebknecht consistently opposed the admission of anarchists into the workers congresses. "We must," he said, "fight them as we would our worst enemies, not admitting them into any of our communities or gatherings." The one who most brutally and openly revealed the extent of the fraternal love socialists profess for anarchists was the French deputy Chauvin in the presence of two or three thousand citizens: "The first act of the democratic socialists on the day of their triumph should be to shoot all the anarchists."

Think about it, then, and try not to forget it, especially all you naive anarchists who equate socialism with anarchy and see in each socialist a good-natured, loving brother.

Strikes

(1906)

If we were asked our opinion about strikes, we would say: Every strike should be general and armed. *General*, in order to combat and besiege the capitalist world from all sides and force it to surrender. *Armed*, to prevent the interference by the authorities in struggles where they should play no other part than witness.

Partial strikes don't always succeed in benefiting the worker because the strikers, abandoned to their own forces, without the aid of their companions, are beaten separately and have to give in to the owner.

Unarmed strikes also fail because the decisive intervention of the authorities in the struggle between masters and servants always means alliance with the former.

When all the workers of a town declare themselves on strike, from the butcher to the lamplighter, the bourgeoisie, trembling at the thought of not having a piece of meat in the stew or a lamp lighted in the street, becomes compassionate and reasonable. When everyone is armed, from the man with a revolver to the woman with her scissors, the authorities become docile because a strike like that isn't far from a revolution.

In Peru, when a strike is called by a trade union or a group of workers, the other unions and the other workers remain as unconcerned as if it were a matter alien not only to the working class but to the planet. They leave their companions dangling between the claws of the owner and the rifles of the authorities.

In the strikes of Callao all the workers associations observe with utmost indifference how workers are regarded as slaves in the barbarous decrees.

Of course, currently the workers associations of Lima and Callao have two grave matters to concern themselves over: the municipal elections and joining the Catholic Union. . . .

The Soldier's Rebellion

(1906)

There are two irreconciliable concepts, however subtly and persuasively we strain to reconcile them: internationalism and patriotism. We have no country if we love all countries equally; we aren't patriots if we stop preferring the citizens of our country to a Laplander, a Frenchman, or a Chinese.

Socialism, despite its detachment from all religions, is based on a Christian maxim: *we are all brothers.* Consequently, if this is a truth engraved in the most intimate place in our hearts, if we rule all our actions by this maxim, we have the right to protest when they oblige us to violate it so they can turn us into murderers of our brothers.

The propaganda of the socialist internationalists, urging desertion in case of a war, is the most logical consequence of this doctrine. Not so logical is the attempt by some French and German socialists to reconcile internationalism with patriotism, human freedom with military service. Such advocates remind us of casuistical Jesuit theologians. In theory, they condemn military service and war; in practice, they neither oppose passive obedience nor accept insubordination or rebellion in the individual soldier.

In the vigorous resolve of the recruit, in his refusal to become a mere cog in the blind, collective machine, we have the most enlightened resolution to the problem. Armies will only cease to exist, and consequently wars, when men refuse to suffer the military yoke, when the majority of those drafted into the service have enough courage to rebel, invoking the generous principle of brotherhood.

And this mass, collective protest cannot come about without first being initiated by a series of individual protests: many will follow the example, once a few begin to provide it. The well-paid diplomat drawing up protocols in the Conference at The Hague can make a bit of progress toward ending wars; but surely the poor *Doukhobor* on the Russian steppes who refuses to serve in the military and is willing to endure the *knut*, prison and exile in Siberia, can do much more.

The First of May (1907)

(1907)

We don't know whether the workers, not just those in Peru but throughout the world, are capable of thinking and acting in concerted fashion today. If they commemorate past rebellions and show a determination to bring about a radical transformation in all spheres of life, we have nothing to say. But if they merely limit themselves to celebrating May Day, assuming that the desideratum of social demands can be reduced to an eight-hour day or Sundays off, then we can't help smiling and lamenting the naïveté of the proletariat.

Labor Day! What does that mean? Why should the worker rejoice about toiling so others can rest and producing so others can reap the profit? The owners of factories and ranches, those with a monopoly on capital and land, those we call industrialists because they practice the art of growing rich on the sweat and blood of their fellow men, they're the ones who should be organizing street demonstrations, decorating buildings with streamers, setting off fireworks, and giving speeches. But it's the workers who are out there rejoicing and congratulating themselves, without considering that the ironic phrase *Labor Day* really means *Slavery Day.*

At the dawn of societies, when war broke out between two groups, the victor inexorably killed the vanquished; in later times, he reduced him to slavery so that he would have in him a work machine. In even later times, slavery was transformed to servitude and last, servitude was replaced by the proletariat. So slavery, servitude, and proletariat are the same thing, modified by the effect of time. If we could reconstruct the genealogy of the proletariat in all nations, we would see that they descend from slaves or serfs, that is, from the vanquished.

True, the fact that the earth is habitable and life is comfortable is a function of the double labor of muscle and mind: let's hold off for a while working against the hostile forces of nature, and then we'll see whether divine providence comes to our aid. You could say, then, that Jesus Christ was talking nonsense when he said "do not be anxious about . . . what you shall eat or what you shall drink. . . . Look at the birds of the air; they neither sow nor reap nor gather into barns, and yet our heavenly Father feeds them."

But the daily and exclusive use of the muscle also dulls the mind of half of humanity. Those who drive a yoke of oxen or wield a hammer from morning to night aren't living the intellectual life of mankind, and in stifling their cerebral functions they end up converting their actions into *a simple automatism of the lower faculties.* Thanks to the constant depressive effect of the rulers over the ruled, today we literally have human animals who possess only enough intelligence to tie off the threads of a spool or break up the lumps of clay in a field. They're like the products of natural selection, like the beef cow or the race horse.

If vigorous work of the muscle cheers the heart, wards off bad thoughts, and makes the body strong, if it produces all the benefits boasted by our professional moralists, why don't the children of the bourgeoisie, instead of grabbing their books and heading off to the universities, hook up the oxen and go off to plough the field? Because societies have one set of morality and hygiene for those at the top, another set for those at the bottom. There are two kinds of workers: those who really work and those who just seem to, calling it work to watch their fellows sweat and cripple themselves. Thus the rancher who climbs on his beautiful horse at eight in the morning and spends two or three hours riding through the cane fields where the peasants are sweating their asses off, him we call a *working man;* likewise, the industrialist who from time to time gets up from his cushioned desk chair to look in on the sweatshop where the woman and child work nonstop for twelve or even fifteen hours a day, him we call a *working man.*

We'll say it again: today the only ones who should be celebrating are the exploiters of human labor; perhaps the man who ploughs a field with the expectation of harvesting the crops, or the woman who spins a few pounds of wool, knowing she'll get to use it to make a dress, perhaps they have some reason to celebrate. But what possible reason does the poor devil who lives his life sawing wood, driving oxen, or working in a mine from January to January and from dawn to dusk have to celebrate? The man who's going to be a member of the proletariat tomorrow just as he is now and just as he was yesterday ought to be screaming out in rebellion, regarding this peaceful *Labor Day* as a cruel irony, a public demonstration by the slave to sanction his slavery.

Antipoliticians

(1907)

Happily, amid the hubbub raised by wretched and despicable interests, a new cry has been unleashed, a redeeming cry that is echoing through the working classes: *Down with politics!*

In addition to the existence in Lima of publications that openly call themselves antipolitical, conferences and meetings of an antipolitical nature are beginning to be held, as for example the one celebrated in this city on May 19.

Ten years ago, a meeting like this would not have been possible, for lack of both a public and speakers. Today it is possible because workers groups have produced conscious individuals who are eager to bring light to the minds of their comrades, and because even the most ignorant are beginning to sense that there is light beyond the subterranean darkness where they vegetate and die.

Nothing so degraded Peruvian workers, nothing continues to degrade them so much as politics: politics divides them, weakens them, and reduces them to impotence, leading them to squander in useless and counterproductive struggles the energies they ought to be using to organize and grow strong. What have the workers gained by going off to drop their votes into the amphora in the public square? They haven't even managed to choose their own masters, because every national election is decided by fraud or violence.

The interest taken in the worker by the politician every time a serious conflict breaks out between capital and labor can be seen today, not far from here, in the case of the workers from Darsena: what are the parties doing while the strikers from Callao struggle to win a salary increase or the fulfillment of conditions solemnly guaranteed in their contracts? Nothing; and it's bound to be the same tomorrow as it is today because the interests of the politicians are one thing, the interests of the proletariat another.

Although equality and brotherhood are preached, the world remains divided into enemy classes that live by exploiting and savaging each other. In countries that most pride themselves on being civilized, Christianity spills from people's lips, but it doesn't reach the depths of their hearts. All are *brothers*, but some live in castles while others sleep on the streets; all are *brothers*, but some wear fine woolen clothes while others die from the cold; all are *brothers*, but some eat while others starve. And who are the ones who get to play the role of victims or brothers stripped of their inheritance? The workers.

They are the law, they are justice, they are the masses. Then why aren't they the unstoppable army or the irresistible force? Because they are disunited; because in face of the homogeneous and compact block of the executioners and exploiters, they form heterogenous, soft groups, because they divide and subdivide themselves into selfish and adversarial factions.

One of the great agitators of the nineteenth century never stopped repeating: *Workers of the world, unite.* That's what we should be saying at every moment, everywhere, and we'll say it now: *Disinherited workers of Peru, unite.* Once you are united into a great community and can organize a strike including everyone—from the baker to the janitor—then you'll see if there are enough policemen and soldiers to stop you and shoot you.

Revolution

(1907)

The life and death of societies obey a determinism as inflexible as the germination of a seed or the crystallization of a salt. If sociologists had been able to enunciate laws similar to those formulated by the astronomers, we would now be able to announce revolutions the way we fix the date of an eclipse or a full moon.

Everything follows the law. But in this universal determinism in which innumerable unknown forces act, are we capable of measuring the human factor? If we can promote germination and impede crystallization, shouldn't we be able to influence the development of events or phenomena related to collectivities? "Social forces," says Engels, "work the same as those of nature, blindly, violently, destructively, as long as we don't understand them or know how to use them."

All of man's power resides in understanding or, more precisely, in discovering the laws. What is called our *fall* in Christian legend ought to be called our *ascent* because when we ate the fruit of the tree of knowledge we became (as the serpent predicted we would) equal to the gods.

The will of man can itself change, or it can act effectively to bring about social phenomena, thus initiating evolution, that is, producing revolutions. Just as we can use artificial heat to evaporate in a few hours a body of water that would take weeks and even months to dry with the simple rays of the sun, so can we help countries to do in a few days the work that would otherwise take them years to achieve. We shouldn't regard evolution and revolution as two diametrically opposed phenomena, like light and darkness or stillness and movement, but rather as a single line drawn in the same direction, though sometimes taking the form of a curve, at other times a straight line. Revolution could be called evolution accelerated or unleashed, rather like a forced march at full speed.

Let's not be frightened by the word. Men who had nothing in common with anarchists and who never dreamed of radical and violent transformations of society have said, "Peoples become educated in revolutions" (Lamartine); "There's something good about every revolution" (Chateaubriand); "The worst aspects of revolutions vanish; the good remains" (?). Such ideas are so deeply rooted in the mind of the masses that even barracks revolts or pronouncements by the most unremarkable leaders—simply because they smack of revolution—often enjoy popular support. With the exception of the parasites who live in the shadow of a social or political regime, and with the further exception of those addicted to the status quo, who are afraid of being asphyxiated by every cleansing of the atmosphere, the rest of the people regard revolutions as heroic remedies. It could be said that the noblest and most generous part of humankind comes into the world knowing intuitively that the earth has to grow, not by peaceful fluctuations but by violent upheavals. The comparison between storms (which purify the air) and revolutions (which bring bounty to the people) isn't new, but it's valid.

In every popular movement we can see where it begins but not where it will end: what starts out as a strike by a few workers or a protest by a few women can conclude in political or social liquidation. Even the people who in 1789 began by attacking the Bastille may not have expected that in 1793 they would end up guillotining Louis XVI. Hence, governments fear nothing so much as outbursts in the street. You can buy congressmen, judges, journalists, and even your political rivals, but you can't buy off an angry crowd; a people aroused to rebellion will burn, pillage, or kill, but it won't sell out. Today as never before the oppressors are conscious of how important it is to them to lull to sleep the *monster known as the people* with dusty religious hymns and moral fables. If the masses sleep like groundhogs, they've been known to awaken like lions.

Since the Reformation and especially since the French Revolution the civilized world has been living in a state of latent revolution: the revolution of the philosopher against the absurdities of dogma, the revolution of the individual against the omnipotence of the state, the revolution of the worker against the exploitations of capital, the revolution of women against the tyranny of men, the revolution of one sex or another against the enslavement of love and the prison of matrimony; in short, the revolution of everyone against everything.

In Russia and France we can observe today two magnificent explosions of that great *latent revolution*. No one can guarantee that the struggle of the state against the Church in France won't end up in a war of the proletariat against the capitalist, or that the uprising of the people against the autocracy of the czar in Russia won't end up as a rebellion by that same people against the fanaticism of the pope.

The First of May (1908a)[1]

(1908)

The strike in Iquique is proceeding just the opposite of what usually happens with movements of that sort when a conflict breaks out between workers and police. The first news is always exaggerated and events are characterized as a hecatomb, when in fact only a few people are slightly wounded or pushed around. In the current situation, the events that were communicated by telegraph a few hours after they happened were more serious and more brutal than what had been thought at first. It has been verified, beyond the slightest doubt, that more than a thousand peasants were killed by the soldiers without any threat or provocation on the part of the strikers.

And to add insult to brutality, charges are being brought against the guilty parties, that is, against the poor workers who, driven by necessity and having been rudely turned down by the bosses whom they asked for a raise, had gathered peacefully and were marching toward a village, not to use it as a fortress or a military post but just to have a centralized place to meet for the purpose of agreeing on the best way to resolve the frightful economic crisis. Unarmed and trying to avoid any disorder that would provoke violent intervention by the soldiers, they had even taken the precaution of forbidding the sale of alcohol. Never had there been a less bellicose strike. Then why such cruelty to stifle it? Because

[1] 1908.

they wanted to make an object lesson; because they wanted to show the workers that they should obey and keep quiet.

If today, May 1, we recall the inexcusable slaughter in Iquique, it is to demonstrate to the proletariat that in the struggle against the capitalists they should expect neither justice nor mercy. For blacks on the hacienda there was the stock and the whip; for the workers in the factories or the mines there's the rifle and the machine gun. Even worse, if the owner of the hacienda respected the life of the slave because it represented a certain value to him, the industrialist of our times has no such scruples because he loses nothing by sacrificing the life of a worker. If one disappears, he's replaced on the spot, perhaps profitably.

What we call the *right to work* is nothing but a cruel joke to the man whose only capital is the strength of his arms and who stops eating the day he stops working. There are only two roads open to the proletariat: work hard and earn a less than living wage or rise up and be mowed down by soldiers' bullets.

There is no lack of lyric hacks devoted to celebrating the good fortune of the worker who gets to do his work without having to worry about whether the product will sell or not; who sleeps peacefully every day of the week and on Saturday, after receiving his pay, goes off humming to dine happily in the company of his wife and children. A lovely fantasy! Through association of contrary ideas, that *good fortune* makes these hacks think about the *misfortune* of the wealthy boss who, without resting for a single moment of the day goes about his mental labor and stays up nights, worrying about bills that must be payed, warehouses overflowing with stock, the difficulty of sales, ruinous competition from his rivals, and so on. His bread is bitter and his drink even more so.

Still, we never see (nor in all likelihood will our descendants ever see) the poor boss trading places with the happy worker. What a lovely spectacle it would be to see the Yankee multimillionaire giving up his millions to become the happy worker who supports his wife and six kids on the honest wage of eighty cents a day!

No, the capitalist will never give up an inch of what he claims is rightfully his. When he does give up something, it's not by virtue of reason but by virtue of force. Hence there's no better way to obtain justice than to resort to armed strikes and sabotage.

This is what, on this May 1, needs to be repeated to the deluded workers who continue to trust in the humanity of the capitalist, believing that the arduous conflicts of social life have to be resolved by peaceful accord: the capitalist never gives what he's begged for, only what's demanded of him with threats.

The Police[1]

I

Taine, a philosopher who was neither revolutionary nor anarchist, wrote: "Because there are so many gendarmes and urban policemen in France, we would be inclined to regard them as more of a nuisance than helpful. Any time a few passersby gather on the street to look at a dog with a broken leg, a man with a moustache comes up and tells them: 'Gentlemen, groups are prohibited; disperse'" *(Philosophie de l'art).* And everyone disperses on the spot, as if shot from a spring. Anyone interested in knowing a people submissive to the orders of the authorities, don't visit Russia or Turkey, but the land of the great revolution, France. The guillotiners of kings, the conquerors of allied Europe, tremble and hush at the slightest gesture from a mere policeman. Looking at it carefully, they're quite right to do so because woe to the rebel or deaf person who falls under the full weight of official proceedings and—following those—a fine and jail sentence. We'll say nothing of police brutality or the running of the gauntlet; Baudin, Jaurès, and some other French deputies know a bit about those matters. Not in vain were they born in "the loveliest kingdom this side of heaven."

According to George Sand, if the street cops are abhorred when they

[1] Unpublished.

serve political passions, they generally win admiration for their good sense and fairness in exercising the functions proper to their institution. When the police—she adds—clearly demarcate the boundaries of their authority, which are confused today by human discord, they will fulfill a mission so paternal even in their severity that men will be proud to belong to that profession *(La Filleule)*. We aren't going to await the coming of the era in which policemen turn into guardian angels and people are proud to belong to the most odious of social institutions, based on espionage, arrest, bribery, and torture, the institution responsible for providing jails, penitentiaries, galleys, and gallows.

Even if, by virtue of autonomous organization, the police came to constitute the fourth power of the state, it would never stop succumbing to the influence of political passions, which even affect the courts of law from time to time. It's difficult to imagine a society in which individuals lacked opinions and simply vegetated year after year, alien to party struggles, maintaining their equanimity during tremendous social upheavals. Is selfishness some kind of invulnerable shield? The egotist moves along confidently when the river runs smoothly; but, when we least expect it, the river overflows its banks and drags him in. Because wherever men breathe, passions are at work, and politics dominates universities, charities, municipalities, police stations, and monasteries; as long as there are states and governments, there will be politics in every meeting of citizens, even if they gather together for scientific, religious, artistic, humanitarian, industrial, financial, or sporting purposes. A sickness not only hereditary but contagious, politics infects the organism of modern man.

Why even even dream, then, of the advent of an institution formed by men without human weaknesses? Since the police are a force as powerful as the army, and since the gendarme is sometimes more useful than the soldier, it's not conceivable that the politician will refrain from using guards and burly cops. But even if they are somehow detached from politics, assigned only to protecting lives and property, the policemen will imitate Offenbach's carabineers: they'll always show up late. If they could prevent accidents and crimes, they'd be performing a humanitarian function; but, generally, they're thinking only of pursuing the criminal when they crash into the innocent passerby. The murder victim, what good does it do him if the murderer is captured or brought to trial? The woman who's been raped, how is she benefited by the punishment of the rapist? Public vengeance, moral sanction, public example . . . are these any more than words?

II

From childhood on, almost from the cradle, the policeman embitters and saddens our lives, and if we used to frighten our children with devils, boogymen, and witches, now we threaten them with the corner policeman. When we walk past a school, many of us rejoice at having escaped the ferule of the teacher, the master, the pedant; but which of us is confident of getting through the day without having to contend with a cop? This individual has the ubiquity of providence and the tenacity of a fly: he doesn't leave us alone day or night. Awake and in the street, we see his phantom at every step; half-asleep and in our own bedrooms, we hear him blowing his whistle hour after hour. For all we know, when we're dead and buried we'll hear his boots tromping over our graves.

If the police don't deserve much love or sympathy even in well-organized nations, what can we say of them in chaotic or embryonic societies? Here, in Peru, from the government minister down to the police informant (without leaving out all the magistrates, supervisors, deputies, inspectors, guards, or jailors), they're all alike, they all conceal a poison of equal virulence. They do not serve to preserve public order but to defend abusive goverments because presidents, instead of handing certain individuals over to the law, entrust them to carry out functions in the police force. The tax collector is made a magistrate; the torturer, a supervisor; the ruffian, a deputy, and so on. A most select corporation, it persecutes the adversaries of the government, invents conspiracies, practices blackmail, provokes mutinies, beats writers, destroys printing presses, rapes women, tortures prisoners, steals what was stolen, murders guilty and innocent alike on our highways . . .

The members of such a corporation, which might well be called mafia or Camorra, deserve neither love nor sympathy. If we had the wolfish instinct of those born to be gendarmes or urban police, we'd yell "Good shot!" anytime we heard that a striker's or revolutionary's bullet hit a magistrate. But since we lack such depraved instincts, we condemn the effusion of blood and take our satisfaction from less tragic scenes. Thus, when Guignol grabs a billy club and knocks the cop for a loop, we applaud and feel happy, sharing the feelings of children, housewives, cooks, servants, workers, in short, all the innocent masses of people. A "Long live Guignol!" fights its way to our lips. So too, when a youth with strong fists punches out a guard, we feel like shouting, even if we don't know who's in the right, "Hit him again!"

The policeman, the functionary known in Lima by the nickname *cachaco,* represents the lowest link in the ominous chain made up of government ministers, magistrates, subprefects, deputies, and inspectors. However, no one is more abusive, more arrogant, or more inexorable than the *cachaco*—an ant with pretensions of an elephant, a tail with the pride of a head. This is his law: humility toward his superior, arrogance toward his inferior. He's all servility before the grand lady and the great lord, all arrogance toward the timid *chola,* the poor Negro, and the wretched Chinese. He's born of the people, lives in the intimacy of the masses, knows the miseries of the dispossessed, and declares himself their implacable enemy. With what enormous satisfaction does he bloody his club on the head of an unconscious drunk! With what joy does he fire his rifle into the breast of a helpless striker! With what delight does he push a defeated and fleeing revolutionary from the top of a tower! He senses the just hatred of the masses, and he takes his vengeance.

We can't understand, since there are so many honorable ways to make a living, how a man can join the police force. What can we say of the poor frizzy-headed Indian, planted on a corner and imagining he's engaged in some glorious and enviable function? We'd like to grab him by the neck, shake him, and shout at him, If you have any sense of decency and dignity left, if you haven't lost the last shred of shame, be anything a man can be in the world, anything, except a policeman. Dedicate yourself to the lowest, filthiest job: clean chimneys, sweep streets, collect garbage, herd pigs, unclog sewers, and spread lye. In dispersing foul odors or wallowing in filth, you'll stink less and look cleaner than in patrolling a street corner in your khaki uniform, white cap, and billy club.

The Two Nations

Liebknecht said, "In the world there are but two nations: the land of the rich and the land of the poor." It can be said too that in every nation, whatever its level of culture and its form of government, there are only two clearly defined social classes: the possessors and the dispossessed. Since money separates men more effectively than race, it's no exaggeration to say that *the poor are the blacks of Europe*.

This grand division of classes is felt as well in our republican America, where the wealthy families are beginning to constitute an aristocracy even more insolent and abhorrent than the nobility of the monarchic states. Because they are nouveaux riches, our false aristocrats take presumptuousness and pride to such extremes that the feudal lord of gallows and sword pales by comparison.

Descendants (by twisted lineage) of those Spaniards who were obsessed by gold fever, our hidalgos of master key and picklock have but one desire: to accumulate money. Having monopolized the exercise of authority, they have given us at best republics of fraud and intrigue, at worst republics of shame and blood.

But in none of the former Spanish colonies is this division of society into rich and poor more exacerbated than in Chile. Nowhere does the man in the frock coat look with more scorn or treat more inhumanely the man in the cotton shirt and poncho; in few is the domination more harsh. We have recourse to the testimony of the Chileans themselves. In issue 8 of *La Razón* of Chañaral, we read the following:

In Chile, mainly in the seaports, we've met *aristocratic families* who started out as lawyers, shysters, witch doctors, messengers, carpenters, tinsmiths, tailors, tobaccanists, cobblers, bricklayers, laundresses, and cooks. There's nothing odd about them having had a trade; we're simply focusing on these details to discover quickly the origin of the *middle class,* which is the worst enemy of the workers.

We deduce that the cradle of the aristocratic bourgeoisie, secular as well as clerical, is to be found in the shops, in the *chicha* bars, and in the pigsties where our laundry is washed and our food is cooked.

The middle class in Chile is the product then of the commonfolk, who as soon as they become educated, take on the comical manners of the aristocrats, learn as monkeys do to dress properly, growing intoxicated on the fumes of pride and vanity, and forgetting that their parents sold dog piss as mineral water, percale by the yard, sugar in five-pound sacks, cheap wine by the gallon, wax candles as counters, and had even been usurers, thieves at such and such a percent.

From these passages from *La Razón,* we see that in Chile the same thing happens as in Peru: the two aristocracies of "late emergence" (the one from Mapocho and the one from Rímac) are alike in forgetting their origins and in their low regard for the class from which they come. Thus, Vicuña Mackenna, who was the half-breed son of an Anglo-Saxon and an Araucanian Indian, once said that the Chilean peasant carries in his blood the instinct for robbery and murder.

If this Vicuña Mackenna were to come back to life, he would have a hard time answering the following questions: What instincts does the Chilean pseudo-aristocracy carry in its blood? Is it the peasants who are stealing from the national treasury and driving the nation toward financial collapse? Was it the peasants who created the War of the Pacific and unleashed on their neighbor a devastating and barbaric invasion? True, the peasant-turned-soldier proved to be as ferocious in Peru as the Turkish soldier in Armenia and the Cossack in China. But leading the soldier the officer was there to incite him, to get him drunk and send him out to rob, burn, rape, and murder. And the officer wasn't making war on his own behalf: he was obeying orders from the ruling class.[1]

---

[1] This article was written in the decisive hours of the recent dispute between Chile and Peru, and it is good to remember that the author participated in the Peruvian youth protest during the war of 1879. The eminence of González Prada and the significance of

This ferocity of the Chilean *possessor* was recently confirmed for us in the strike in Iquique. There it was demonstrated for the thousandth time that if the laws are somewhat valid for resolving questions of the privileged among themselves, they have absolutely no validity for settling disputes between poor and rich, or proletariat and capitalists; in such cases, there's no law, no judge, no arbitrator, other than force.

We won't persist on bringing up the stupid and cowardly massacre of the saltpeter workers (who could be unaware of those bloody episodes?) and we'll simply point out a significant fact, since it helps reveal the state of mind that's beginning to develop among the workers. In some of the saltpeter mines, following the horrific massacre, the Chilean workers trampled underfoot, spat on, and burned the Chilean flag.

Thus the victims of international hatred are beginning to see through the gross farce of patriotism and to recognize *that in the world there are but two nations—the land of the rich and the land of the poor.* If the two *enemy* armies could remember this truth when the firing starts, they would change the direction of their fire: they would proclaim that their real *enemies* are not the ones in front of them.

his total work make it indispensable to preserve the integrity of his thought, keeping in mind the circumstances mentioned. (Editor's note)

The First of May (1908b)
(1908)

In a recent congress held by the socialists it was decided that May 1 would be commemorated as May Day or Labor Day.

This measure would seem quite enlightened to us, if those attending the congress had taken the precaution to specify who were the ones who were meant to celebrate that grand date with greatest joy.

As we see it, it's not the workers but the bosses, not the proletariat but the capitalists, who should be celebrating it. To whose advantage does work redound? Surely it isn't the cobbler who goes around half barefoot, or the tailor, who goes around almost naked, or the bricklayer, who lives in some hole without air or light.

Those who parade about in elegant goatskin boots, who wear magnificent woolen overcoats and live in veritable palaces with fresh air and sunlight wafting and smiling through the rooms, they're the ones who ought to be thronging to the city squares today to sing panegyrics to the glories and virtues of work.

As for the worker holding the red banner aloft as if he were blandishing on high his parish cross and who sings a hymn to the first of May as if he were chanting the Miserere, he inspires neither anger nor scorn in us. We feel sorry for him: he's the turkey celebrating Easter.

Work implies honor and provokes legitimate pride when it is undertaken freely and for one's own benefit; but it signifies humiliation and shame when performed on behalf of a stranger and in conditions of virtual slavery. We don't see much difference between the man who wears himself out for a miserly wage to make the capitalist wealthy and the ox who sweats and strains for a few pounds of hay to fatten the owner of the hacienda.

Happily, humanity today is not made up of humble, resigned masses bent over the fields from dawn to dusk and lifting up their heads only to kiss the hand of their bosses. A great army of the proletariat, scattered throughout the world, now understands the irony of commemorating Labor Day and regards May 1 as symbolic of the coming together of the oppressed and exploited to tell their stories, to share their aspirations, and to prepare for the definitive demolishment.

Today, the enlightened worker celebrates the revolution.

The Individual[1]

Classical Rome bequeathed the God-state to us; medieval Rome imposed the God-Church. Today the revolutionary in Catholic nations is struggling against these two myths. He wants to raze the Church (already staggering from the blows of the Reformation, the encyclopedists, and the French Revolution) in order to raise up the monument of science in its rubble. He wants to dethrone the state (already shaken by the pounding of anarchist propaganda) in order to establish the sole autonomy of the individual. In short, the modern revolutionary seeks to emancipate man from every human and divine power, without presuming, as some freethinkers do, that it's enough to subject religion to civil authority or uproot religion from a country to achieve the greatest possible number of freedoms. Conceding to the state what's been whittled away from the Church, we diminish the celestial tyranny only to augment the profane, we escape the priest's fanaticism only to fall under the superstitious sway of the politician, we give up the God-Church only to idolize the God-state.

Simply from mouthing absolutist ideas, some theologians of the Middle Ages ended up believing them to be as real as beings and tangible objects: simply from musing about the state, contemporary politicians end up granting it a personality more tangible than the in-

[1] Unpublished.

dividual's. The modern statist incarnates the medieval realist and can hold his own with Duns Scotus. Since there is no reality beyond the individual, the state is nothing more than an abstraction, a metaphysical concept. However, that abstraction—that concept—on becoming incarnate in certain men, seizes control of us from the cradle, usurps our life, and only stops oppressing and exploiting us when it sees us converted into something nonproductive, a corpse. With its triple organization of barracks, office, and monastery, the state is our worst enemy. The wise man says, "The species is nothing; the individual is all." The politician responds: "The state is everything; the individual is nothing."

The consequence of this principle, the idea of humanity as a huge entity, as a living organism where individuals play the part of organs or even simple cells, can lead to monstrous conclusions. If there are brain-individuals and heart-individuals, why shouldn't there be hair-individuals and fingernail-individuals? We could divide the social body up into noble parts and lower parts: some worthy of being kept because they're necessary, others being eliminated because they don't affect the life of the encompassing entity. As human beings, we do not constitute unconscious cells or organs subject to the control of a central and collective soul. We are decentralized organisms, with our own autonomous lives and wills. True, we can't exist outside of society; we're organized for living within it. But it's also true that in the midst of others we can enjoy a relative isolation and exercise the right of Segregation.

Above all powers and all hierarchies, the individual stands out, with the right to integrally disengage his person, rejecting the yoke of the strong and the superstition of the ignorant. He doesn't have to subject himself to parliamentary or popular majorities or enslave himself to the service of a country. He is absolute master of himself. "There is," says Alfredo Calderón, "an ownership, primary, spontaneous, eternal, that carries its own legitimacy within, that requires no social recognition to survive, that is born in the womb of human nature: the ownership that each man has over himself, his body, his mind, his senses, and his faculties, his hands, his feet, his eyes, his limbs, his thoughts, and his affections" *(Palabras)*. "No," writes Pompeyo Gener. "This life we own we owe to no one, we can use it as we please. Everything in me, thought, feeling, desire, my energies, my actions, all my efforts belong to me, I owe them to no one nor to any personification, to no phantasm, to no imposed idea, call it Virtue, Duty, or Superman . . . I don't want them to lift me up or to oblige me to lift myself up. I want to lift myself up; and if I lack the strength, at that moment I'll ask for help" *(Inducciones)*. Yves Guyot condenses into a single line the words of Gener and Calderón: "Chaque être humain est propiétaire de sa personne."

We belong then to no man, to no collectivity, in a word, to no one, only to ourselves or to those we love and to whom we give ourselves willingly. If we're altruistic, we live for others and even sacrifice ourselves for them; if we're selfish, we live idolizing ourselves and making our self the center of the universe.

But what good does it do for the individual to own himself in theory, if he lacks the means to maintain and perfect himself? In creating us, nature imposes on us the obligation to live. We have the right to breathe, not vegetating wretchedly and pitifully but achieving the most intense and expansive life. Whoever lacks what he needs and who cannot acquire it through work should appropriate the excess and superfluous property of the privileged. Everyone well or everyone ill: if the products of the earth are sufficient to let humanity thrive, let everyone thrive; if not, let us all suffer deprivation. No one should stuff himself and live in luxury while others suffer hunger and exposure. When he resigns himself to misery, when he fails to fight to obtain a place at the feast, the individual betrays his human dignity and loses his right to complain. Aren't the usurpers few? Aren't the usurped many? Why, then, if both right and might are on our side, do we not take possession of the earth? Because humanity is made up of innumerable commoners and only a tiny aristocracy: the commonfolk, submissive and resigned; the aristocracy, unbowed and rebellious.

To proclaim individualism in its true sense is not the same as advocating the rebirth of barbarism. The emancipated human being doesn't worship creeds or respect codes, but rather professes an ethic: to proceed in conformity with his own ideas about the universe and life. No one has the right to coerce us with the ineluctable necessity of certain obligations. To Kant's categorical imperative we can respond with another, diametrically opposed. Since man changes with time and his degree of enlightenment, there can be no immutable ethic, not even for the individual himself. His standard of morality adjusts to each period of life. We don't derive moral obligations from nature, only facts and laws: power prevails, the weak succumb. Reciprocal protection among some animals of the same species does not constitute a universal or cosmic law. Justice and compassion seem to be exclusive to man or, more precisely, to certain men in the social state.

We make no apology for the human species. In the heart of the civilized man a savage is always lurking, more or less asleep. Even the most peaceable cannot belie the jungle where his ancestors devoured one another. But isn't it possible for humankind to exist without drinking blood? Will the state have to exist forever as restraint and punishment? Will the judge, the jailer, the policeman, and the executioner rule eternally? With the exception of a few refractory individuals, perverse by nature and sicker than delinquents, the human species is educable and corrigible. If the atavism of evil abounds, it can't be said that good is entirely absent. Our thousands of progeny, do they not evince some good traits? Assuming human perfectibility, the existence of a society based on Anarchy, with no sovereignty beyond the individual, is conceivable. Modern man is further removed from prehistoric savagery than from the genuine *individual* of the future anarchist society.

The state with its penal codes and the Church with its posthumous threats, both instill neither positive change nor moral behavior. Morality doesn't reside in bibles or codebooks, but in ourselves: it must be extracted from man. Our love of self and our repugnance for suffering and dying instill in us respect for the lives of others and the avoidance of pain, not only in man but also in animals. Through a kind of reflexive selfishness, the negative Christian precept, "Do not unto others what we would not have them do unto us," is transformed into the positive human dictum: "Do good to all creatures without anticipation of gain."

The Paris Commune

(1909)

If anything can make us doubt the infallibility of historical affirmations, it is surely the swift modification of the judgments concerning the Paris Commune. Execrated yesterday by almost every bourgeois writer as an explosion of evil passions or the sinister masquerade of a few plundering, bloodthirsty bandits, it is considered today by many writers of the same ilk as a premature movement for social reparation or as the violent but just insurrection of men inspired by generous ideals. Hardly any fail to condemn the implacable rage of the victors or to stand aghast at the result of an unequal contest in which the Versailles army suffered some five hundred casualties while the communists or members of the confederation had more than thirty thousand victims, including among them a large number of women, old men, and even children.

Even the politicians—who always were and are still the mystifiers of the people and the chief beneficiaries of the improvements brought about by revolutions—even they resort today to subtle distinctions, *separating the good from the bad,* and acknowledge that the Paris Commune created the Republic of France.

An ironic and romantic acknowledgment, since it doesn't lead them to express their gratitude or to treat their benefactors humanely. Under the republican government of Fallières the worker endures the same economic servitude he suffered under the imperial regime of Napoleon

III. Today as before, the politician is the ally of the boss; today as before, the worker on strike has to retreat before the praetor's guns. If the communist of 1871 created the republic, the republicans didn't make him any more free or happy.

Examining things in the light of experience and with the perspective of distance, today we can see what caused the failure and where the roots of the evil are to be found. The commune suffered the grave consequences of having been a political movement rather than a social revolution; and if it had not died drowned in blood, it would perhaps have disappeared in a coup d'état, as happened to the republic of 1848. Its men, however frightening and destructive they may have seemed to their honorable neighbors, felt a real bourgeois respect for social institutions and for property. Not daring to provoke a financial crisis of colossal dimensions, they became guardians of the wealth hoarded in the banks; they defended the *capital*—inhumane and selfish—that incited and unleashed the fierce Versailles army against them.

As for the crimes and horrors of the commune, what were they, with the exception of the execution of Archbishop Darboy, the priest Deguerry, and a few Dominican friars? That act, however worthy of censure it may be, is mitigated if we bear in mind that it came as a reprisal and was carried out during the last moments of the struggle, when the despair over the imminent and inevitable defeat enraged their hearts and stifled all sense of humanity. Why be horrified about a dozen executions carried out by the communists and not about the thousands of murders perpetrated by the forces of law and order? No doubt, it's because of the nature of the victims, since it's believed that the life of a bishop is worth as much as the lives of ten thousand workers. We don't see it that way; we don't understand why the blood of a clergyman has to be more sacred than that of a bricklayer. Life for life, we regard the worker's as more useful than that of the vendor of masses and muttererer of Latin gibberish.

Although many may think it an exaggeration to repeat it, we insist that if the commune sinned at all, it was surely in leniency: it made many threats but seldom followed through. One witness, not at all partial to it, wrote in mid-May (a few days before the taking of Paris) "For seven weeks the commune issued terrorist decrees, and during that same period none of them were put into effect. They seemed to be affected by a kind of sweet madness, compatible with a relative sociability . . . The only ones really doomed were the poor devils the commune sent out to man the barricades" (Ludovic Hans).

Force

(1901)

When someone first said, "Might Over Right," sentimental souls in both worlds cried out in horror, as if they had been born on a planet of thornless roses, where animals had no claws and men no remnants of their bestial origins. However, that famous phrase (attributed unfairly to Bismarck) did not sanction a principle; it acknowledged a fact.

The same thing happened recently with the affirmation by the Chileans: "Victory is the supreme law of nations." We South Americans, mainly the children of Peru, have drawn back in horror, proffering cries of indignation. If victory is not the supreme law of nations, if it concedes no rights, what does it grant, then, to those conquered? Will the victor be obliged to cover the costs of war, to pay compensation for damages and injuries, to give up a slice of territory and sign the treaty imposed by the defeated? Ever since mankind has existed, right has been regarded as a luxury of the strong, victory as the supreme law.

In the realm of reality, things don't function as they do in the world of imagination and sentimentality. We men breathe in an atmosphere of crimes and abominations. And since we think we're living in a land of glorious beatitude, we confuse the real with the fantastic and expect to find in people and countries what only exists in the cells of our brain. Happily, daily experience teaches us that a syllogism is insufficient to hold back a treacherous attack, and that two belligerents aren't going to lay down their arms just because some well-meaning mediator preaches the benefits of arbitration to them.

We ourselves, the moaning, tearful victims of today, why speak of justice and rights, when it could well happen that tomorrow we would become the plunderers and executioners of our neighbors? If we aren't aggressive or abusive abroad it's because weakness reduces us to the role of the inoffensive and benevolent. We who burned villages and executed prisoners in the civil wars, who coldly whipped and tortured in barracks and cells; we who proved to be hyenas toward our own people, are we going to turn into sheep when we're confronted with an enemy nation? A patriotism of convenience and opportunism shouldn't cause us to throw a veil over the abominable pages of our history. If there is perfidy and iniquity on the part of the Chileans, there was also perfidy and iniquity on the part of Peruvians, who weren't always generous and loyal to Bolivia or Ecuador.

Let's talk without hypocrisy or stereotyped formulas. Why expect men to be better than they usually are? Why imagine nations to be more civilized than they really are? True, we're heading toward a land of peace and mercy, but we aren't there yet. Along the way we attack and wound and devour each other. Mankind, individually, strives to perfect itself to the point of semidivinity; collectively, it hasn't gone much beyond idiocy, bestiality. Moral elevation doesn't seem to be a characteristic of the species, but rather the exceptional endowment of a few individuals. There's never been a Socrates-land or an Aristotle-nation. At critical moments, the most civilized nations betray the churlishness of their souls, resolving and settling their most delicate and serious disputes with their fists. Among international fauna, all hands grasp, all jaws bite, even if the hand is named England, even if the jaw is named France.

Let's not glorify debility and weakness in deference to the traditions of a depressing and corrupting religion. On the contrary, let's go back to the good old days of paganism and exalt the simultaneous development of intellectual and physical force, positing the supreme ideal of perfection in a careful balance between the two. What good is the physical constitution of a Hercules if we're endowed with the cerebral mass of a cretin? What good is the intelligence of a Plato, if our body is degenerate and sickly?

The weak decrying strength is like the eunuch renouncing virility. If force can overcome iniquities, it also serves to win rights. All privileges and all abuses are based on force, and they have to be destroyed by force. Are we to imagine that a banker from City Bank is going to give up his fortune just because we arouse his sense of Christian charity? Or that a czar of all Russia will turn into a human being just because we invoke his philanthropic sympathies? We can expect nothing of charity or philanthropy; they're bankrupt now. Let's expect everything of justice—not justice armed with the sociologist's simplistic arguments but justice incarnate in the power of the masses.

We'll say it again: physical strength is insufficient. The old maxim "a sound mind in a sound body" needs to be changed today to "a strong mind in a strong body." Because force isn't just the steam that moves the propellor of a ship, the ax that bites into the trunk of a tree, or the dynamite that pulverizes rocks. Force is honest, rational writing; it is eloquent, free speech; it is disinterested, generous action. Our inner strength is enhanced by the prestige of the unknown and mysterious; we can estimate the power of the muscle, but how do we measure the power of a mind? How can we know what a thought tossed out to germinate today in the cranium of the masses might bring about tomorrow? How many times has humanity been moved to march forward, unconsciously, by the force of an idea sown three or four thousand years ago!

As evidence of the enormous disproportion between the power of the mind and the power of the body, behold the workers of both worlds—the servants of capitalist feudalism. Their muscles are strong, but because their minds are weak they serve as eternal playthings to those who are knowledgeable and shrewd. Instead of joining together to hasten the hour of social reparation, they remain divided, destroy each other, and prostitute themselves in contemptible political squabbling. They don't exercise their human rights, but clamor for citizen perquisites; they lack bread, but they demand the right to vote; they don't eat, but they vote. Poor flock, complacent and congratulating themselves on their right to choose who gets to shear them!

No. The workers still haven't figured out that if they practiced class solidarity, if they concentrated their power, if they struck just a few blows with pick and ax, it wouldn't take long to bring down the entire edifice of abuses and iniquities. But they don't dare. Fear of what need not be feared and respect for what deserves no respect keeps them eternally in place and in chains. Not so much a flock of sheep, the masses are giants chained by spiderwebs.

VI

Under Opprobrium

Caporalismo
(1914)

Mired in our mediocrity, which grows ever more intense and widespread, we should remember that individuals and nations acquire their value only through their moral elevation, and that no lofty feeling can germinate in a country resigned to the imposition of force and ruled by the doctrine of accepting conventional ideas. Where Cashibo thugs or African despots rule, there is only room for herds of mindless servants.

In Peru today we put up with everything, and everything is sanctioned by virtue of being in effect for a few days: it doesn't take years or months for a Judas reconstituted into a Gil Blas to be transformed into a celebrity. Today we take for granted indefinite prison terms, exile, and the rape of women; today we remain silent about summary executions in rivers and nocturnal assassinations in military barracks; today revolutionaries are threatened by examples of unmitigating repression from high places in government; today people go about saying as if they had finally discovered the panacea for all our ills: "What we need here is a good tyrant." This phrase, obligatory in the mouths of many poor wretches, reveals a state of mind equivalent to that summed up in the cry "Long live our chains!" shouted in Spain by the subjects of Fernando VII.

And it isn't only the soldier or professional animal who uses this phrase as a boast; the peasant or novice animal also uses it; the drawing room tiger sings the chorus to the jungle tiger. The divinization of brute force can be understood in the military, among those atavistic beings of inferior mentality who observe the kind of justice practiced by the cave bear; it can't be understood, however, among doctors, lawyers, engineers, and university professors, men who claim to be exponents of civilization. We wouldn't think of asking the professional animal for his opinion about the benefits derived from tyrannizing nations because that would be like consulting the horsefly about biting mules. But it would be good to ask the novice animal which nations were ever ennobled and made prosperous through tyranny, even if the tyrant was named Caesar or Napoleon.

Tyrannies, however much they brag about honesty and the economy, distribute the gold among favorites and praetorians; tyrannies function on behalf of a class, a caste, and sometimes a family, to the detriment of the masses; tyrannies, after a momentary and illusory period of well-being and a lethargic tranquility, produce hunger, internecine conflicts, and foreign wars. Tyrannies diminish everyone: some through the servility with which courtiers pay for their livery, others through fear, by reducing them to the condition of resigned and trembling subjects. Tyrannies, in short, feed on the weakening of our wills and the emasculation of our minds, stifle all free expression of the pen or the word, and try to impose a long, tomb-like silence, interrupted only by the sound of the sword being dragged along the ground. And this is what people are asking for and praising, this clamor for the advent of *a good tyrant.*

But something even worse is being asked and praised. Since there isn't sufficient substance in Peru to put together a Caesar or a tyrant in the grand classical mode, some petty tyrant will have to emerge, some Apache colonel, a rat with epaulets, a beribboned troglodyte, in other words, a *caporal,* or village strongman. Anytime we use the word *tyrant* or *tyranny* in reference to a governor or to the national government, you should read *caporal* and *caporalismo.* Not the Napoleonic or German variety of *caporalismo,* but the South American, consistent with the autocracy of the ordinary, rapacious army thug who with one hand raises his sword to salute the Constitution and with the other slices open the national treasury.

Caporalismo, then, signifies the degeneration of militarism, which is like saying a double degeneracy or a regression. This professional of death, whether he's called Napoleon or Frederick II, is little more than a throwback who can benefit us in some small way but can surely cause us serious harm. When the military man saves us through an act of unjust foreign aggression, he fulfills his duty and earns the gratitude of his compatriots. But when he doesn't limit himself to practicing his trade of international policeman and serves instead to support illegal governments, then he deserves our scorn and hatred for having transformed himself into the blind instrument of the *caporal.* He instills even more scorn and hatred when, aligning himself with the *krumiro,* the cop, and the boss, he resolves strikes expeditiously by shooting the strikers.

This liking for the *caporal* and for bloody solutions isn't something new today: it already had its sporadic manifestations. What redskin from our army hasn't dreamed of being a Porfirio Díaz, at the very least? There is always been a defensive alliance between the *caporal* and the lawyer: the *caporal* behaved like a *caporal,* and the lawyer justified his crimes of sword and claw. A few years ago, a judge from the Civilist Party advocated exile and confiscation of property, while a senator of the Democratic Party pushed for the use of the guillotine. Let's try to imagine a confiscation carried out by the pseudo-aristocracy of the Civilist Party and a guillotine operated by the necrocracy of the Democratic Party.

Have we enjoyed so many freedoms that today, through some sort of morbid curiosity or political sadism, we hanker for a taste of tyranny? Have we grown bored with our superabundant production of superior specimens like Aristides, Cincinnatus, and Marcus Aurelius? Are we running into a Washington or a Lincoln everywhere we turn? No. But our blood waxes nostalgic for slavery. Our faces long to be slapped, we long to be kicked in the ass. According to the Asians, the European stinks of corpses; we don't know what the Chinese and Japanese smell in us when they come sniffing around, but just as the sun emits light and the flower disperses fragrance today Peruvian flesh emits the effluvia of abjection. Our moral geometry knows no vertical lines. Horizontal is the favorite position of prostitutes and hordes of Peruvians: the former, face up and embracing the man who pays, the latter face down and licking the feet of the petty tyrant who tosses them their scraps.

Those who go beyond the boundary of voluntary servitude in this way deserve nothing, not even our pious disdain. People with a hunger to endure *good tyrants* are ripe for conquest: since they bellow like oxen for the national yoke, they deserve a foreign yoke. Anyone willing to tolerate a *caporal* can endure conquerors.

Peru should be depicted by a black horizon, pitch black, with a bloody sword as emblem.[1]

[1] The publication of "El Caporalismo" in *La Protesta* (Lima) in October 1914 led to the closing of this newspaper by the government of Colonel Benavides. See the article "La Protesta," p. 119.—A.G.P.

The Good Revolution

I

We condemn national revolutions because they impoverish us, dishonor us, bleed us, and turn us into savages. If in normal times the only guarantee of safety rests in the will of the satrap hunkered in his palace, during a civil war the law of Lynch prevails, applied to honest people by criminals. In cities like Lima and Callao, where the diplomatic corps keeps close watch on the actions of the government and exercises an ostensibly moderating restraint, there's some pretense of respect for lives and property. But in the towns and villages of the interior, where they can operate in their own backyards and without fear of bothersome witnesses, no one is respected or treated with human decency. Everyone suffers from abuse of power, those with the least suffering most; thus, the poor Indian ends up crucified between the crook in a frock coat and the brute wearing a poncho. What the soldier doesn't confiscate the guerrilla will, and the poor devil who eludes the government panther can't escape the revolutionary wolf.

How do we achieve positive change if the criminals themselves lead the revolutions? When they don't initiate them, they foment them; and when they don't foment them, they jump on board at the moment of victory to reap the benefits, ousting the naive souls who risked everything to defend the constitution and the laws. Our civil wars turn out bad, not because they aren't justified but because the wicked lead them or take advantage of them. Veritable cannibalistic orgies, they start out with the perpetration of every variety of crime in the provinces and end up with the execution of three or four thousand men in the streets of Lima. We erect a mountain of skulls and install at the top a democratic clown, an androgyne from the Civil Party, or a three-cornered hat and a sword.

Once the new satrap is seated at the top, there's no movement to resuscitate a single former institution or to correct even one of a thousand inveterate abuses. The regime remains the same, consisting of a single power—the executive—with two equally servile appendages—the parliament and the judicial power. There's not even a radical change of personnel, since the same judge goes on selling sentences and the same congressman goes on selling votes to the highest bidder. Even the defeated gradually end up enlisted in the ranks of the victor, while a few intransigent revolutionaries cut ties with the satrap and go off to set up an opposition government without a plan, headless, counterproductive. Convictions, parties—words with absolutely no meaning in Peru: the civilist deifies the soldier, the democrat shoots the worker, the constitutionalist grinds the constitution underfoot. The parties are nothing but officer corps without armies; convictions, mere opportunism in a larval stage, ready to emerge in a realignment of gunsights on the national treasury. After every revolution, all we have are mobs camped out in the governmental palace. Yesterday the civilist mob, the constitutional mob, or the democratic mob; today the praetorian/roadblock mob; tomorrow . . . what mob will assault us tomorrow?

II

You'll say it's the same everywhere, that the same monsters crawl from beneath the stones and the same iniquities are repeated whenever people revolt. It may be that way in Spanish America; but not all civil wars are financial operations conducted by a clique, not all revolutionaries degenerate into bloodthirsty knights of industry. In the French Revolution and the Paris Commune, those unfairly called beasts or bandits were fighting for an idea and didn't die with their pockets stuffed with gold. Robespierre died owning nothing but a few worthless paper bills; the secretary of the treasury during the Commune had his clothes washed by his own wife. There is an enormous difference between revolutionaries: those in France might be depicted as a cross between a cat and an apostle; those here, as a cross between a crow and a tiger. We're separated from European nations by entire geological ages: we don't produce social and revolutionary specimens, but political, praetorian, bandit gorillas.

Just because we haven't yet achieved a true revolution, does that mean we never will? Will we always be a pack of muzzled dogs ruled by the whip of a festooned *caporal*? Will we always live doomed to an endless servitude more humiliating and shameful than the slavery of old? Who's to say that Peru, surrendering to its instincts for survival, won't sooner or later offer a virile demonstration of its latent power? People aren't like the ox or the colt who, once tamed, live and die obedient to the spur or the rein. They have periods of lethargy like the marmot, but moments of awakening like the lion. They stop, they inch forward timidly or retreat; but when it's least expected they burst into a run and go forward, recuperating in a day the ground lost over years. Japan and China surprised the theorists of slow, peaceful evolutions.

True, the masses usually go where the clever push them and wreak havoc with the irresponsible blindness of the child and the madman; but they also know how to lead themselves, consummate tremendous social liquidations, and carry to the point of sacrifice their faith in ideas or in men. More perhaps in men than in ideas. Perhaps once the clarion call is sounded and the spark initiated, the necessary leader will emerge in Peru today. Humankind has surprising intellectual and moral reserves that appear when revolutions break out. During the Spanish domination, who would have thought that in South America men like Bolívar, Sucre, San Martín, Córdoba, and a hundred others would emerge? For the revolution of 1854 we had Castilla; in 1865, Gálvez.

The true popular revolution, the one dreamed of and longed for by sane men, the one feared and abhorred by the decadent clowns of politics, the one we need more than anything today, will come some day, perhaps quite soon, perhaps tomorrow. It won't be the torrential flood that washes everything away, turning the fertile fields into a wasteland, but an inundation that will drown the leeches and spread fecundating alluvial slime over the impoverished soil. It will be, too, the dawn of the great day. Some blood will be spilled. Dawns are always tinged with red.

The Rotten Core

(1914)

I

Someone said that "Peru isn't a nation but an occupied territory," and someone else affirmed that "our republic is little more than a geographic name." In the former, at least for now, there's a modicum of truth. If Peru wants to boast that it's a nation, it should point out where the citizens are to be found, since they are the essential elements of any nationality. Citizen means free man; here, what we have are herds of slaves vegetating: there's not much distance from this to Dahomey or the Congo. If human groups are to be judged by the leaders they choose or endure, we would deserve to be called a camp of bedouins, a Gypsy fair, or a settlement of savages. We earn no more glorious label when we let ourselves be ruled by a Benavides.

Great nations behave with utmost benevolence when they send their ministers to meet with our Behanzines; although they treat us as equals (carrying diplomatic courtesy to extremes), they nonetheless appraise us at our proper value. If now and then a statesman from one of the great nations resorts to a map to pinpoint our geographical situation and make sure we don't border on Japan or Canada, others are aware that until recently our principal export was guano and that today we're still known mainly for starting revolutions, taking out loans, and not paying our debts. Spain regards us as ungrateful, rebellious children; the other states look at us from the commercial perspective—buyers and sellers: sellers of copper, cotton, and sugar; buyers of garish products, trinkets from bazaars, and cheap novels by Montépin and company.

Peru was Spain's favorite colony in South America. In Peru she spent lavishly, taking pains to leave the greatest number of public works. To compensate the lack of schools, she filled us with churches and convents; but she couldn't bequeath us anything else, given the epoch and the Spanish character. Those convents and those churches attest to the expenditure of extraordinary human effort. If the Spaniards collected much gold, they didn't take it all away. We don't know what the result would be if we compared the value of what was left us by the viceroys with the value of what was constructed by the presidents. When we won independence, we weren't regarded as the least important nation on the continent. Could you say that today we're the first? None of our cities can compare with Buenos Aires, Montevideo, or Santiago. Stagnation or ruin is palpable in all of them; an atmosphere of hospital or cemetery presses down on them all.

Lima, of lyric fame, is comparable to a third- or fourth-rate European city. It has an ancient look about it, an air of something that has been dug up, the appearance of a medieval Pompey. Any man conditioned to breathe in a modern environment will die of asphyxiation here; it's not a place where you can savor "that good air of Paris, which according to Flaubert seems to be laden with fragrances of love and intellectual emanations." Thanks to inept and rapacious municipal authorities, the air of Lima seems laden not with those sweet fragrances and emanations but with the stench of open sewers, the aroma of pollution and garbage dumps, the dust from streets paved laughably or not at all, and the putrid smell of stagnant water standing in ditches. And this we call "the Pearl of the Pacific" and "the South American Seville." With the ludicrous modernization of antiquities that utterly resist modernization and its new rasta-style houses, our capital is a dirty old man who thinks he's very cool and modishly dressed in his second- or third-hand suit, his faded ribbons, and his slow, damp voice like mold dissolved in naphthalene. When we return to Lima after residing for a while in a modern city, we suffer such a depression and become so dispirited that we feel like heading for the cemetery, climbing into a grave, and having a slab laid over us. Alive or dead, aren't they about the same here? Those living in our streets and plazas, are they any more alive than the dead in the mausoleum?

II

According to Edgar Quinet, "the Spanish American republics were born with the wrinkles of Byzantium already in place . . . Here the morning breeze of the universe wafts across the forehead of man but can't revive the old fellow." We doubt that these words (spoken around the middle of the nineteenth century) are still accurate for all the American nations of Spanish origin: some are evolving in midyouth. No one would dare call Mexico, Argentina, Uruguay, and so on, youths prematurely aged, incapable of being rejuvenated "by the morning breeze of the universe."

Unfortunately, we are not included in the list of republics that have been able to erase the Byzantine wrinkles from their foreheads. We are stubbornly Byzantine but without the erudition and art of Byzantium, having traded gladiator and rhetorician for bullfighter and shyster lawyer. Our modest material progress, does that compensate for the lack of progress in higher matters? If through some cataclysm, like the one that befell Atlantis, we were to vanish overnight, the world wouldn't suffer any great loss: only a few shopkeepers and peddlers would lament our passing. We're a nonentity in the intellectual wealth of the human species: we have initiated no reform, created no institution, enunciated no scientific discovery, and produced no literary masterpiece. We have no men who aren't echoes of other men, and we don't express ideas but simply repeat wornout, moth-eaten platitudes. The voices of our parliament, our universities, and our literary or scientific associations buzz like the hum of insects around a swamp. Now and then something rises above the buzzing: the croaking of a frog with delusions of being a nightingale.

In political terms, we now live under conditions even more degrading than under Spanish domination. If yesterday we groveled under the protection of a king who had a modest understanding of justice, today we're on the verge of falling under the tyranny of an adventurer of shameful stock. The viceroys were far less abusive than our presidents. The servitude we experienced in colonial times seemed almost natural:

we were born vassals and died vassals; the servitude we are now experiencing, ninety years after independence, is inconceivable and nauseating: we are born free but choose to live as slaves. And slaves of what lords! The regime of violence and plunder inaugurated by the military on May 15 would have produced a general uprising in any other nation, and the petty tyrant would have been immediately trampled underfoot by the angry masses. Our gutless, bloodless masses react only with fright before the audacity and crimes of the incipient Peruvian Melgarejo. The sight of the corpses of the victims sacrificed in Santa Catalina, el Napo, Llaucán, Vitarte, Arequipa, and so on, make men tremble (if the term men can be applied to spiritual eunuchs, lacking all virility above the waist). And if they don't succumb to fright, they can be bought.

But nothing should surprise us in a country where corruption gushes nonstop, where we live in moral bankruptcy, where men have become not just mercenaries but merchandise subject to the fluctuations of supply and demand. A conscience can be bought and sold in Peru today the way a horse, a car, or a piece of furniture is bought and sold. What *is* surprising is that the current price of a minister, judge, congressman, mayor, magistrate, colonel, or journalist, isn't listed on the stock exchange.

And we're referring in particular to Lima, which functions within the national organism as the infected nucleus. Here are born the pathogenic germs that spread throughout the republic, here healthy men who come from the provinces to become involved in politics grow sick. The provincial, caught up in the dance of Lima conspiracies, starts out by acquiring a false vision of things and ends up suffering the utter obliteration of his moral sense. The vices he brings from his village are unchecked, and he becomes contaminated by the vices of the capital. An outsider who adapts to Lima becomes worse than the Limeño of pure blood.

Even the name of our capital embodies an irony: they give the name City of Kings to a miserable town where a half-breed president or viceroy governs in a court of free men or emancipated slaves interbred with Frenchmen, Germans, Japanese, Italians, Chinese, and so on. That motley court forms a kind of masonic chain made up of old men practiced in crooked politics and young men who are even more venal and rotten than their elders. Skilled at starting revolutions, but not at staying with them at the cost of their blood, Limeños turn their streets into battlefields, bury the dead, and fraternize with the victors. It is always been this way; when our splendid grandfathers set fire to a castle to celebrate the advent of the patriots, they kept another to celebrate the return of the royalists. Remember how the victors of San Juan and Miraflores were received in 1881? Our proud Limeños aren't exactly paragons of courage or integrity.

However, the provinces live in awe of the capital, their eyes fixed on it, as if awaiting inspiration from the infallible oracle: they neither think nor act without first consulting the opinion or receiving instructions from the Peruvian Delphi. In effect, "What do they say in Lima?" is what the republic asks before making any decision. The good provincials, through some kind of optic aberration, see tiny things as large from a great distance, mistaking the illiterate, inane journalist for Girardin, the bewigged mulatto for Talleyrand. Worse, they mistake the officers corps without armies for huge political parties, receive as gospel the hollow programs of bewitched candidates, and are convinced the Messiah will be born in the classic land of deserters and moneylenders. Provoking laughter and pity, they imagine that Lima is the flourishing center of a youthful society inspired by the most sublime ideals and eager to sacrifice themselves for national regeneration. As if from one generation to the next the blood of traitors and thieves were going to be transformed into the blood of heroes and noblemen! As if children were not the image of their parents! As if wolves didn't sire wolf cubs, vipers baby vipers!

National disinfection can't come from the rotten core; the necessary and saving action must be initiated outside of Lima so as to lift from the other towns the odious domination exercised by small parties from the capital.

Tyrannicide

B lood horrifies us; but if some must be shed, let it be the blood of the wicked. Who knows but that from a perspective on justice less narrow than human justice it might not be a greater crime to wound a helpful animal than to exterminate an evil man. Perhaps we would be right in concluding: before shedding the blood of a pigeon or a lamb, kill the tyrant. Why not come right out and say it? The spilling of certain blood produces no stain. Hands that free us from despots and petty tyrants bear no stain, are worthy of being clasped by honest men. To strike down such a culprit, him alone, without sacrificing innocent people, is an end to be desired. The Angiolillos, the Brescis, the assassins of Grand Duke Sergio, and the executioners of King Carlos deserve more sympathy than Ravachol, Emile Henry, and Moral.

An inveterate prejudice leads us to abhor the elimination of the tyrant with revolver, dagger, or dynamite, but not to condemn the undoing of that same tyrant by means of a devastating and bloody revolution. In other words, the tyrant can assassinate the people, but the people aren't supposed to kill the tyrant. This is certainly not how the ancients looked at it when they glorified tyrannicide.

When the entrenchment of the status quo makes any popular uprising impossible, when the only way to end tyranny is to eliminate the tyrant, should we put him to death or go on indefinitely enduring an ignomious and brutal oppression? Should we value all that highly the life of a person who has no respect for the lives of others? True, "man should be sacred to man," but let the despot set the example.

When tyrannicide ends a degrading regime and saves many lives, its perpetration should be included in the list of praiseworthy and beneficent acts. It even deserves to be called a sublime manifestation of Christian charity in the best sense of the word. If a Francia, a Rosas, a García Moreno, and a Porfirio Díaz had been eliminated in the first days of their dictatorships, how much pain and how many crimes could have been avoided in Paraguay, Argentina, Ecuador, and Mexico! There are countries where removal alone is not enough. In the Spanish American republics the overthrown boss or petty tyrant usually recoups his seat of power or goes on burdening the nation for some twenty or thirty years, reborn as a professional revolutionary or even the restorer of public freedoms. If each Spanish American despot had only had his timely appointment with the executioner, we wouldn't have had to watch the repugnant series of ignorant soldiers filing down through our history, all of them vulgar, all of them brutes. This excessive respect for the lives of criminal rulers can make us enemies of the people.

We put to death a rabid dog or a panther escaped from its cage, so why not do the same to a tyrant every bit as threatening and frightening as the panther and the dog? Being human doesn't consist in simply having human form but in harboring notions of mercy and justice. A man with the instincts of a gorilla isn't a man, he's a gorilla. We aren't committing homicide when we put him to death. Montalvo, the most unhypocritical of men, put it quite frankly: "The life of a wretched petty tyrant without virtues personal or ancestral, the life of one who devours human flesh out of sheer instinct, for no reason, perhaps even unaware he's doing it . . . is of no value . . . and it's allowable to kill him as we would a tiger, a snake." Blanco-Fombona, after witnessing the uselessness of revolutions and civil wars in Venezuela, writes with an endearing sincerity: "Does this mean we should simply cross our arms in the face of the excesses of despotism or weep like women about our bad luck? No. It means we should put away our old ways, that we should become men of our time, that we should remember there's such a thing as dynamite. Tyrannicide should replace revolution . . . Let's be concrete, let's personalize the punishment of the guilty. That is justice. To start a civil war just to overthrow a tyrant is like setting fire to the palace to kill a mouse" (*Judas Capitolino*, "Prólogo").

Whether or not we approve of violence, we can't fail to acknowledge the generosity and heroism of the avengers who offer their lives to punish outrages and injuries they themselves did not suffer. They strike without personal hatred toward the victim, for the sheer love of justice, knowing they'll die on the scaffold. Perhaps they're wrong, and what does it matter? The merit of the sacrifice doesn't depend on the truth of one's conviction. Those who in good faith took the wrong path, sacrificing themselves for the lie of country or the lie of religion, today constitute the glorious pleiad of our heroes and saints.

The great avengers of today, will they not be the Christs of tomorrow?